The Jewish Journey Haggadah

Connecting the Generations

הגדה של פסח

Rabbanit Adena Berkowitz

Photography by Shira Hecht-Koller

gefen
publishing house · בית הוצאה לאור גפן
JERUSALEM ◆ NEW YORK · Est. 1981

Cover and Page Design: Ben Herskowitz
Typesetting: Ben Herskowitz

ISBN: 978-965-229-912-3
1 3 5 7 9 8 6 4 2

.Gefen Publishing House Ltd   Gefen Books
Hatzvi Street 6   Edison Place 11
Jerusalem 94386, Israel   Springfield, NJ 07081
972-2-538-0247   516-593-1234
orders@gefenpublishing.com   orders@gefenpublishing.com

www.gefenpublishing.com

Printed in Israel

Library of Congress Cataloging-in-Publication Data

Names: Berkowitz, Adena K., editor.
Title: The Jewish journey Haggadah : connecting the generations = Mi dor
    l'dor : hakol b'Seder / [edited by] Adena K. Berkowitz.
Other titles: Mi dor l'dor : hakol b'Seder | Haggadah. English. | Haggadah.
    Hebrew.
Description: Jerusalem : Gefen Publishing House, [2018]
Identifiers: LCCN 2018038295 | ISBN 9789652299123
Subjects: LCSH: Haggadot–Texts. | Seder–Liturgy–Texts. |
    Judaism–Liturgy–Texts. | Haggadah.
Classification: LCC BM674.643 .B475 2018 | DDC 296.4/5371–dc23 LC record
available at https://lccn.loc.gov/2018038295

In loving memory of
Rabbi William Berkowitz and Rebbetzin Florence Berkowitz
Beloved parents and grandparents
~The Berkowitz-Brenner Family

In memory of
Nessie Chana bas Minna Leah
~Michael, Allison, Rebecca, and Avi Bromberg

In loving memory of my father
Dr. Milton S. Steinberg, Shmuel Mordechai ben Yitzchak Gedalya
~Dr. Alissa Grill and family

We dedicate this to our children,
David, Sophia, and Isaac:
May you continue to transmit our heritage from generation to generation.
You are our redemption.
With everlasting love from your parents,
~Sharon and Dr. Bart Inkeles

In loving memory of
our beloved Shele Danishefsky Covlin, *z"l*
~The Karstaedt and Danishefsky families

In memory of
our dear parents and grandparents Miriam Shuchat and Rabbi Wilfred Shuchat
~Bryna and Joshua Landes and family

In honor of
our children, grandchildren, and great-grandchildren, who will, God willing,
retell the story of Passover for generations to come
~Tiki and Simcha Lyons

In memory of
my beloved mother
Eleanor Sutker, Etta bat Yitzhak v'Rifka
~Barbara Messer

In loving memory of
Henrietta Milstein and Sheldon Ohringer
~Eve and Stephen Milstein and family

In loving memory of
Judge Paul P. E. Bookson, *z"l*
beloved father and grandfather, respected jurist and community leader
forever in our hearts
~Shoshana, Saul, Michael, and Drew Stromer
~Alexandra and Michael Farbenblum

In memory of
Mordechai ben Avraham Sutton
remembered by his son and daughter-in-law
~Dr. Leon and Dr. Karen Sutton

How to Use This Haggadah

This Haggadah contains the traditional Hebrew text with an English translation and transliteration. In addition, on each page you will find instructions for conducting the Seder. Other features include:

LEADER. Introductory paragraphs that the Seder leader can choose to read out loud or assign to one of the participants.

BACKGROUND. Longer pieces that provide more in-depth insight into practices and themes of the Seder.

REFLECTION. Interesting stories or points designed to stimulate greater thought and spiritual connection.

SUGGESTION. Ideas to share with those present.

QUESTIONS FOR DISCUSSION. Designed to pique conversation and participation from Seder guests.

HUMOR CORNER. Jokes or stories to make everyone laugh.

KIDS' CORNER. Suggestions to help further engage children at the Seder.

Additionally, in each section you will be directed to the appendix for fun sing-along songs and additional readings. At the back of the Haggadah you will also find Seder recipes, as well as a glossary of commentators with brief biographical sketches.

A note on spelling, transliteration, and translation: In this Haggadah, transliterations are written with modern Israeli Hebrew pronunciation in a simplified style using *ch* (and not *kh* or *h*) for the Hebrew letters *chet* and *chaf*. The English translations are gender neutral. For the most part a literal reading is provided in English, but at times a metaphoric explanation of the Hebrew text is used.

I am constantly mindful of the injunction not to depart from *"matbei'a shetav'u bo Chachamin"* (the formulaic language that the Sages created). Therefore, all traditional texts in the Haggadah remain as they are. However, influenced by the inclusive and sensitive philosophy of Rav Hisda in *Berachot* 49a, I have incorporated that approach in the Grace after Meals to the extent halachah permits.[1] Hence, I have suggested that people reciting the Grace after Meals have our Matriarchs Sarah, Rebecca, Rachel, and Leah in mind. In addition, I have also provided a phrase to note when saying the phrase *"v'al b'rit'cha shechatamta bivsareinu"* (for sealing Your covenant in our flesh). The note

provided, "*v'al mitzvotecha shechatamta b'libeinu*" (and for Your mitzvot that You sealed in our hearts), is an adaptation from the verse in Song of Songs 8:6, "*Simeini kachotem al libecha*" (Set Me as a seal upon your hearts), and from Deuteronomy 30:6, "*U'mal Hashem Elokecha et levavecha*" (And Hashem your God will circumcise your heart), as well as influenced by Maimonides and Saadya Gaon, who eliminated "*shechatamta bivsareinu,*" only retaining "*v'al b'ri'tcha.*"

The name of God is spelled out to read "A-do-nai." For those conducting the Seder in Hebrew and using the English only for understanding a particular word or phrase, God's name in the English should be scanned or read as "Hashem." However, for those who are actually conducting the Seder in English, God's name is spelled out so that prayers in English have an equivalency to the Hebrew. Tradition teaches us that our prayers are heard by God no matter what language we use. May we all merit that our prayers soar to heaven and bring about the Redemption speedily in our day.

Chag sameach – Happy Passover!

Acknowledgments

While I began work on this Haggadah many years ago, along the way, there were many happy interruptions – raising children, day-to-day work, going back to school, preparing *shiurim*, sermons, lectures, articles, and other book projects. Finally in the last three years, I was able to turn back to this long-overdue project and bring it to fruition. However, this journey has not been a solitary one. Along the way, this Haggadah has moved along with the help of family and friends, in the form of both moral and financial support. First and foremost, I am grateful to my husband, Rabbi Zev Brenner, and our dear children Menachem Leib, Lizzy (and her husband Sam Zakay), Pammy, Aderet, and Jessica for allowing me, literally across the years, to share with them Passover ideas and thoughts and jokes and stories. Our family Sedarim have served as the testing ground for so much of what is in this Haggadah and helped birth this work almost as a collaborative project.

It goes without saying that the groundwork for seeing the beauty of Pesach and the Seder experience was started in the home in which I was raised and at the feet of my beloved parents, Rabbi William and Rebbetzin Florence Berkowitz, of blessed memory. My parents shared at our Seder table the traditions of their parents and grandparents, but always with an added insight, song, joke, or story – or, courtesy of my mother, a unique Galitzianer pronunciation.

I am very grateful to Shira Hecht Koller for her magnificent and spectacular photographs, which transport the reader and make the pages of this Haggadah come alive. Amy Rosen's creative and mouthwatering recipes leave the reader asking for more, as each one is tastier than the next. Warning – you may gain weight just from reading them! Thank you both for allowing me to include your creative work.

Additionally, this Haggadah is enhanced by the inclusion of parody songs and stories that so many authors and publishers happily provided permission for me to include. I am very grateful to Rabbi Sharon Cohen Anisfeld, Yeshaya Douglas Ballon, Bangitout, Joyce Bohnen, Chabad.org, Feldheim Publishers, Rabbi Binny Freedman, Isaac and Seth Galena, Dr. Mendy Ganchrow, the Ghetto Fighters' House Museum, Jewish Lights Publishing, Jonathan Glick, Rabbi Howard Goldsmith, Doug Gordon, Shy Held, Cantor Deborah Katchko Gray, *JOFA Journal*, Koren Publishers, Dr. Yael Levine, Rabbi Daniel Liben, Live Science, Stuart Malina, Anna Morrison Markowitz, Alan Morinis, Aaron Naparstek, Barbara Sarshik, Natan Sharansky, Barbara Sofer, Randi and Murray Spiegel, Gary Teblum, Dr. Warren Tessler, Marnie Winston-Macauley, and Dr. Ronald Wolfson. I am deeply appreciative to Rabbi Marc Angel, who provided a proper Ladino version of the Four Questions, as well as to my daughter Pammy Brenner for her expertise with the Yiddish version.

Profound thanks to my dear friends Paula Gantz, whose publishing expertise and assistance helped jump-start this project; Lauren Klein, who never tired of hearing me

describe some new addition; and the following wonderful friends whose support made this publication financially possible: Gail Asper, Allison and Michael Bromberg, Dr. Alissa and Steven Grill, Sharon and Dr. Barton Inkeles, Eve and Marc Karstaedt, Bryna and Joshua Landes, Tiki and Rabbi Simcha Lyons, Barbara Messer, Eve and Stephen Milstein, Shoshana and Dr. Saul Stromer, and Dr. Karen and Dr. Leon Sutton. My heart overflows with gratitude.

I am also grateful to those who over the years read excerpts of this Haggadah and made suggestions, including Rabbi Daniel Fridman; Rivka Haut, of blessed memory; and Rabbi Ariel Rackovsky. I also thank the many attendees of Kol HaNeshamah, where I serve as Scholar in Residence, and the loyal attendees of my Nosh and Drash *shiur*, who over the years heard me share Passover themes that are now reflected in this work.

Finally I would like to extend my deep appreciation to Ilan Greenfield, the Publisher of Gefen Publishing House, for believing in this project, with all its complexity, together with his wonderful team: Senior Editor Kezia Raffel Pride, an editor's editor, who was meticulous and thorough to a fault, never tiring of the many revisions and additions; Project Manager Emily Wind (who also helped compile the Hebrew text, transliteration, and translation of the Haggadah text); Project Manager Devorah Beasley, who stepped in when Emily went on maternity leave; and thanks to designer Ben Herskowitz, whose beautiful layout makes the text jump off the pages. *Rav todot!*

I have been blessed to always feel every year that I am on a Passover journey, excited to learn new things from my family and those joining us at our Seder table. I now invite you to experience an exciting Passover with *The Jewish Journey Haggadah*.

With supreme gratitude to Hashem Yitbarach, to Whom all praise is directed, for reaching this milestone.

Tam v'nishlam — hakol b'seder! and as the Haggadah concludes: *L'shanah haba-ah birushalayim habenuyah!*

Rabbanit Dr. Adena Berkowitz
Rosh Chodesh Shevat 2019/5779

If there is a shmurah matzah bakery in your area, find out if they allow members of the public to participate in the baking of matzah.

Why Is This Night Different from All Other Nights?

This question, which is recited at the Passover Seder, has evoked a range of emotions and memories for Jews across the ages and around the world. The Passover Seder is the quintessential moment to host a meal in the company of dear family and friends as the assembled recall and retell the Jewish people's liberation by God from Egypt and discuss the meaning of freedom and the ability to triumph over adversity. Since Passover is a time of questions, it is natural to begin our journey with a few questions of our own.

The First Question

Why the need for a new Haggadah?

In some families, a Haggadah distributed by a leading coffee company might suffice. For others, further insight and explanation of the text is needed to make the Passover story come alive. This Haggadah has been designed to

- **FOSTER** a deeper connection to Passover to enable participants from all backgrounds, from generation to generation, to be comfortable using a Hebrew or transliterated text, together with an inclusive English translation

- **PROVIDE** a user-friendly format with suggestions for preparing for Passover and internalizing its messages afterwards

- **SHOW** the central role played by women in the Passover story
- **SPARK** discussion and sharing of insights, teachings, anecdotes, and stories

In our family, my husband and I and our children have always come to the Seder laden with numerous Haggadot. (In fact, so many that we literally need another table just to accommodate them!) The various Haggadot we bring have different commentaries and points of emphasis from which we may learn. In this Haggadah, I have brought together diverse commentaries as well as incorporated my own thoughts and family customs. The word *Haggadah* is based on the Hebrew word *l'haggid* (to tell). One rabbinic interpretation explains that often the Hebrew letters *heh* and *alef* are interchangeable. Hence instead of reading it as a Haggadah, we can read it as though it begins with an *alef*: *agudah*, which means a united entity. On Seder night, as we read the Haggadah, we hopefully will feel the sense of unity, the chain of Jewish faith and tradition.

The Second Question

What sets Passover preparations apart from all other holidays?

Unlike the usual hustle and bustle that goes with cleaning for other holidays (or even on a weekly basis for Shabbat), Passover is all-encompassing. Ridding one's house of chametz (leaven) requires much energy and stamina. The process of turning one's house upside down, with a thorough scouring of the kitchen, means not only getting rid of bread but any leavened product and by extension anything produced in a non-Passover-cleaned kitchen or factory.

My mother, Florence Berkowitz, of blessed memory, always joked that at Passover, God freed the Jews but enslaved the women! The context of this remark is that often the responsibility for cleaning and preparing for Passover has rested primarily on women, not to mention the challenge of preparing the Seder and holiday meals as well. (That might explain the burgeoning numbers of families now choosing to go away for the holiday.) The work involved can be overwhelming.

Preparing for Passover traditionally begins one month before the holiday, after the conclusion of Purim. Observant Jewish families immediately start to cut down on the purchase of chametz (leavened products including bread, pasta, cereals, and grains) and products containing *kitniyot* (legumes and rice). Traditionally, Ashkenazim have not eaten *kitniyot* during Passover; Sephardim have different customs as to the type of *kitniyot* they will eat. In Israel, more and more Ashkenazim have embraced eating *kitniyot* or *kitniyot*-based derivatives.[2]

What we celebrate is a uniquely Jewish symposium, with a set order, filled with foods and symbols designed to pique the curiosity of the youngest among us.

The word Haggadah is based on the Hebrew word l'haggid (to tell).

The Third Question

How did the Seder come about and how did it take on the structure we have today?

In the Torah, in the Book of Exodus, God commands the Jewish people to bring a Passover sacrifice, mark their doors with the blood of a lamb, and eat the sacrificed animal along with bitter herbs. We are to eat unleavened bread for seven days and tell the Passover story to our children. As we recall the Exodus from Egypt and our escape to freedom, we are also to sing songs of praise. In the time of the Temple in Jerusalem, the Passover sacrifice would be offered by each head of family and eaten after the meal along with wine, a vegetable that had been dipped, bitter herbs, and matzah. Then the children would be encouraged to ask their questions based on what they had seen (including a question pertaining to the roasted meat). After the Temple was destroyed, Jews were no longer able to bring and eat the Korban Pesach (the Passover sacrifice). The rabbis realized that an educational initiative was required to keep the Passover story and experience fresh and ever important. The Seder had to be restructured and formalized, taking into account the lack of the Passover sacrifice. Renewed emphasis was placed on prayers, discussions, and rituals to engage participants; the essence of the Seder is *seder* (order).

The Seder would now begin with the four questions along with a change in the questions asked.

The question pertaining to roasted meat was omitted and later replaced by one concerning reclining. In addition, the rabbis of the Talmudic age added in the requirement of four cups of wine. While the Babylonian Talmud references a Haggadah, the evening's format was primarily based on an oral tradition. A more formalized version would not appear until several hundred years after the destruction of the Temple, based on the format found in the Mishnah, the Oral Law codified by Rabbi Yehudah Hanasi in 200 CE. The earliest version of a Haggadah appears in the siddur (prayer book, a word also related to *seder*) of Rav Amram Gaon, the head of the Babylonian Sura Academy, who lived in the ninth century. The Haggadah he prepared was sent throughout the Diaspora and was further developed a century later by Rav Saadia Gaon, who was then the head of the Sura Academy. By the Middle Ages, other Haggadot began to appear in France, Germany, Spain, and Prague. With the advent of the printing press in the fifteenth century, the Haggadah became more standardized, leading to the format we have today, with more than seven thousand versions in print.

The Fourth Question

What has the Seder come to represent?

What we celebrate is a uniquely Jewish symposium, with a set order, filled with foods and symbols designed to pique the curiosity of the youngest among us.

As with so many Jewish customs, influences from the surrounding culture show up even in this most central Jewish ritual. The Greco-Roman symposium, a time for eating and reclining, intellectual conversations, and discussions with questions and answers, has seemingly influenced the Seder. Some of the food consumed, such as parsley and other foods that are dipped, could remind us of the appetizers served at such feasts. Yet there are important distinctions that make us realize the key differences between those symposiums and our Seder.

A Seder is a religious event commemorating a Jewish historical event. While a symposium was designed around discussion, it was geared toward the elite. A Seder is to be open to all, especially with a focus on involving and engaging children. Symposia ended with going from place to place, with wild entertainment. This provides one interpretation for the word *afikomen*, which is derived from the Greek word *epikomion*, which means "after dinner revelry/entertainment." While drinking and singing are all part of a Seder, the rabbis made sure that a Seder would never degenerate into licentiousness. Rather, a Seder would stand out as an educational, religious, and spiritual gathering, with the afikomen taking on a completely different role as the dessert or final food consumed to remind us of the Korban Pesach.[3]

The Fifth Question

Why is this night different from all other nights?

What makes this night unique is the rabbinic objective to truly experience Passover as if we were there too. At the Seder, we must actually feel the backbreaking work and heat of Egypt, the suffering of our fellow slaves, the terror of the plagues unfolding around us, the rush to leave Egypt, the water lapping at our feet as with trepidation we cross the Sea of Reeds, and our exhilaration to be liberated by God and to face the future in the Land of Israel. What we recite at the Seder has to be more than dry history. It has to be an evocation of our experience. If that feeling has been conveyed, then we can say our Seder was complete.

The rabbis of old were so concerned that participants, especially children, not fall asleep on Seder night that rituals were moved up before the meal, with the conclusion of the Seder to follow. Today, many of us may also feel the pull of rushing through much of the ritual to get to the meal. We should always bear in mind, no matter how long our Seder lasts, that we have to make it a night to remember, a night to recall our liberation and exodus to freedom.

Fifteen Steps before Passover

The number fifteen has special significance in Jewish tradition. For example, Passover begins on the fifteenth of Nisan. There were fifteen steps leading to the Temple in Jerusalem, which correspond to the fifteen Songs of Ascents in Psalms. So too, the Seder follows a fifteen-stage process of ascent. To help make the holiday even more meaningful and to echo the theme of the fifteen steps in the Seder, here are fifteen suggestions for before Passover – some even months before. (Fifteen suggestions for after the Seder has concluded are found in the appendix at the back of this Haggadah.)

1. **SEPTEMBER/OCTOBER:** Take a lulav (palm branch) used during the festival of Sukkot and put it in a safe place to save for pre-Passover. The night before the start of Passover, during Bedikat Chametz, the search for leaven, use it to sweep the crumbs into the collection bag that will be burned the next morning with leavened products. This represents a nice continuity from one holiday to the next.

2. **JANUARY/FEBRUARY:** Until the introduction of machine-made matzah in the late 1800s (with a resulting argument as to whether such matzah was kosher for Passover), all matzah was made by hand. Today, most Jewish consumers buy square machine-made matzah. For a more authentic taste, one can purchase round *shmurah matzah* (literally "watched matzah," as the wheat is watched before production to make sure it does not become wet, possibly causing it to become chametz). If there is a *shmurah matzah* bakery in your area, find out if they allow members of the public to participate in the baking of matzah. You might be able not only to watch the process at work but to have a hand in the baking and get to bake your own matzot for the Seder. Often this means signing up to visit a bakery in January or February. If you don't get a chance to actually bake your own *shmurah matzah*, purchase at least enough for yourself and your guests to have at the Seder.

3. **JANUARY/FEBRUARY:** On Tu b'Shevat, the Jewish "new year" holiday for trees, plant parsley that will bloom/bud in time for use at the Seder.

4. **FROM AFTER PURIM UNTIL PASSOVER:** Collect leavened products from your kitchen that can be donated to a local food pantry for

The number fifteen has special significance in Jewish tradition.

Take a lulav (palm branch) used during the festival of Sukkot and use it during Bedikat Chametz to sweep the crumbs into the collection bag.

donation to needy non-Jews. When you food shop for the holiday, purchase Passover food suitable for donation for kosher-for-Passover food drives.

5. **Listen to Passover music** to get into the holiday mood. Start visiting websites and checking out apps for Passover and downloadable material to enhance the experience of your Seder guests. Prepare a series of tweets to send out to family and friends and followers that tells something very short about the holiday or an idea to share. #getintheholidayspirit.

6. **When you begin to clean your house,** remember to check pockets in coats and jackets, and other places chametz could be hiding (for example tefillin and tallit bags). If there are children at home, make sure they help clean their rooms. Have them empty and clean out their backpacks in addition to their clothing. The following story illustrates what can happen when parents forget to do that: A family was invited to the home of their rabbi for a Seder. Shortly after they arrived, with the Seder not yet started, their five-year-old felt hungry and whipped out a bag of pretzels from the backpack she'd brought with her. Needless to say, the following year, the parents did a thorough search everywhere, including all school bags.

7. **In the weeks before Passover,** contact a rabbi to sell the chametz in your possession, even if you are going away for the holiday. Before Passover, the rabbi arranges a sale of chametz to a non-Jew, thus ensuring that even leavened products one would find onerous to get rid of (that expensive bottle of single malt) or other chametz you may be unaware of will not be considered to have stayed in your possession. After Passover, the rabbi buys it back for you.

8. **Some suggested arts and crafts projects:**

   - Purchase inexpensive wine glasses or heavy-duty plastic cups. Have children decorate them with waterproof paint and stencil in figures related to Passover. This can be a wonderful memento for each guest to use at the Seder. They can also decorate glasses or cups for Kos Eliyahu and Kos Miriam, or design pottery or ceramic Seder plates at a local craft store or at home.

   - Have children prepare afikomen bags by making a template out of a larger piece of felt. They can use felt pieces, markers, glue, and sparkles to decorate them. Younger children can cut out and make individual rings from construction paper and join them together as a chain, to be used later in the Seder.

   - Children can also make paper bricks for the Seder table or accompany an adult to buy some bricks for the table to represent the bricks the children of Israel used as slaves in Egypt.

- Purchase white pillowcases and have children design them for use at the Seder. They can use waterproof magic markers to make a design or tie-dye them to create special family heirlooms.

- Prepare a coupon book that lists fifteen things your children like about the Seder or fifteen fun things that can happen at a Seder. Tell them this list can be read at each of the fifteen steps of the Seder, or prepare a mock newscast during which each item can come in like a news flash.

- Prepare inexpensive (clean for Passover!) backpacks filled with some matzah and a Haggadah at each place setting. Guests can follow Sephardic custom by putting them over their shoulders to reenact leaving Egypt with only the matzah on their backs.

- Buy plastic washing cups for each guest that children can decorate and personalize with permanent waterproof markers.

9. **Before the Seder,** send out trigger questions on themes connected to the Seder or questions found in the Haggadah to help guests be prepared to participate. If you invite guests who speak a foreign language, ask them to prepare the Mah Nishtanah in their native language. At our Passover Sedarim, in addition to the youngest reciting the Mah Nishtanah in Hebrew, we have had adult guests and our older children recite the Mah Nishtanah in Arabic, Ladino, Russian, and Yiddish.

10. **Buy a kittel** or prepare white clothes to wear to the Seder.

11. **To keep kids involved** in preparation for the Seder as well as engaged during the Seder itself, try the following activities:

- Have adults and children write a short play together about any aspect of the Passover story to put on for fellow guests.

- Organize props ahead of time. Pick up Pharaoh and Cleopatra wigs and masks in a costume store or museum shop. If you have an inner artist, design costumes and masks. Wrap a doll to look like baby Moses and place it in a basket. Pre-assign roles for a skit.

- Buy a plastic blow-up mic to use and have guests go around and interview each other in talk-show-host style: What did

you take with you when you left Egypt? What was the worst part of being a slave? What will you do when you are free?

- Prepare charades cards for guests to use for each other to guess what characters they represent in Passover history.

- Prepare a news broadcast or tweets beginning with Joseph being sold into slavery. Periodically interrupt the Seder with news updates on the Exodus from Egypt.

- Print up mock newspapers or tweets that reflect each aspect of the Passover story.

- Prepare a family history to share with guests. Some examples: the escape from pogroms in Europe; fleeing to America and the struggle to survive economically and stay Jewishly connected there; experiences of family members during the Holocaust, in the former Soviet Union, or fleeing modern-day Egypt or Ethiopia.

- Purchase a "plagues" kit from your local Judaica shop or online, so the children at the Seder can act out the plagues. Just watch out for your tablecloth when it comes to simulating the red color that the Nile turned!

- Check websites/Facebook/Twitter/other social media for recipes and interesting articles to print out and distribute or other ways to make the Seder more engaging for guests.

- If you are going away for Passover, bring a bit of home with you. Take along some inexpensive wine goblets, and any of the arts and crafts projects that will travel well in a suitcase.

- If any relatives or friends immigrated, ask them to bring expired passports that show the journeys they took on their road to freedom, or copies of visas or passports showing your family's journey. The custom of the Adler family in Jerusalem has been to place next to the Haggadot facsimiles of German Reich passports. Each great-grandchild receives a copy of the original transit visas granted to their great-grandfather Leo Adler and great-grandmother Bella that reflected their journey during the Holocaust. They read out the cities stamped in the visas: Ansbach, Mir, Kedan, Vilna, Kobe, Shanghai, Gorki, Karaganda, Kok Uzed, Odessa, Vienna, Brooklyn, New Jersey, and Basel. And one more stop has been added: Jerusalem, where every single great-grandchild lives.[4]

- In advance of the Seder, ask guests to think of a modern-day manifestation of slavery, relevant to their daily lives. (For example, feeling as if one is a slave to fashion, to cultural norms, societal expectations, etc.)

12. **PREPARING THE SEDER TABLE** is a task unto itself. Don't feel obligated to do it by yourself – ask for help from those coming to your Seder. If you are joining family or friends, volunteer to help with any aspect of the Seder, bringing one of the food items or wine (there are so many delicious kosher wines available beyond the traditional heavy Malaga), or designing place cards. Children in the family can usually be counted on to provide a school project, such as a matzah cover or Seder plate. Even those with little time to help can send flowers before the holiday to decorate the table. It could be fun to come up with a particular theme or schematic to coordinate the décor, table, and place cards. For example, vases with flowers, blue tissue paper running down the middle of the table to reflect crossing the Sea of Reeds, pyramids and/or a depiction of the splitting of the sea made out of (clean for Passover) children's building toys, etc. Asking children to help set the table is a wonderful opportunity to emphasize the Jewish idea of preparing (*hachanah*) for a holiday, and an important lesson in seeing all the steps leading up to the holiday. In essence, Jewish life is not only about the eating (or the reward!) but shows the importance of the preparation as well.

13. **PEOPLE HAVE DIFFERENT CUSTOMS** related to the afikomen. For an additional twist on the practice of searching for the afikomen and redeeming it for a gift, Rabbi Michael Strassfeld suggests writing the names of various charities on pieces of paper prior to the holiday. At the Seder, place them in envelopes and hide them. Have the adults search for them. Each guest is then responsible for making a donation to the cause he or she finds. Children can participate as well. Put categories of mitzvot in envelopes that children pledge to do – visit a sick friend, prepare Shabbat food for donation to the poor, etc.

14. **SOMETIMES A LITTLE BRIBERY** goes a long way – encourage children to nap in the afternoon before the Seder and promise them a reward for cooperating. Make sure to feed the kids a light snack beforehand as well.

15. **AND LAST BUT NOT LEAST** – be happy, it's Passover!

Passover becomes almost like a second Yom Kippur when we rid ourselves of all chametz, not only in our cabinets, but in our spiritual lives and relationships.

Be happy, it's Passover!

What Comprises the Seder Table?

Three whole matzot are placed in a holder or between separate folds of a cloth, one on top of the other. These three matzot are said to represent the three categories of Jews: the Kohanim (priests), Leviim (Levites), and Yisraelim (Israelites). In our day of fractured communities, this is a good symbol of unity – for the Seder is not complete without all three.

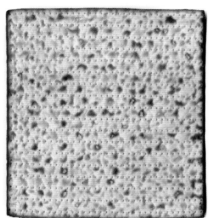

Matzah will be eaten three times at the Seder: when we make the blessing over it, when we eat the Hillel sandwich with maror (bitter herbs) and charoset, and a third time as dessert (the afikomen). Matzah and chametz are closely related. From a food standpoint, all that separates the two is the leavening agent (yeast). Chametz is analogous to ego, puffery, sourness, bitterness, and the evil inclination. Passover becomes almost like a second Yom Kippur when we rid ourselves of all chametz, not only in our cabinets, but in our spiritual lives and relationships. Out goes conceit and puffery and anything that causes us to rise like fermented yeast. We then have the opportunity to turn inward, as we do on the High Holy Days, and ask ourselves: Who are we? How do we change and grow? How do we balance success with inflated ego? What do we want our lives to be about? How can we remain positive despite the challenges we encounter? How can we avoid negativity and emotional bitterness?

Linguistically, the two words *chametz* (*chet, mem, tzadi*) and *matzah* (*mem, tzadi, heh*) are different only in two letters – *heh* (ה) and *chet* (ח) – that resemble each other so strongly there is only a tiny space between the two. So too only a moment separates matzah from becoming chametz, which makes us realize how quickly we can turn sour. One thing we can learn from this is that when we have the chance to do a mitzvah, we should strive to do it happily and not with a sour, "*chametzdik*" face!

Along with the matzah, we prepare a Seder plate consisting of five items:

1. **Maror and chazeret,** the bitter herbs, consisting of romaine lettuce for maror and horseradish root for chazeret; these are a visceral reminder of the bitterness and hardship of slavery. They will not only be eaten alone but will also be used in the Hillel sandwich.

2. **Karpas,** a vegetable to be dipped in salt water. Parsley or celery is often used, but many families dip potatoes.

3. **Charoset,** a mixture of chopped nuts, apples, cinnamon, and other spices that are minced and made into a paste with sweet wine or grape juice. Sephardic Jews use a slightly different recipe, such as raisins, figs, and dates mixed together with nuts, wine or grape juice, and spices (see appendix for a recipe). No matter

The rabbis of old were so concerned that participants, especially children, not fall asleep on Seder night that rituals were moved up before the meal, with the conclusion of the Seder to follow.

what the ingredients, its purpose is to remind us of the mortar our ancestors used to lay bricks in Egypt. Apples are also a symbol of Jewish female resistance during the enslavement in Egypt. A rabbinic teaching reminds us that women convinced their husbands to build families despite slavery, and then gave birth surreptitiously in the fields under apple trees.[5]

4. **BEITZAH,** a roasted egg, hard-boiled and scorched to evoke memories of the festival offering (the Chagigah) along with memories of the destruction of the Temple. Eggs are also traditionally used by mourners, designed to evoke for us our pain at the destruction of the Temple, and with it, the end of the ability to bring the Korban Pesach.

5. **ZEROA,** a roasted shank bone (chicken or turkey neck) to remind us of the Paschal Lamb. For vegetarians, substitute a broiled beet, which evokes the color of the blood.[6]

Some suggest placing at the Seder table a brick as a visceral reminder of the bricks that the Jews used in their backbreaking labor in Egypt. Another reclaimed custom is to place fish next to the shank bone and egg on the Seder plate, as a reminder of Miriam and her association with water. In the tenth century, the people of Kair Ovan (in North Africa) asked Rav Sherira, the Gaon of Pumpedita in Babylonia, regarding the two foods placed on the Seder table. He responded that they symbolize the two messengers, Moses and Aaron, whom God sent to Egypt. He told them that "there are those who place a third food – fish – on the Seder table in memory of Miriam, as it says, 'And I will send before you Moses and Aaron and Miriam' (Micah 6:4)."[7] Tradition teaches us that these three food items (egg, meat, and fish) will be eaten in the world to come.[8]

The rabbis saw drinking wine as derech cherut, a symbol of freedom.

The Abarbanel explains that the four cups are connected to four different types of redemption.

Four Reasons We Have Four Cups of Wine

The custom of drinking four cups of wine during the Seder was introduced by the rabbis in post-Temple times.[9] The rabbis saw drinking wine as *derech cherut*, a symbol of freedom.[10]

REASON 1. In the Jerusalem Talmud,[11] Rabbi Yohanan says in the name of Rabbi Benayah that the four cups of wine of the *Seder* correspond to the four phrases of redemption found in Exodus 6:6–8: "Hence say to the children of Israel, I am the Lord, I shall *take you out* from the pressure of work in Egypt; I shall *save you* from their service, I shall *redeem you* with an outstretched arm and great judgments. I shall *take you* as a people for me." In the Talmud the rabbis remarked that in the absence of the Temple

in Jerusalem, with the inability now to bring the paschal sacrifice, there was no joy except with the drinking of wine.[12] Unlike Roman feasts, which tended to revolve around three occasions to drink (before, during, and after the meal), the rabbis made the Seder have four cups but made sure they revolved around holy ideas. The first cup would be Kiddush – recited before the start of the meal and reminding everyone of the Exodus from Egypt and their status as God's people. The second cup would be drunk right before the main meal. The third cup would be drunk following the grace after meals, and the fourth cup almost at the conclusion of the Seder, after Hallel.

REASON 2. The Abarbanel explains that the four cups are connected to four different types of redemption. The first is when Abraham was chosen as the founder of the Jewish people, the second represents our liberation from the slavery in Egypt, the third represents our survival and perseverance, despite attempts to annihilate the Jewish people throughout our years of exile, and the fourth is the messianic redemption yet to come.

REASON 3. The Bnei Yissaschar viewed the four cups as a reward for what the rabbis viewed as the four heroic acts the Jewish people traditionally performed in Egypt: they never changed their names (and distinctive Jewish dress), they never forgot the Hebrew language, they retained their moral values, and they never betrayed one another to their slave masters.

REASON 4. The Maharal said that the four cups or *kosot* (a word that takes the feminine form) of wine represent the memory of the four Matriarchs – Sarah, Rebecca, Leah, and Rachel. As noted on page 19, it was for the sake of the righteous women that the children of Israel were redeemed from Egypt. The four cups then are a salute to the founding mothers of Judaism. As the Maharal points out, Sarah influenced many people in the surrounding culture to convert and become part of the Jewish people; Rebecca because she left her idols behind her; Rachel was the mother of Joseph, who kept his faith in God even during all the years of his imprisonment; and Leah was the first woman to praise God and was the mother of Judah, who became the head of what would become the Jewish people.[13]

Kos Eliyahu/Kos Miriam

On the table we place Kos Eliyahu, Elijah's Cup, to be filled later with wine. Tradition teaches us that Elijah the prophet will return to announce the messianic era. On Seder night, when we celebrate our liberation from Egypt, we also have the opportunity to express our hope in the coming of the Messiah, the one who will lead us out of our current state of exile and bring about the complete redemption and return to Israel . Since tradition teaches us that it will be the prophet Elijah who will announce the messianic era, we are so confident of our imminent redemption that we actually pour a cup for Elijah to reflect the fifth expression of redemption found in the Torah: "And I shall bring you into the land..." (Exodus 6:6–7). One twentieth-century rabbi, Rabbi Menachem Kasher, proposed that the fifth cup should be drunk in honor of the establishment of the State of Israel, which religious Zionists believe is the beginning of the redemptive age. Later in the evening we will open up the door to "welcome" him in. Seder night is Leil Shimurim, a night of watching or protection, in which we show we are unafraid and we open our doors to those who are in need of physical and spiritual sustenance.

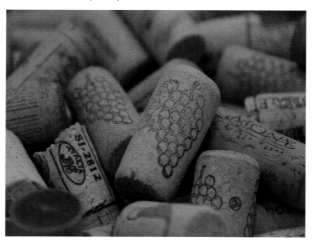

One contemporary addition to the Seder table is Kos Miriam, Miriam's Cup, which is filled with water. This cup is to remind us of Moses's sister, who is a central figure in the Passover story. Miriam saves her brother's life by placing him in a basket to float in the Nile and watching over him until he is rescued by Pharaoh's daughter. After the Jewish people cross the Sea of Reeds, she leads the women with her tambourine in song. We are taught that God gave to Miriam a well of water that sustained the Jewish people throughout their sojourn in the desert and had curative powers. When Miriam died,[14] we are told, the well dried up and with it its spiritual cures, leading Moses to hit a rock for water. That incident led him to be unable to enter the Land of Israel.[15]

This cup also serves as a reminder of the heroic women in the Passover story. The women insisted on having children despite Pharaoh's decree. A midrash tells us that after Pharaoh's decree, Moshe's father decided to divorce his wife, Yocheved. Soon, all the Jewish men followed suit. Miriam turned to her father and said, *You are worse than Pharaoh. He only decreed against the boys; but by your action you have decreed against the girls*

as well.[16] The brave midwives Shifra and Puah defied Pharaoh's decree and helped these women deliver their children. And Yocheved's determination to save Moshe prevailed.

In Exodus 15:20–21, we read the Shirat Hayam (Song at the Sea), which includes the following: "Miriam the prophetess, the sister of Aaron, took the tambourine in her hand; and all the women followed her with tambourines and dances. And Miriam called to them, 'Sing to God, the most exalted; horse and rider God cast in the sea.'"

As the Lubavitcher Rebbe, Rabbi Menachem Mendel Schneerson, points out, "The men sang, and then the women. The men sang…they sang their joy over their deliverance, they sang their yearning for a more perfect redemption – but something was lacking, something that only a woman's song could complete…. Miriam and her chorus brought to the Song at the Sea the intensity of feeling and a depth of faith unique to womankind."[17]

According to Tosafot, the miracle of the Exodus occurred because of the righteous women.

Pillows at the Seder are a symbol of aristocracy and heighten the interest of children, who will immediately see that this is no ordinary meal.

Women and Passover Customs and Rituals

Jewish firstborn males are required to fast as acknowledgment of the divine intervention that spared the Jewish firstborn in Egypt during the tenth plague.[18] However, if they attend a *siyum* (celebration of the conclusion of learning a tractate of the Talmud) on the morning of Passover eve, that is an occasion for feasting and not fasting. Are firstborn women required to participate, as the men do, in the fast of the firstborn? A midrash teaches us that firstborn girls were killed as well.[19] For example, Batya, the daughter of Pharaoh, was a firstborn, but the rabbinic commentaries tell us that she was spared because of the merit of her saving Moses. The *Shulchan Aruch* (*Code of Jewish Law*) tells us that "some say that even a woman fasts if she is a firstborn."[20] In fact, according to Sephardic authorities, firstborn women should fast or participate in a *siyum*. In contemporary times, Rabbi Ovadiah Yosef, the leading Sephardic rabbinic decisor of the late twentieth and early twenty-first centuries, provided leniencies for pregnant or nursing women, but he encouraged others to go to a *siyum* if it is not too much trouble. While the sixteenth-century Ashkenazic halachic authority Rabbi Moshe Isserles (known as the Rema) rejects this custom for women, he does indicate that where a woman is married to a firstborn, and they have a firstborn son, the woman should fast or participate in a *siyum* for their firstborn son until he becomes a bar mitzvah.[21]

Are women bound by the commandments to eat matzah, drink four cups at the Seder, eat maror and afikomen? The rabbis answered that women are required to partake of all these rituals, since they were saved by the same miracle as the men.[22] According to Tosafot (medieval commentaries on the Talmud), the miracle occurred because of the righteous women.[23]

Should everyone bring a pillow to the Seder? We are reminded that in order to evoke a feeling of aristocracy and freedom, we are to recline (on the left side) when we drink the four cups and while eating, with certain exceptions. Many bring pillows to the Seder as a symbol of reclining and aristocracy and to heighten the interest of children, who will immediately see that this is no ordinary meal.

Until recently, it was customary only for men to bring pillows to fulfill this tradition of reclining. Today more women are doing so. According to the Talmud (and later adapted by the *Shulchan Aruch*), "A woman who is in the presence of her husband does not recline but important women should."[24] The Mordechai ruled that "today all women are important and must recline" and this was accepted as an option by the Rema.[25] In fact, according to Sephardic tradition, this view prevails and women are required to lean.

It is customary for the Seder leader to wear a *kittel*, a long white robe. A *kittel* is also worn on Yom Kippur and is a symbol of both festiveness and holiness; some add that it reminds us of the white robe that the High Priest wore in the days of the Temple in Jerusalem. We no longer have a Temple, but wearing a *kittel* is another reminder of how we transform our tables into holy space, akin to an altar. Even those who are not leading a Seder may have the custom to wear white.

The Kli Yakar teaches us that we wear white to demonstrate our remorse over the behavior of Joseph's brothers, who resented Joseph's coat of many colors. It was this resentment and jealousy that led Joseph down to Egypt and the eventual enslavement of the Jewish people.

Until recently, it was customary only for men to bring pillows to fulfill this tradition of reclining. Today more women are doing so.

On the night before Passover Eve, after nightfall, all the leaven in the home is searched for and collected.

Bedikat Chametz: Searching for Leaven

On the night before Passover Eve, after nightfall, all the leaven in the home is searched for and collected. To make sure that the blessing is not said in vain, a few pieces are placed in various parts of the house. Kabbalistic custom encourages us to place ten pieces of bread throughout our home, representing the ten Sefirot (God's emanations), and search for them with candle in hand (or use a flashlight for safety if searching with children) and a feather to sweep up the crumbs. Many Judaica stores and Jewish organizations have such kits available prior to the holiday. Another option is to use the lulav that you saved from Sukkot to sweep the chametz into the bag. Check with a rabbi for the different procedures if you will be celebrating Passover away from your home.

Before the search say:

Baruch Atah Adonai, Eloheinu	בָּרוּךְ אַתָּה יְיָ אֱלֹהֵינוּ
Melech ha-olam,	מֶלֶךְ הָעוֹלָם,
asher kid'shanu b'mitzvotav,	אֲשֶׁר קִדְּשָׁנוּ בְּמִצְוֹתָיו,
v'tzivanu al bi-ur chameitz.	וְצִוָּנוּ עַל בְּעוּר חָמֵץ.

Blessed are You, Adonai, our God, Ruler of the universe, Who sanctified us with Your commandments and commanded us concerning the removal of leaven.

After the search, say:

Kol chamira vachami-ah d'ika	כָּל חֲמִירָא וַחֲמִיעָא דְּאִכָּא
virshuti d'la chamiteih ud'la	בִרְשׁוּתִי דְּלָא חֲמִתֵּהּ וּדְלָא
vi-arteih ud'la y'dana leih libateil	בְעַרְתֵּהּ וּדְלָא יְדַעְנָא לֵיהּ לִבָּטֵל
v'lehevei hefkeir k'afra d'ara.	וְלֶהֱוֵי הֶפְקֵר כְּעַפְרָא דְּאַרְעָא.

Let any leaven within the vicinity of my home, even if I may not have seen and removed it, be considered null and void and as public property, like the dust of the earth.

Suggestion

For safety, if children are present, consider using a flashlight instead.

Kids' Corner

After hiding the bread, join in a rendition of "A-Searching We Must Go" sung to the tune of "A-Hunting We Will Go."

Reflection

The following teaching reminds us that even in the seemingly mundane task of cleaning, holiness resides: "When Pesach was coming, [Rabbi Levi Yitzchak of Berditchev] would go and watch the Jewish women toiling, scrubbing, rinsing, and chasing after every crumb of *chametz*. Then he would lift his eyes toward Heaven and, just as on Rosh Hashanah we ask that the angels that are born of *Tekiah*, *Shevarim*, *Teruah*, and *Tekiah* [the various shofar blasts] should speak on our behalf, he would say, 'Master of the world! May it be Your will that the angels born of *Toiling*, *Scrubbing*, *Rinsing*, and *Tidying* come before Your Throne of Glory and speak on our behalf.'"[26]

Reflection

In the Talmud Yerushalmi (Jerusalem Talmud), we are taught that all are trusted with the responsibility of *biur chametz*, including women.[27]

Reflection

Throughout the ages, chametz has been described as not only representing physically leavened products but also symbolic of a spiritual type of yeast, of sourness and puffery, pride and arrogance that we should rid ourselves of as well. As we search our homes, think of ten types of spiritual chametz that need to be purged from our inner selves. Unlike edible chametz, commit to not reintroducing the spiritual chametz after Passover ends.

Even in the seemingly mundane task of cleaning, holiness resides.

We begin our liberation on Egyptian time, but we conclude on Jewish time as free people following our own calendar.

Biur Chametz: Burning the Leaven

Ridding our homes of chametz during Passover is connected to the commandment in the Torah to eat matzah in remembrance of the bread that didn't rise when the Jews left Egypt in such haste. Yet a historic note provides a deeper meaning. Egyptians were the first to perfect bread baking. How ironic then that when we experienced liberation from Egypt, what we left behind was not only the actual bread but metaphorically the very essence of Egypt. Another unusual custom is that we stop eating chametz not at the start of the holiday at sunset, but before noon, on the eve of the holiday. However, as with Shabbat and all the festivals, Pesach ends at nightfall. Why then is the prohibition brought on this early? One explanation is that historically, by late morning, the Passover Sacrifice, the Korban Pesach, could begin to be prepared. However, we can find a deeper spiritual explanation; in essence, we begin our liberation on Egyptian time – as the Egyptian day began in the morning – but we conclude on Jewish time as free people following our own calendar.[28]

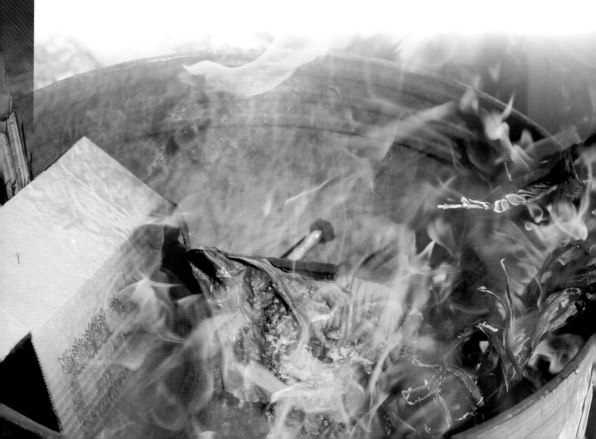

(When Passover begins on Saturday night, there is a different procedure for the disposal of chametz on Shabbat morning, which does not involve burning it. Please check with a rabbi for the correct times and procedures.)

On the following morning, burn the leaven and say:

Kol chamira vachami-ah d'ika	כָּל חֲמִירָא וַחֲמִיעָא דְּאִכָּא
virshuti dachaziteih ud'la	בִּרְשׁוּתִי דַּחֲזִתֵהּ וּדְלָא
chaziteih, dachamiteih ud'la	חֲזִתֵהּ, דַּחֲמִתֵהּ וּדְלָא
chamiteih, d'vi-arteih ud'la	חֲמִתֵהּ, דִּבְעַרְתֵּהּ וּדְלָא
vi-arteih, libateil v'lehevei	בְעַרְתֵּהּ, לִבָּטֵל וְלֶהֱוֵי
hefkeir k'afra d'ara.	הֶפְקֵר כְּעַפְרָא דְאַרְעָא.

Let any leaven within the vicinity of my home, whether I have seen it or not, whether I have removed it or not, be considered null and void as public property, like the dust of the earth.

Let any leaven within the vicinity of my home...be considered null and void...like the dust of the earth.

Eiruv Tavshilin:
Preparing for Shabbat

One is allowed to cook and do various types of work on a holiday for that day alone. When Passover begins on a Wednesday night, in the Diaspora the second day of yom tov *is Friday. Since we cannot do work on Shabbat, and the laws of* yom tov *dictate that we cannot do work on Friday for the following day, we have a dilemma as to how to prepare food and candles and the like for Shabbat. Hence, before the start of the holiday (on Wednesday before sundown), we make an Eiruv Tavshilin. This is a ritual in which the Shabbat preparations are begun in advance, with a stipulation that they may then be continued on the holiday (Friday) for Shabbat. Matzah and another cooked food, such as a hard-boiled egg, are placed on a plate, which one raises while reciting the following blessing. The food should be put aside and eaten on Shabbat together with the rest of the meal.*

Baruch Atah Adonai, Eloheinu	בָּרוּךְ אַתָּה יְיָ אֱלֹהֵינוּ
Melech ha-olam, asher	מֶלֶךְ הָעוֹלָם, אֲשֶׁר
kid'shanu b'mitzvotav, v'tzivanu	קִדְּשָׁנוּ בְּמִצְוֹתָיו, וְצִוָּנוּ
al mitzvat eiruv.	עַל מִצְוַת עֵרוּב.

Praised are You, Adonai, our God, Sovereign of the universe, Who sancti-fied us with Your commandments and commanded us concerning the eiruv.

Bahadein eiruva y'hei sharei lana	בַּהֲדֵין עֵרוּבָא יְהֵא שָׁרֵא לָנָא
la-afuyei ul'vashulei ul'atmunei	לַאֲפוּיֵי וּלְבַשׁוּלֵי וּלְאַטְמוּנֵי
ul'adlukei sh'raga ul'takana	וּלְאַדְלוּקֵי שְׁרָגָא וּלְתַקָּנָא
ul'mebad kol tzar'chana, mi-yoma	וּלְמֶעְבַּד כָּל צָרְכָנָא, מִיוֹמָא
tava l'Shabata lanu u'lchol	טָבָא לְשַׁבַּתָּא לָנוּ וּלְכָל
Yisra-eil hadarim ba-ir hazot.	יִשְׂרָאֵל הַדָּרִים בָּעִיר הַזֹּאת.

With this eiruv, it is allowed for us to bake, cook and keep the food warm, to light the candles, and to make any needed preparations on the holiday for Shabbat. This is permitted to us and to all Jews who reside in this city.

Lighting the Candles

On the Sabbath, women light candles first and then make the blessing, while their hands are over their eyes. This is done because by making the blessing we acknowledge the ushering in of the Sabbath, after which we can no longer light a match. When we uncover our eyes, it is as though we just "lit" the candles. On a holiday such as Passover (exclusive of the Sabbath), when we can transfer fire from a preexisting source, it is permissible to make the blessing over the candles first and then light the candles. In the sixteenth to seventeenth centuries, Rebbetzin Baila Edels Falk found the sources that indicated on holidays it would be appropriate to follow this custom, and her findings were accepted by the rabbis. (However, for many, in order to avoid confusion, the same format that is used on the Sabbath is retained.)

In the Diaspora, where we add an additional day and thus have two Sedarim, we are told to wear a new outfit on the second eve to provide a definite reason for making the *shehecheyanu* blessing. (The rabbis were concerned that we not make any blessing unnecessarily. Since we already said this blessing on the first night, there is doubt whether we are obligated to say it on the second night. Therefore the rabbis suggested saying the blessing over a new garment and having in mind the second night of the holiday as well.)

SUGGESTION

In many families, as each child is born, a candle is added to the two lit for each spouse. Many people follow a Lubavitch custom that girls beginning at age three light their own candles.

Prior to the start of the festival, holiday candles are lit and the following blessing is said. If it is the Sabbath, the bracketed words are added. As on all festivals, we add in the shehecheyanu *prayer, the blessing of thanksgiving to God for helping us reach this point and celebrate another Passover. Before the Sabbath, we light the candles first and then cover our eyes as we make the blessing. If you are lighting candles, please note that when making Kiddush you should not repeat the shehecheyanu.*

On the second night of Passover, the candles should be lit only after nightfall and from a preexisting flame. When lighting candles on Saturday night, remember to say the verse Baruch Hamavdil bein kodesh l'kodesh *before transferring the fire. This is the phrase that denotes the transition from Shabbat to just the holiday.*

Baruch Atah Adonai, Eloheinu

בָּרוּךְ אַתָּה יְיָ אֱלֹהֵינוּ

Melech ha-olam, asher

מֶלֶךְ הָעוֹלָם אֲשֶׁר

kid'shanu b'mitzvotav, v'tzivanu

קִדְּשָׁנוּ בְּמִצְוֹתָיו וְצִוָּנוּ

l'hadlik ner shel

לְהַדְלִיק נֵר שֶׁל

(Shabbat v'shel) yom tov.

(שַׁבָּת וְשֶׁל) יוֹם טוֹב.

Blessed are You, Adonai, our God, Ruler of the universe, Who sanctified us with Your commandments and commanded us to kindle the (Shabbat and the) festival light.

The shehecheyanu is to be recited on both Seder nights.

Baruch Atah Adonai, Eloheinu

בָּרוּךְ אַתָּה יְיָ אֱלֹהֵינוּ

Melech ha-olam, shehecheyanu

מֶלֶךְ הָעוֹלָם שֶׁהֶחֱיָנוּ

v'ki'manu v'higi-anu

וְקִיְּמָנוּ וְהִגִּיעָנוּ

laz'man hazeh.

לַזְּמַן הַזֶּה.

Blessed are You, Adonai, our God, Ruler of the universe, Who kept us alive, sustained us and enabled us to reach this season.

Many use candle-lighting time as an opportunity for adding personal prayers of well-being for the family and loved ones. The following is a techinah *– a personal petition that many choose to recite after candle lighting.*

Y'hi ratzon milfanecha, Adonai

יְהִי רָצוֹן מִלְפָנֶיךָ, יְיָ

Elohai v'Elohei avotai,

אֱלֹהַי וֵאלֹהֵי אֲבוֹתַי,

shet'chonein oti [v'et ishi/

שֶׁתְּחוֹנֵן אוֹתִי [וְאֶת אִישִׁי

ishti/yakiri, v'et banai, v'et

אִשְׁתִּי\יַקִּירִי, וְאֶת בָּנַי, וְאֶת

b'notai, v'et avi, v'et imi]

בְּנוֹתַי, וְאֶת אָבִי, וְאֶת אִמִּי]

v'et kol k'rovai, vatitein lanu

וְאֶת כָּל קְרוֹבַי, וְתִתֶּן לָנוּ

u-l'chol Yisrael chaim tovim וּלְכָל יִשְׂרָאֵל חַיִּים טוֹבִים

v'aruchim, v'tizk'reinu b'zichron tovah וַאֲרוּכִים, וְתִזְכְּרֵנוּ בְּזִכְרוֹן טוֹבָה

uv'rachah, v'tafk'deinu bifkudat y'shuah וּבְרָכָה, וְתִפְקְדֵנוּ בִּפְקֻדַּת יְשׁוּעָה

v'rachamim, u-t'varcheinu b'rachot g'dolot, וְרַחֲמִים, וּתְבָרְכֵנוּ בְּרָכוֹת גְּדֹלוֹת,

v'tashlim bateinu, v'tashkein Sh'chinat'cha וְתַשְׁלִים בָּתֵּינוּ, וְתַשְׁכֵּן שְׁכִינָתְךָ

beineinu. [V'zakeini l'gadeil banim u-vanot בֵּינֵינוּ. [וְזַכֵּנִי לְגַדֵּל בָּנִים וּבָנוֹת

u-v'nei vanim chachamim v'chachamot וּבְנֵי בָנִים חֲכָמִים וְחַכָמוֹת

u-n'vonim u-n'vonot, ohavei Hashem, וּנְבוֹנִים וּנְבוֹנוֹת, אוֹהֲבֵי יְיָ,

yirei Elokim, anshei u-n'shei יִרְאֵי אֱלֹהִים, אַנְשֵׁי וּנְשֵׁי

emet, zera kodesh, ba-Shem d'veikim, אֱמֶת, זֶרַע קֹדֶשׁ, בַּיי דְּבֵקִים,

u-m'irim et ha-olam ba-Torah וּמְאִירִים אֶת הָעוֹלָם בַּתּוֹרָה

u-v'ma-asim tovim, u-v'chol m'lechet וּבְמַעֲשִׂים טוֹבִים, וּבְכָל מְלָאכֶת

avodat ha-Borei.] Ana shema et עֲבוֹדַת הַבּוֹרֵא.] אָנָּא שְׁמַע אֶת

t'chinati ba-eit ha-zot, biz'chut תְּחִנָּתִי בָּעֵת הַזֹּאת, בִּזְכוּת

imoteinu Sarah v'Rivkah v'Rachel אִמּוֹתֵינוּ שָׂרָה וְרִבְקָה וְרָחֵל

v'Leah, v'ha-eir neireinu shelo yichbeh וְלֵאָה, וְהָאֵר נֵרֵנוּ שֶׁלֹּא יִכְבֶּה

l'olam va-ed, v'ha-eir panecha לְעוֹלָם וָעֶד, וְהָאֵר פָּנֶיךָ

v'nivashei-ah. Amen. וְנִוָּשֵׁעָה. אָמֵן.

May it be Your will, oh God and God of our ancestors, that You be gracious unto me (and my husband/my wife/my dear one, and my child/children, my mother/father) and all my relatives and all those who are close to me. And grant to us and to all Israel good health and long life, and remember us for good and bless us with compassion, salvation, and many worthy blessings. Grant peace in my/our home and let Your Shechinah reside among us. [May I merit to raise children and grandchildren, wise and learned,

God-fearing lovers of Torah and holy people of truth, clinging to mitzvot and lighting up the world with Torah, good deeds, and service of God]. Dear God, please hear my prayer and plea now. In the merit of our fore-fathers and foremothers, may the light of these candles shine forever, and may Your glory be reflected upon us so that we may merit the Redemption.

Blessing of Children

FOR A SON

Y'simcha Elohim

יְשִׂימְךָ אֱלֹהִים

k'Ephraim v'chi'Menashe.

כְּאֶפְרַיִם וְכִמְנַשֶּׁה.

MAY GOD make you like Ephraim and Menasheh.

FOR A DAUGHTER

Y'simeich Elohim k'Sarah,

יְשִׂימֵךְ אֱלֹהִים כְּשָׂרָה

Rivka, Rachel, v'Leah.

רִבְקָה רָחֵל וְלֵאָה.

MAY GOD make you like Sarah, Rebecca, Rachel, and Leah.

FOR ALL CHILDREN

Y'varech'cha Adonai v'yishm'recha.

יְבָרֶכְךָ יי וְיִשְׁמְרֶךָ.

Ya'eir Adonai panav eilecha vichuneka.

יָאֵר יי פָּנָיו אֵלֶיךָ וִיחֻנֶּךָ.

Yisa Adonai panav eilecha

יִשָּׂא יי פָּנָיו אֵלֶיךָ

v'yaseim l'cha shalom.

וְיָשֵׂם לְךָ שָׁלוֹם.

MAY ADONAI bless you and watch over you. May Adonai shine upon you and be gracious to you. May Adonai look toward you and grant you peace.

SUGGESTION

Even if you are not at home with your parents, or your children are away for Passover, try to call before the holiday to receive a blessing from your parents or bestow blessings upon your children. This allows a personal con-nection with family even if you are not physically connected for the holiday.

The Order of the Seder

*The person conducting the Seder opens with the following explanation
of the order — which is what the Hebrew word* seder *means — of the
Passover night service.
(This is especially helpful if anyone at your table may be unfamiliar with
what is going to unfold.
It is also a good time to explain the Seder plate.)
It is customary to have a communal chanting of the Order of the Seder.*

KADESH	Inaugurate the festival over wine	קַדֵּשׁ
UR'CHATZ	Wash your hands without saying a blessing	וּרְחַץ
KARPAS	Eat vegetables dipped in saltwater	כַּרְפַּס
YACHATZ	Split the middle matzah	יַחַץ
MAGGID	Recite the Haggadah	מַגִּיד
RACHTZAH	Wash your hands and say the blessing	רָחְצָה
MOTZI-MATZAH	Say the Motzi and Matzah blessings over the matzah (the Matzah blessing is only said at the Seder)	מוֹצִיא-מַצָּה
MAROR	Eat the bitter herb	מָרוֹר
KORECH	Eat the bitter-herb sandwich	כּוֹרֵךְ
SHULCHAN ORECH	Eat the festival meal	שֻׁלְחָן עוֹרֵךְ
TZAFUN	Eat the afikomen	צָפוּן
BARECH	Say the Grace after Meals	בָּרֵךְ
HALLEL	Chant the Hallel praise and thanksgiving Psalms	הַלֵּל
NIRTZAH	Pray that God accept our supplications and prayer.	נִרְצָה

LEADER: As we begin our Seder with the recitation of Kiddush, which proclaims the holiness of this holiday, we express our gratitude to God for the opportunity to join with family and friends, dear ones and loved ones for this unique holiday feast. We are all grateful to be together to celebrate this special religious celebration of freedom. (We recall with love those family members and friends who are no longer with us. The holes in our hearts remain, yet the memory of their lives fills the void within us along with the impact of their lasting good deeds and good name.)

As this is an evening devoted to remembering the great national experience that the Jewish people had in leaving Egypt, we are ever mindful of what the rabbis teach us — we too must feel as if we were freed from Egypt. As we are about to embark on this unique spiritual, intellectual, and culinary experience this evening, may we use this occasion to renew our connection to the great moment of our liberation from Egypt. May it be a time to renew our commitment to our faith, tradition, and community.

We are all grateful to be together to celebrate this special religious celebration of freedom.

The rituals and foods at the Seder are designed to pique the curiosity of the children and prompt them to ask questions.

REFLECTION

One of the features of the Seder is the importance of four. We have four cups of wine based on the four Torah verses connected to the Exodus, four questions comprise the Mah Nishtanah, and four children are described in the text.

REFLECTION

The rituals and foods at the Seder are designed to pique the curiosity of the children and prompt them to ask questions. The fifteen steps at a Seder give order to the Haggadah. We start with the blessing over the wine and proceed to washing our hands without a blessing, dipping a vegetable in salt water and eating it, breaking the middle matzah for the afikomen, telling the exodus story, washing our hands with a blessing and eating matzah, eating bitter herbs dipped in charoset, eating a "Hillel sandwich" consisting of bitter herbs dipped in charoset and chazeret on matzah, the festive meal, grace after meals, recitation of praise for God, and the concluding blessing and songs.

REFLECTION

The Exodus from Egypt took place thousands of years ago. The Seder is meant to make that historic experience real and visceral. And yet, we have no firsthand survivors to tell us what it was like to toil at backbreaking slave labor in Egypt, facing death every day, or the fear of standing at the shore of the Sea of Reeds with the Egyptian army pursuing from behind and the water in front. In our modern lifetime, tragically we see millions who are still enslaved, who every day seek freedom to live and freedom to practice their faith and thousands who have had to flee, seeking refuge elsewhere. Within the Jewish world, we still have within our midst the dwindling number of witnesses who survived modern genocide – the Holocaust. We can encounter thousands who survived spiritual enslavement in the former Soviet Union. Or those who escaped Ethiopia to seek their brothers and sisters in Israel. It behooves us, then, on this night of historic remembrance, to hear their stories of survival. How did Holocaust survivors experience Passover within the darkness of Auschwitz? How did Russian Jews observe Passover when the observance of any mitzvah was a crime punishable by years in prison, and neighbors were always waiting to inform? What was it like to flee Ethiopia or North Africa, traveling over deserts with insufficient water at the mercy of smugglers always willing to take advantage of weary and vulnerable travelers?

*See pp. 213–14 for songs "There's No Seder Like Our Seder,"
"Our Passover Things," "The Order of the Seder," and "We Didn't Start the Seder"*

KIDS' CORNER

Here's a song to help children remember what's on the Seder plate, sung to the tune of "Ninety-Nine Barrels of Beer": "Maror in the middle, Pesach at the top, zeroa, charoset, chazeret and karpas."

REFLECTION

The nineteenth-century rabbi Yechiel Epstein was concerned that the custom of each guest pouring for each other would lead to wives being exploited to only pour wine for their husbands. Instead, he suggested that everyone pour the wine for himself or herself. A good way to avoid this potential problem is to make sure that both the hosts and guests pour for their other guests, and in the case of husbands and wives, they pour for each other.[29]

REFLECTION

Passover is a time when we remember those who are in need and strive to help them in a way that also preserves the recipient's dignity. A man once came to see the Beis Halevi, the nineteenth-century rabbi Yosef Dov Soloveitchik, on the eve of Passover. He asked the rabbi if it was permissible for him to use four cups of milk at the Seder instead of four cups of wine. Rabbi Soloveitchik asked why the man would want to use milk. Was he ill? The man replied that he just couldn't afford to buy wine. Rabbi Soloveitchik responded by giving the man twenty-five rubles. When the man left, the rabbi's wife asked Rabbi Soloveitchik why he'd given him so much money when two or three rubles would have been sufficient for wine. Rabbi Soloveitchik replied that if the man had to ask if he could use milk at the Seder, it meant he also didn't have enough money for matzah and meat and fish...[30]

Passover is a time when we remember those who are in need and strive to help them in a way that also preserves the recipient's dignity.

One of the unusual features of the Seder is the requirement that each participant must drink four cups of wine.

Questions for Discussion

Why don't we recite a blessing over the recitation of the Haggadah?

On the one hand it would seem that we don't because a Seder has no fixed length and its scope is not defined. It would then seem inappropriate to make a formal blessing as we do before we drink or eat.

On the other hand, it seems that we do – when we make Kiddush. At that moment, we are recognizing the central theme of the Seder: God liberating us from Egypt. Thus, when we make Kiddush, it can give extra meaning and sanctity to the blessing over the wine.

Reflection

One of the unusual features of the Seder is the requirement that each participant must drink four cups of wine. Normally one may fulfill one's obligation for Kiddush by listening to the leader. Here at the Seder, each of the four cups is a distinctive mitzvah that requires all participants to join in each of the blessings and drink as much of a cup of wine as possible. What also makes Passover different from Friday nights and other holidays is that beyond recalling the Exodus from Egypt in the Kiddush, on Passover we are required to go beyond that and tell the story, in addition to remembering it.

Furthermore, unlike at a Sabbath meal or other holiday meal, we don't begin by ritually washing our hands and then eating bread or matzah. Instead we will wait till much later during the course of the Seder to make the blessing over the matzah.

Suggestion

Ask one of your guests to pour the water for Kos Miriam and invite everyone to sing "Miriam Haneviah" to the melody of "Eliyahu Hanavi."

Miriam Haneviah

Miriam Haneviah, im hanashim	מִרְיָם הַנְּבִיאָה עִם
rakdah. Miriam shirah,	הַנָּשִׁים רַקְדָה
limdah otanu. bimheirah	מִרְיָם שִׁירָה לִמְדָה אוֹתָנוּ.
b'yameinu, nizkeh l'mayim	בִּמְהֵרָה בְּיָמֵינוּ נִזְכֶּה
chayim, mayim chayim	לְמַיִם חַיִּים
mi'be'erah.	מַיִם חַיִּים מִבְּאֵרָהּ.

Miriam the Prophetess led the women in a dance.

Miriam the Prophetess led the women in a dance. Miriam sang to us, taught us. Speedily, soon in our day, may we merit to drink from the living waters drawn from her well.

REFLECTION

As we pour a cup to honor Miriam, reflect on any heroic women and men who have made a difference in your life.

KIDS' CORNER

Go around the table and ask children if they can think of other categories of four in Jewish or general tradition. (Some examples: four *tzitzit* [ritual fringes], four seasons of the year, four corners of the earth.)

KIDS' CORNER

Have you ever heard of a chocolate Seder? One way to reward children at the Seder is to give out a tiny chocolate bar with each cup of wine. By the end of the Seder, the kids will have four bars (or maybe not!) – a good treat to spread over the holiday!

Kadesh: Recitation of the Kiddush

Each guest should pour the first cup of wine for his or her neighbor. Creating the impression that each of us has a butler or personal sommelier to care for us evokes a sense of aristocracy and nobility and adds to the special nature of the evening.

Everybody stands. Recite the Kiddush and shehecheyanu *holding the cup in the upraised palm of the right hand. (If it is Saturday night, the* shehecheyanu *is said after the Havdalah prayer. Those who said it at candle lighting should not repeat this blessing.) Some begin with this:*

FIRST CUP

Hineni muchan u-mezuman l'kayem	הִנְנִי מוּכָן וּמְזוּמָּן לְקַיֵּם
mitzvat kos rishon me'arba	מִצְוַת כּוֹס רִאשׁוֹן מֵאַרְבַּע
kosot. L'shem yichud kudsha	כּוֹסוֹת. לְשֵׁם יִחוּד קוּדְשָׁא
brich hu u-shechinteh al	בְּרִיךְ הוּא וּשְׁכִינְתֵּיהּ עַל
yedei hahu tamir v'neelam	יְדֵי הַהוּא טָמִיר וְנֶעֱלָם
b'shem kol Yisrael.	בְּשֵׁם כָּל יִשְׂרָאֵל.

Here I am ready and willing to fulfill the mitzvah of drinking the first of the four cups of wine, as is the will of the Holy One.

On Friday night, begin here.

Vay'hi erev vay'hi voker yom	וַיְהִי עֶרֶב וַיְהִי בֹקֶר יוֹם
hashi-shi. Vay'chulu hashamayim	הַשִּׁשִּׁי, וַיְכֻלּוּ הַשָּׁמַיִם
v'ha-aretz v'chol-tzva-am. Vay'chal	וְהָאָרֶץ וְכָל-צְבָאָם: וַיְכַל
Elohim bayom hashvi-i,	אֱלֹהִים בַּיּוֹם הַשְּׁבִיעִי,
m'lachto asher asah, vayishbot	מְלַאכְתּוֹ אֲשֶׁר עָשָׂה, וַיִּשְׁבֹּת
bayom hashvi-i, mikol-	בַּיּוֹם הַשְּׁבִיעִי, מִכָּל-
mlachto asher asah. Vay'vareich	מְלַאכְתּוֹ אֲשֶׁר עָשָׂה: וַיְבָרֶךְ
Elohim, et-yom hashvi-i,	אֱלֹהִים אֶת-יוֹם הַשְּׁבִיעִי,

vay'kadeish oto, ki vo shavat mikol-

mlachto, asher-bara Elohim la-asot.

וַיְקַדֵּשׁ אֹתוֹ, כִּי בוֹ שָׁבַת מִכָּל-

מְלַאכְתּוֹ, אֲשֶׁר-בָּרָא אֱלֹהִים לַעֲשׂוֹת:

And there was evening and there was morning, the sixth day. Heaven and earth were completed, and all they contain. On the seventh day, God completed all the work that God had been doing, and blessed the seventh day and declared it holy, because on it God desisted from all the work of creation that God had done (Bereishit 1:31–2:3).

On weekday nights, begin here.

Savri maranan v'rabanan

v'rabotai, ug'virotai.

סַבְרִי מָרָנָן וְרַבָּנָן

וְרַבּוֹתַי וּגְבִירוֹתַי.

Attention, our masters and teachers and gentlemen and ladies.

Baruch Atah Adonai, Eloheinu Melech

ha-olam, Borei p'ri hagafen.

בָּרוּךְ אַתָּה יְיָ, אֱלֹהֵינוּ מֶלֶךְ

הָעוֹלָם, בּוֹרֵא פְּרִי הַגָּפֶן:

Blessed are You, Adonai, our God, Ruler of the universe, Creator of the fruit of the vine.

(The passages in parentheses are said only on Friday night.)

Baruch Atah Adonai, Eloheinu Melech

ha-olam, asher bachar banu mikol-am,

v'rom'manu mikol-lashon, v'kid'shanu

b'mitzvotav, vatiten-lanu Adonai

Eloheinu b'ahavah (*On Friday night

add:* Shabatot limnuchah u)moadim

l'simchah, chagim uz'manim l'sason

et-yom (*On Friday night add:* ha-

בָּרוּךְ אַתָּה יְיָ, אֱלֹהֵינוּ מֶלֶךְ

הָעוֹלָם, אֲשֶׁר בָּחַר בָּנוּ מִכָּל-עָם,

וְרוֹמְמָנוּ מִכָּל-לָשׁוֹן, וְקִדְּשָׁנוּ

בְּמִצְוֹתָיו, וַתִּתֶּן-לָנוּ יְיָ אֱלֹהֵינוּ

בְּאַהֲבָה (שַׁבָּתוֹת לִמְנוּחָה וּ)

מוֹעֲדִים לְשִׂמְחָה, חַגִּים וּזְמַנִּים

לְשָׂשׂוֹן אֶת-יוֹם (הַשַּׁבָּת הַזֶּה

וְאֶת-יוֹם) חַג הַמַּצּוֹת הַזֶּה. זְמַן

Shabat hazeh v'et-yom) Chag Hamatzot	חֵרוּתֵנוּ, (בְּאַהֲבָה,)
hazeh. Z'man cheiruteinu, (On Friday	מִקְרָא קֹדֶשׁ, זֵכֶר
night add: b'ahavah,) mikra kodesh,	לִיצִיאַת מִצְרָיִם. כִּי
zeicher litzi-at Mitzrayim. Ki vanu	בָנוּ בָחַרְתָּ וְאוֹתָנוּ
vacharta v'otanu kidashta mikol-ha-	קִדַּשְׁתָּ מִכָּל־הָעַמִּים.
amim. (On Friday night add: v'Shabat)	(וְשַׁבָּת) וּמוֹעֲדֵי קָדְשֶׁךָ
umo'adei kod'shecha (On Friday night	(בְּאַהֲבָה וּבְרָצוֹן)
add: b'ahavah uv'ratzon) b'simchah	בְּשִׂמְחָה וּבְשָׂשׂוֹן
uv'sason hinchaltanu. Baruch Atah	הִנְחַלְתָּנוּ: בָּרוּךְ אַתָּה
Adonai, m'kadeish (On Friday night add:	יְיָ, מְקַדֵּשׁ (הַשַׁבָּת וְ)
haShabat v') Yisra-eil v'hazmanim.	יִשְׂרָאֵל וְהַזְּמַנִּים:

Blessed are You, Adonai, our God, Ruler of the universe, Who chose us and exalted us and sanctified us with Your commandments. And lovingly You gave us, Adonai, our God, (Sabbaths for rest and) set times for celebration, festivals and occasions for rejoicing, this (Sabbath day and this) Matzot Festival, and this holiday, this holy convocation, the occasion of our liberation (with love): a holy convocation in remembrance of the Exodus from Egypt. Indeed, You chose us and sanctified us from among all the peoples, (and Sabbaths) and Your holy set times (lovingly and gladly,) happily and joyously did You bequeath to us. Blessed are You, Adonai, Who sanctifies (the Sabbath and) Israel and the festivals.

(If the Seder takes place on Saturday night, add the following two blessings.)

Baruch Atah Adonai, Eloheinu	בָּרוּךְ אַתָּה יְיָ, אֱלֹהֵינוּ
Melech ha-olam, Borei	מֶלֶךְ הָעוֹלָם, בּוֹרֵא
m'orei ha-eish.	מְאוֹרֵי הָאֵשׁ:

Blessed are You, Adonai, our God, Ruler of the universe, Creator of the lights of fire.

Baruch Atah Adonai, Eloheinu Melech ha-olam, hamavdil bein kodesh l'chol bein or l'choshech, bein Yisra-eil la-amim, bein yom hashvi-i l'sheishet y'mei hama-aseh. Bein k'dushat Shabat likdushat yom tov hivdalta. V'et-yom hashvi-i misheishet y'mei hama-aseh kidashta. Hivdalta v'kidashta et-am'cha Yisra-eil bikdushatecha. Baruch Atah Adonai, hamavdil bein kodesh l'kodesh.

בָּרוּךְ אַתָּה יְיָ, אֱלֹהֵינוּ מֶלֶךְ הָעוֹלָם, הַמַּבְדִּיל בֵּין קֹדֶשׁ לְחֹל בֵּין אוֹר לְחֹשֶׁךְ, בֵּין יִשְׂרָאֵל לָעַמִּים, בֵּין יוֹם הַשְּׁבִיעִי לְשֵׁשֶׁת יְמֵי הַמַּעֲשֶׂה. בֵּין קְדֻשַּׁת שַׁבָּת לִקְדֻשַּׁת יוֹם טוֹב הִבְדַּלְתָּ. וְאֶת- יוֹם הַשְּׁבִיעִי מִשֵּׁשֶׁת יְמֵי הַמַּעֲשֶׂה קִדַּשְׁתָּ. הִבְדַּלְתָּ וְקִדַּשְׁתָּ אֶת-עַמְּךָ יִשְׂרָאֵל בִּקְדֻשָּׁתֶךָ. בָּרוּךְ אַתָּה יְיָ, הַמַּבְדִּיל בֵּין קֹדֶשׁ לְקֹדֶשׁ:

Blessed are You, Adonai, our God, Ruler of the universe, Who distinguishes between the holy and the mundane, between light and darkness, between Israel and the other peoples, between the seventh day and the six workdays. You have distinguished between the sanctity of the Sabbath and holiday sanctity, and the seventh day You declared holy above the six workdays. You set apart and hallowed Your people, Israel, with Your holiness. Blessed are You, Adonai, Who distinguishes between one sanctity and another sanctity.

The following blessing is always said:

Baruch Atah Adonai, Eloheinu Melech ha-olam, shehecheyanu v'ki'manu v'higi-anu laz'man hazeh.

בָּרוּךְ אַתָּה יְיָ אֱלֹהֵינוּ מֶלֶךְ הָעוֹלָם שֶׁהֶחֱיָנוּ וְקִיְּמָנוּ וְהִגִּיעָנוּ לַזְּמַן הַזֶּה.

Blessed are You, Adonai, our God, Ruler of the universe, for keeping us alive, and sustaining us, and enabling us to reach this occasion.

Drink the first cup, reclining to the left.

BACKGROUND

The Use of Grape Juice at the Seder

Can we substitute grape juice for all or part of the four cups drunk at the Seder? During Prohibition in the 1920s and early 1930s, this question became particularly relevant as well as controversial. In the non-Orthodox world, Professor Louis Ginzberg of the Jewish Theological Seminary was disturbed by reports of abuse by bootleggers and bogus rabbis who relied on the sacramental wine exemption given to Jews and religious institutions (for the right to use wine for ritual purposes). In January 1922, he wrote a rabbinic responsa validating the use of grape juice.[31]

In response, he received threatening letters from those angry that this could impact their illegal alcohol smuggling. His wife feared for his life and did not want him going out at night alone.[32]

A contemporary question on the use of grape juice in Catholic ritual was once asked by a priest and resolved by a rabbi! Rabbi Dr. Abraham J. Twerski, a renowned psychiatrist and Chasidic rabbi, directed a substance abuse clinic in Pittsburgh, Pennsylvania. After successfully treating a priest who suffered

from alcoholism, Rabbi Twerski was approached by the priest with the following question: How was he to lead Mass if he could no longer drink wine? Dr. Twerski told him to substitute grape juice. But the priest protested that it contravened canon law. He asked Rabbi Twerski to talk to the head of the diocese, which he did. When the head of the diocese asked him on what this was based, Rabbi Twerski replied that it was a great rabbinic decisor, Rabbi Moshe Feinstein, who wrote the decision allowing unfermented wine for Sabbath use. (Rabbi Feinstein, however, required on Passover that a little wine be mixed into grape juice to fulfill the Jewish legal obligation of "*derech cherut*" – the path to freedom/aristocracy.)[33] This information was sent off to the Vatican, and a short time later the priest was informed that based on Rabbi Feinstein's reasoning and Rabbi Twerski's intervention, an acceptable form of grape juice would be considered a legitimate substitute for wine!

REFLECTION

When the Seder falls on a Saturday night, to help us with the "order" of Kiddush and Havdalah (the prayer we make to separate Shabbat from the rest of the week, including a festival) a mnemonic was devised called Yaknehaz (*yud, kuf, nun, heh, zayin*). It stands for *yayin* (wine), Kiddush, *ner* (candle), Havdalah, and *zman* (time, i.e., the blessing on time, *shehecheyanu*). We make Kiddush and then Havdalah (we turn to the lit holiday candles or any light source in the room), skip the blessing over the spices, and then make the *shehecheyanu*. In some medieval Ashkenazic Haggadot, we can find pictures of a scene of hunters and hares – the German term for hare hunt is *jag den Has* (hunt the hare), which is quite similar to the mnemonic of Yaknehaz.

REFLECTION

When Shabbat precedes or marks the end of the first day of a festival, we don't use spices at Havdalah when we mark the conclusion of Shabbat. Ordinarily when the Sabbath concludes, our spirits sag and we use spices to revive the *neshamah* (soul) to face the coming week. But when a festival follows, our hearts remain in a happy state, and we don't need that extra spark of spices.

Ur'chatz: Handwashing without a Blessing

Pour water from a washing cup over each hand three times without saying a blessing.

REFLECTION

One reason we wash without a blessing is that in the time of the Temple, people were required to ritually wash their hands prior to eating any vegetable or fruit that came in contact with water. There is a question as to whether this is still required, however, and we do not make a blessing when there are rabbinic authorities who differ in whether or not to make a blessing. This is based on the rule of *safek b'rachot l'hakel* (when in doubt, we skip the blessing so as not to take God's name in vain). Another purpose for this is that it serves to arouse the curiosity of the children present.

Could this ritual also be a reminder to practice good hygiene? To quote an old saying, "Cleanliness is next to godliness!"

QUESTIONS FOR DISCUSSION

Are there certain foods we should "wash our hands of," if they were procured in an unethical manner (for example, unfair labor conditions)? In the Talmud we find concern not only with what goes into our mouths but the manner in which food comes to our tables.

REFLECTION

The nineteenth-century rabbi Israel Salanter was visiting a matzah bakery to check on its *kashrut*. Witnessing the deplorable working conditions, he said he would declare all the matzah non-kosher for Passover if the working conditions for the matzah bakers didn't improve. "What have I done wrong?" the owner protested. Rabbi Salanter's answer was that there was blood in the food. "Blood! Where is the blood?" protested the owner incredulously. "Your sense of efficiency, together with the unacceptable

Use this moment to reflect on those who are not yet free and hope for their redemption.

demands placed upon your workers, shows that their blood is mixed into the food produced in this bakery," Rabbi Salanter answered. Even though there wasn't actual blood mixed into the matzah, Rabbi Salanter would not certify its *kashrut*.[34]

In contemporary times, rabbis have debated whether external issues can also affect the *kashrut* of animals and products. For example, should a certificate of ethical *kashrut* be required, to confirm that animals were treated humanely prior to slaughter or that workers in factories or restaurants were treated ethically? Should eco or ethical *kashrut* standards be a factor in the acceptability of what we eat?

In the late 1960s, numerous rabbinic organizations in a variety of cities declared California grapes non-kosher because of the conditions related to their picking (due to *oshek*, the exploitation and abuse of workers.)[35] More recently, the Orthodox organization Uri L'Tzedek has given out ethical certificates (Tav HaYosher) to restaurants and kosher food establishments that treat their workers with proper labor standards.

Karpas: Dipping in Salt Water

LEADER: If the green of the parsley evokes the hope of spring and redemption, the salt water we dip it in is to remind us of the tears shed at the pain, bitterness, and hardship of our slavery in Egypt. We also can use this moment to pause and reflect on those in our own time who are not yet free and hope for their redemption.

If you planted parsley on Tu b'Shevat, use it here. If you are eating eggs, make the blessing shehakol. *Dip your vegetable of choice into saltwater and say the following blessing before eating:*

Baruch Atah Adonai, Eloheinu Melech

ha-olam, Borei p'ri ha-adamah.

בָּרוּךְ אַתָּה יְיָ, אֱלֹהֵינוּ מֶלֶךְ

הָעוֹלָם, בּוֹרֵא פְּרִי הָאֲדָמָה:

Blessed are You, Adonai, our God, Ruler of the universe, Creator of the fruit of the soil.

(Ashkenazic Jews follow the custom described in the Shulchan Aruch *to dip the karpas into salt water. Sephardic and Yemenite Jews follow Maimonides, who said karpas should be dipped into charoset. We make sure to have in mind that this blessing includes the maror we will eat later.)*

SUGGESTION

When eating the vegetables, have in mind that the blessing recited is also to cover the eating of the maror later in the Seder. According to some authorities (such as Maimonides), one should eat just under a *k'zayit* – a quantity about the size of one-third of an egg. Eating a larger amount would necessitate making an after-blessing. Other rabbinic decisors, such as the Rosh and the Rashbam, indicate that one may eat a larger quantity, since more vegetables will be eaten later. If that is your tradition, then go ahead and treat this course as the opening hors d'oeuvres – but remember to leave room to heartily eat matzah later! (Some suggestions: celery, carrots, potatoes, roasted peppers, bananas, kosher for Passover Terra Chips. Some people choose to dip eggs into salt water at this point in the Seder, which would require one to make the *shehakol* blessing and an after blessing.[36])

BACKGROUND

What We Dip and Why

Dipping foods has a historic precedent from Roman times, when it was customary to begin a meal with hors d'oeuvres of vegetables. We begin our Seder with dipping vegetables not merely as a gastronomic choice mimicking a popular Roman tradition, but as an act with a blessing imbued with the memory and meaning of slavery. In addition to parsley or celery, many people have the custom of dipping and eating boiled potatoes. Potatoes have a long Jewish historical connection. A staple in the Jewish diet, they have been immortalized in song (a Yiddish song tells of those who eat *bulbes* [potatoes] every day) and in many ways represent, like the Jewish people, a host of symbols, from their use in latkes at Chanukah, a joyous and happy time of triumph and victory, to the bitter period of

Have in mind that the blessing recited is also to cover the eating of the maror later in the Seder.

Dipping foods has a historic precedent from Roman times, when it was customary to begin a meal with hors d'oeuvres of vegetables.

the Holocaust, in death camps, when many Jews only had potato scraps in watery soup to eat. In fact, for many years after their liberation from the Bergen-Belsen concentration camp, the association of Bergen-Belsen survivors held an annual dinner. My parents attended the dinner annually and told me that at the center of the elegant hotel dining room, the survivors had placed a table filled with potato peels as a reminder of the food eaten during the dark and bitter days of the Holocaust.

We dip the vegetables into salt water to recall the tears of our ancestors as they suffered and died enslaved in Egypt. This is, then, a propitious moment to recall the tears of those throughout time and even in the contemporary era who have faced enslavement, deprivation, and oppression. During the Holocaust, many Jews performed backbreaking slave labor. One Czechoslovakian Jewish woman, Mrs. Gloria Lyon, worked in the salt mines as a slave laborer for the V-2 rocket project. Eventually she was liberated, recuperated in Switzerland, and moved to the United States, where she married and had a family. In 1987, the East German government contacted survivors who had worked there to pay one last visit before they intended to close the mine. (Due to protests from survivors, in the end it remained open as a museum.) Mrs. Lyon made the journey, and when she was in the mine, a German engineer broke off a large piece of salt, which he gave to her. Every year at the Seder she has made it her tradition to use some of that salt for the salt water that they dip the vegetable into.[37] Another survivor, when liberated from a death camp, ran into the dining room of the SS and took two spoons that had the insignia on them. Many years later she gave one spoon to her son and one to her rabbi. She said she took the spoons as a booty, akin to the Jews who left Egypt with booty – but more importantly she took them as a memory of her enslavement. She asked that the spoons be used to serve the maror and charoset at the Seder.

SUGGESTION

Put potato peels on a plate on the Seder table as a visceral reminder of those in recent history who were enslaved and marked for death.

REFLECTION

Who is enslaved today? According to the International Labor Organization, a conservative estimate of the total number of enslaved people worldwide is twenty-one million. Others estimate the number of slaves worldwide to be over forty million! In addition, millions of people worldwide go hungry every day. According to the World Food Program and the US State Department, about 815 million people worldwide are chronically undernourished, and 160 million children under five are stunted due to undernourishment. In the United States, over forty-one million people live in food-insecure homes. Food insecurity is a fancy way of saying people – many of whom are children – go to bed, wake up, and go to school hungry.

Within the United States, concern has grown over the treatment of farm workers who harvest fruits and vegetables. While the tomato industry has reformed its policies, many other farm industries continue abusive labor practices. According to a 2015 Tulane University study for the US Department of Labor, twelve thousand child slaves and over two million children perform dangerous labor in the Ivory Coast and Ghana growing cocoa and harvesting it. Seder night then is an opportune moment to recall modern-day cases of worker exploitation, with some suggesting we place a tomato or a coffee bean on the table to recall the oppression and liberation of farm workers and the hope for fair trade labor practices.[38]

We also call to mind the following people who are enduring forms of enslavement:

- the many women sold as sex slaves in human trafficking across the world
- *agunot*, women whose husbands refuse to grant them a Jewish divorce and who remain chained, unable to marry again until they are freed
- refugees forced to flee and be on the run

All of these situations remind us that freedom is still elusive for so many and serve as a call to action not to be indifferent bystanders but involved activists. For example, in Israel, hundreds of Syrians injured during the Syrian civil war were taken across the border for medical care, despite an official state of war between Israel and Syria.[39]

REFLECTION

As we continue with our freedom feast, we should have in mind at this time the memory of our ancestor Joseph. Karpas, the Hebrew word for the vegetable we dip, can also be an abbreviation for *ketonet pasim* – the coat

of many colors that Joseph wore. We see a hint of this in Rashi, the biblical commentator who looks at the term *ketonet pasim* (Genesis 37:3) as a garment of fine wool, *karpas u-t'chelet* (Esther 1:6). The brothers sold Joseph into slavery and led their father Jacob to believe that a wild animal had killed Joseph by showing him their brother's coat, which they had dipped into the blood of an animal. That first "dipping" led to the odyssey of Joseph's coming down to Egypt and subsequent Jewish enslavement.

Joseph came to Egypt as a slave, yet he emerged as a free man, reunited with his father Jacob and his brothers. When the Jews left Egypt after years of slavery, they remembered to take with them Joseph's bones to be buried in Israel.[40]

Yachatz: Breaking the Middle Matzah

The leader takes the middle matzah and breaks it in half. The smaller piece, representing lechem oni, poor person's bread, is put back for later consumption, and the larger piece, which symbolizes the Korban Pesach, is wrapped up for the afikomen (which we will save for dessert). It is customary for the leader to hide the afikomen for the children to search for and when found, redeem for a prize. (If using envelopes containing the paper afikomen [see p. 10], hide them as well.)

LEADER: As we break the middle matzah, we are reminded of the unusual dichotomy of the Seder. This matzah represents both the bread of affliction and the bread of freedom — one of suffering and one of redemption. Yet we view both of these pieces as one cohesive matzah. As we look at our community, let us dedicate this step of the Seder to the hope that we can surmount the fractures and fissures in our community. On Seder night, may we be inspired to overcome our differences so that we can say of our Jewish community what the rabbis expressed was the feeling at the foot of Mount Sinai as we stood to receive the Torah: all Jews stood *k'ish echad b'lev echad*, as one person with one heart.

REFLECTION

Having three pieces of matzah accommodates the view that we have a broken matzah to reflect "poor man's bread" (Rashi) while simultaneously fulfilling the festival requirement to have two whole matzot (Tosafot).

SUGGESTION

Have guests follow Sephardic custom and "act out" walking around with the afikomen over their shoulders. If you prepared knapsacks, guests might use them now. Here is a suggested script for guests to say: *Where are we coming from? Egypt! Where are we going to? Eretz Yisrael!* This is based on Maimonides' reading of *liharot* (see p. 115), we are required to demonstrate our leaving Egypt.

See p. 214 for song "Don't Sit on the Afikomen"

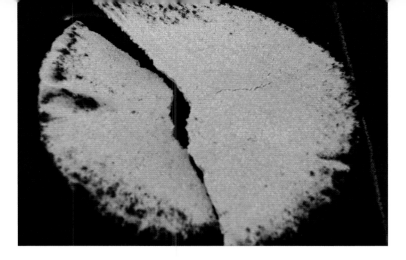

REFLECTION

The rabbis have commented that through this act we can understand the concept of matzah as *lechem oni* (poor person's bread), for only a poor person would save bread for later. Maimonides also points out that sharing one's food with those who are hungry differentiates rejoicing from mere gluttony (which was a central feature of Roman banquets).

HUMOR CORNER

Do you know how the Jews were really able to leave Egypt? Pharaoh announced that he would free the Jewish people if any Jew could win a debate. Everyone was afraid to volunteer except for Shmuel the tailor. Pharaoh told Shmuel the Jews would be free to leave if he refuted three points. If not, they would remain as slaves in Egypt.

Shmuel agreed. Pharaoh held up two fingers and Shmuel pointed with one finger. Next Pharaoh pointed to the sky. Shmuel the tailor pointed to the ground. Finally Pharaoh took out a piece of matzah. Shmuel the tailor then took out a hard-boiled egg. At this point, Pharaoh announced that the Jews were free to leave! Pharaoh's advisors crowded around him and said, "Your Majesty, why did you release the Jews? Did that man really win the debate?"

Pharaoh sadly shook his head and said yes. "You see, I held up two fingers to show that there at least two gods in this world. Shmuel the tailor held up one to say there is only one god – the God of the Hebrews. Next, I pointed to heaven to show that our destiny is totally predestined above. Shmuel the tailor pointed to the ground, reminding us that God created us but has given us free choice on earth to act. Finally I took out a piece of matzah to show that the world is flat. Shmuel took out an egg to disprove that – the world is really round." Pharaoh's advisors sadly shook their heads.

Shmuel the tailor returned and his friends came running, having heard the news. "How did you trump Pharaoh?" they asked with disbelief. "Well," said Shmuel, "it was easy. Pharaoh held up two fingers to say, 'I will poke your eyes out.' I am a proud Jew who won't take that kind of abuse, so I held up one finger to say, 'If you do, I will poke you in the belly.' Next he pointed a finger to heaven to say that was where he was going at the end of days. I pointed down to say, 'You are headed straight for Gehinnom (Hell).' Finally,

he took out a piece of matzah. I figured, if he's going to have lunch, so will I, so I took out my egg…"

REFLECTION

What is the origin of "stealing the afikomen"? The source for this can be found in the Talmud. In *Pesachim* 109a, Rabbi Elazar teaches us to "snatch" matzah on Passover nights so that the small children will not fall asleep. It reminds us that they should try to be kept awake to hear the entire story – not just of our suffering but of the Exodus from Egypt and hope for the ultimate redemption.

Maggid: Recounting the Exodus

LEADER: We dedicate this section, Maggid, to the importance of telling and retelling our story, to asking questions and to making those who feel alienated realize they have a home in our community. May we dedicate ourselves to inspiring those around us to see the beauty of our heritage and to reinspiring ourselves so that the story is ever new.

This is the invitation for all to join in the Seder. The matzot are uncovered and the leader lifts the Seder plate while all participants collectively recite the opening paragraph. This is the first explanation of the purpose of matzah at the Seder.

Ha Lachma Anya

Lift the Seder tray and say:

Ha lachma anya di achalu

avhatana b'ara d'Mitzrayim. Kol

dichfin yeitei v'yeichol, kol ditzrich

yeitei v'yifsach. Hashata hacha, l'shanah

haba-ah b'ara d'Yisra-eil. Hashata

avdei, l'shanah haba-ah b'nei chorin.

הָא לַחְמָא עַנְיָא דִּי אֲכָלוּ

אַבְהָתָנָא בְּאַרְעָא דְמִצְרָיִם. כָּל

דִּכְפִין יֵיתֵי וְיֵכוֹל, כָּל דִּצְרִיךְ

יֵיתֵי וְיִפְסַח. הָשַׁתָּא הָכָא, לְשָׁנָה

הַבָּאָה בְּאַרְעָא דְיִשְׂרָאֵל. הָשַׁתָּא

עַבְדֵי, לְשָׁנָה הַבָּאָה בְּנֵי חוֹרִין:

This is the bread of affliction that our ancestors ate in Egypt. Let anyone who is hungry enter and eat; let anyone who is needy enter and join us in our Passover feast. This year we are here; next year may we be in the Land of Israel. This year we are slaves; next year may we be free people.

REFLECTION

The first paragraph of Maggid is written in Aramaic. Some say this is the only part of the Haggadah written in Babylonia, where this was the vernacular of Jews of the time period when the Haggadah was put together. This was an intentional pedagogic decision to make sure everyone would understand it. Others suggest that it was written in Aramaic during the time of the Romans so that non-Jews who did not speak this language would not think the lines that speak of Jews being free next year would assume that an insurrection was at hand.

BACKGROUND

Ha Lachma Anya

Why, prior to *ha lachma anya*, do we lift the Seder plate? In Talmudic times, the custom was for people to recline and eat at small tables. The prevalent custom, as described in the Talmud (*Pesachim* 115b) was to remove from the room the entire table upon which the Seder plate lay. This unusual practice was bound to pique the curiosity of children. In the *Aruch Hashulchan*, Rabbi Epstein explains (Orach Chaim 473) that when our tables became too big, this was no longer practical, and hence we should move the Seder plate from one end of the table to the other end. Today the custom is merely to raise the Seder plate. Some have suggested reclaiming this age-old practice and moving the Seder plate from one end of the table to the other. One year at a Passover spent in a kosher hotel, my family moved for a short while to the lobby and reclined on the sofas, taking the Seder plate with us. It certainly made our children ask a lot of questions.

Much has been written about the fact that this prayer is written in Aramaic and not Hebrew. Being written in the lingua franca of its day is one hint that this prayer was directed to Jews who did not understand Hebrew. Rabbi Zev Schostak explains that normally we invite somebody for a meal before, not after, the Kiddush has been recited. However, based on the commentary of the S'fat Emet, the words "Let all who are hungry come and eat" can mean that we are directing this toward needy non-Jews as well to join us at the Seder. He explains that this interpretation explains why this invitation is extended in the home after Kiddush has been said, and not in the synagogue.[41] The Abravanel teaches that "*ha lachma anya* should be recited at the entrance to the house, with the door open, so that paupers can hear the invitation and enter."-Some had the custom to open their doors and say it out loud to invite in anyone outside who needed a place to eat.[42] Rabbi Jonathan Sacks, former Chief Rabbi of the United Hebrew Congregations

of the Commonwealth (1992–2014), points out the strange invitation conveyed in *ha lachma anya*. How is it hospitable to offer those who are hungry a taste of the "bread of affliction"? Rabbi Sacks explains this as follows: "[M]atza represents two things: it is the food of slaves, and also the bread eaten by the Israelites as they left Egypt in liberty. What transforms the bread of oppression into the bread of freedom is *the willingness to share it with others*.... Sharing food is the first act through which slaves become free human beings. One who fears tomorrow does not offer his bread to others. But one who is will- ing to divide his food with a stranger has already shown himself to be capable of fellow- ship and faith, the two things from which hope is born. That is why we begin the Seder by inviting others to join us. Bread shared is no longer the bread of oppression. Reaching out to others, giving help to the needy and companionship to those who are alone, we bring freedom into the world, and with freedom, God."[43]

The rabbis also have pointed out a linguistic pun, as the word for "poor person," *oni* (in Aramaic *anya*) can also mean "answer," i.e., this is the bread over which we will answer many things.

Mah Nishtanah

BACKGROUND

The Four Questions

Why do we recite these questions? In the Jerusalem Talmud we find three questions similar to what we recite today (referring to why on all other nights we only dip once but tonight we dip twice, why we only eat matzah tonight, but a different third question – why tonight we only eat meats that have been roasted). The question pertaining to reclining is missing. The two dippings reference the memory of the dipping of the hyssops in blood to put on the door and the second dipping of the bitter herbs into the paschal sacrifice; the matzah was then eaten, followed by the Paschal Lamb.

In the Babylonian Talmud we find four questions: why matzah is eaten, why maror is eaten, why only roasted meats, and why food is dipped twice tonight, when on all other nights we don't even dip once. Our text follows the Babylonian Talmud version, except that the roasted meat question was later replaced in the Geonic period (589–1038 CE) with one referring to leaning.

During the time prior to and during the period of the Jerusalem Talmud, Jews in Israel were accustomed to dipping, as the Romans did for an appetizer. By the time of the compilation of the full Babylonian Talmud around the third to sixth centuries CE, Jews no longer followed that custom at all. The difference between the Jerusalem and Babylonian Talmud versions of the Seder questions has been explained as follows: the Jerusalem Talmud is referring to dipping during a meal, while the Babylonian Talmud version is talking about dipping prior to the meal proper, as we do at the Seder.[44]

Why is there no longer a question pertaining to eating roasted meat? After the destruction of the Temple, we could no longer bring and eat the Passover sacrifice. With the sacrificial system no longer operative in post-Temple times, that question was replaced. Yet, if the Mishnah was compiled in post-Temple times, why would that question be in the Mishnah at all? Wouldn't that custom no longer have been taking place?

One scholarly analysis of the Haggadah poses the theory that the eating of a roasted lamb continued for a period even after the Temple was destroyed as a way of remembering the paschal sacrifice. In fact, we find rabbinic texts referencing this in connection with the first-century head of the Sanhedrin (highest Jewish court) Rabban Gamliel, whose teachings we cite at our Seder. Even after the destruction of the Temple, he had the custom of roasting a lamb on Passover eve. He would tell his servant, "Go and roast the Pesach sacrifice."

It could be that in the post-Talmudic age, the rabbis took out any reference to roasted meat for fear of a slippery slope, concerned that even with

the Temple destroyed, some people might be moved to offer the Passover sacrifice. Perhaps if a figure of the stature of Rabban Gamliel were to eat roasted meat, others could be influenced to try to actually offer a forbidden Passover sacrifice, even in the absence of the Temple in Jerusalem.[45]

Since the destruction of the Temple, various efforts have in fact been made to try to reinstitute sacrifices. In the fourteenth century, Rabbi Ishturi Haparchi sought to reinstitute the Passover sacrifice. In the mid-1800s, Rabbi Tzvi Hirsch Kalisher, considered the father of religious Zionism, wrote to Baron de Rothschild not only to obtain his support for the resettling of Israel but also to reinstitute the sacrificial system. Rabbi Kalisher's proposal was opposed by many, including Rabbis Akiva Eiger, Moses Sopher, and Jacob Ettinger.[46] In recent times, the Temple Mount Institute petitioned the Israeli high court to allow their group to bring a Passover sacrifice on the Temple Mount. In 2017, the Israeli Supreme Court allowed a reenactment of the paschal sacrifice to take place in the courtyard of the Hurva Synagogue in the Jewish Quarter.[47] Today, Ashkenazic Jews continue the tradition of not eating roasted meat at the Seder, while Sephardim do eat it.

How did we end up with a question regarding reclining? As the Vilna Gaon points out, in Mishnaic times it was common practice for people to recline while eating, so that would not have caused a child to think anything unusual, and thus there wouldn't be a reason for that question. Once the question concerning roasted meat was omitted, the question regarding reclining was added in the spirit of keeping the pattern of four questions, because by that time (in Babylonia, where the Talmud was put together), reclining was no longer a common practice, and this would then be considered unusual enough to elicit a child's question.

Why are the questions in this order? The Abarbanel notes it would seem to make sense that the questions concerning dipping and reclining should come before the questions pertaining to matzah and maror, because that is the order in which they happen in the Seder. He explains that we have the current order of the questions because they are grouped in pairs, with the first alluding to slavery and the second to freedom. Furthermore, the food we eat is representative of our experience in leaving Egypt. In one night we went from slaves to free people. Here at the Seder we eat the bread of affliction and the bitter herbs, yet we dip our foods and recline in luxury as aristocracy. That alone is enough to elicit questions from children![48]

REFLECTION

The four Mah Nishtanah questions elicit several other questions (a good Jewish tradition, as we know!). How would a child know to ask questions about dipping twice, when only one dipping has occurred, or to ask about matzah and maror, which haven't yet been eaten? Of course we can say that the children remember it from year to year. A historic answer is that in Talmudic times, the meal was consumed first, and after seeing all the unusual things happen at the table, the child would be inclined to ask the questions.

REFLECTION

Why do we dip twice? As we already referenced, the first dipping reminds us of the first dipping of Joseph's coat into blood, which led him to Egypt and the eventual enslavement of the Jews in Egypt. The second dipping is a reminder of the Jews dipping hyssops into blood to put as a sign on their doors to mark Jewish households.

HUMOR CORNER

A rabbi, when asked why Jews always answer a question with a question, responded, "What makes you ask?"

See p. 214–215 for Top Ten Most Popular Jewish Questions and song "Four Questions"

REFLECTION

Why don't we have four questions at other holidays? For example, it would seem natural at Sukkot, when we sit in a sukkah outdoors, that these and other rituals would equally elicit reactions from adults and children. Rabbi Chaim Alfandari provided an answer: for a Jew to leave his home and sit outside in an unstable dwelling, as we do on Sukkot, would not be an unusual experience, because for two thousand years we have been on the run, suffering, wandering, and in exile. But for a Jew to sit at a beautiful table with abundant special food and plentiful wine, now that is an unusual situation that would elicit questions! But he adds that even with all of this, we call Sukkot our holiday of happiness. It reflects the Jewish ability to embrace the paradox of joy and adversity.[49]

QUESTIONS FOR DISCUSSION

What are four key questions that reflect four issues that our community needs to provide answers to?

HUMOR CORNER

A Jewish man was to be knighted by the queen. He was instructed to memorize a few words in Latin that he was to recite when the queen appeared. When the queen came by, he totally forgot what he was supposed to recite and instead the only foreign phrase that popped into his head was the first line of Mah Nishtanah, which he blurted out. Whereupon, the queen turned to one of her ladies in waiting and said, "Why is this knight different from all other knights?!"

REFLECTION

Why are children asked to read these questions? Rabbi Menachem Kasher explains that Pharaoh aimed his decrees specifically against Jewish children.

Moreover, when Pharaoh agreed to release the Jews, he only wanted to send away the adult Jews but not let the children go. When the children read this passage, this is our way of showing that we have frustrated Pharaoh's plans by saying we, the descendants of the Jews enslaved in Egypt and slated for destruction, are here to tell and retell the tale.

KIDS' CORNER

A good game to play is a Passover storytelling memory challenge. Have the youngest child start by saying, "When I left Egypt, I took with me…" The child names one item. Each succeeding person must repeat the previous choices and then add on a new item. Whoever forgets an item is out, until one person is the winner.

REFLECTION

In the Mishnah we are told that the second cup of wine is filled for the leader and then the child asks the father the Mah Nishtanah. If the child does not have enough understanding to do so, the father teaches the child to ask. The filling of the second cup (in itself an unusual event, as we have already made Kiddush over the wine – a child would wonder why the need for a second cup) and the recitation of the four questions are supposed to be an incentive for the child to be prodded into asking multiple questions.

REFLECTION

As my children came home from school, I always asked them (and continue to!), "Did you ask a good question today?" I was inspired by the experience of Isidore Rabi, who won the Nobel Prize in physics. He said he became a scientist because he learned from his mother to ask good questions. How so? Because when he came home from school she never asked him what he had learned that day but rather what questions he had asked![50]

REFLECTION

Today many Jews are alienated from Judaism. What happened to so fundamentally turn them off? Did parents and teachers turn them away when they had doubts? There is an old Yiddish saying: If you ask a question (on something), the thing will be found to be *treif*. Were they made to feel *treif* or inadequate because of the questions they were asking? The prominent role played by the Mah Nishtanah is an important pedagogic lesson: not only never to be afraid to ask questions, but also to be careful and gentle and wise when answering them.

Rabbi Israel Salanter teaches us to encourage children not to fear asking questions. Rather, we should urge them to ask these questions while they are still at home in the loving embrace of their families – when parents and teachers still have the chance to respond, before they are out in the world at large, unable to respond to those who have different and perhaps negative views of Jewish tradition.[51]

*Put the Seder plate down, cover the matzah, and pour
the second cup of wine.*

*The youngest child is called upon to recite the four questions. If there is no
child present, an adult may recite them. Invite any adult or child who speaks
a foreign language to recite the Mah Nishtanah in another language, in
addition to Hebrew.*

Mah nishtanah ha-laylah	מַה נִּשְׁתַּנָּה הַלַּיְלָה
hazeh mikol ha-leilot?	הַזֶּה מִכָּל הַלֵּילוֹת?
(1) Sheb'chol ha-leilot anu	(1) שֶׁבְּכָל הַלֵּילוֹת אָנוּ
och'lin chameitz umatzah.	אוֹכְלִין חָמֵץ וּמַצָּה.
Ha-laylah hazeh kulo matzah.	הַלַּיְלָה הַזֶּה כֻּלּוֹ מַצָּה:
(2) Sheb'chol ha-leilot anu	(2) שֶׁבְּכָל הַלֵּילוֹת אָנוּ
och'lin sh'ar y'rakot.	אוֹכְלִין שְׁאָר יְרָקוֹת
Ha-laylah hazeh maror.	הַלַּיְלָה הַזֶּה מָרוֹר:
(3) Sheb'chol ha-leilot ein anu	(3) שֶׁבְּכָל הַלֵּילוֹת אֵין אָנוּ
matbilin afilu pa-am echat.	מַטְבִּילִין אֲפִילוּ פַּעַם אֶחָת.
Ha-laylah hazeh sh'tei f'amim.	הַלַּיְלָה הַזֶּה שְׁתֵּי פְעָמִים:
(4) Sheb'chol ha-leilot anu och'lin	(4) שֶׁבְּכָל הַלֵּילוֹת אָנוּ אוֹכְלִין
bein yosh'vin uvein m'subin.	בֵּין יוֹשְׁבִין וּבֵין מְסֻבִּין.
Ha-laylah hazeh kulanu m'subin.	הַלַּיְלָה הַזֶּה כֻּלָּנוּ מְסֻבִּין:

Why Is This Night Different?

Why is this night different from all other nights?

(1) Why, on all other nights, do we eat either unleavened bread or matzah,
but tonight we eat only matzah?

(2) Why, on all other nights, do we eat all kinds of vegetables, but tonight
we make a special point of eating bitter herbs?

(3) Why, on all other nights, do we not make a point of dipping at all, but tonight we make a point of dipping twice?

(4) Why, on all other nights, do we eat either sitting up or reclining, but tonight we all make a point of reclining?

Mah Nishtanah in Yiddish

די פֿיר קשיות

טאַטע לעבן, איך וויל בײַ דיר פֿרעגן די פֿיר קשיות:
מה נשתנה הלילה הזה מכל הלילות? פֿאַרוואָס איז די דאָזיקע
נאַכט פֿון פסח אַנדערש פֿון אַלע נעכט פֿון אַ גאַנץ יאָר?

(1) די ערשטע קשיא איז: שבכל הלילות אנו אוכלין חמץ ומצה,
הלילה הזה כולו מצה? אַלע נעכט פֿון אַ גאַנץ יאָר עסן מיר חמץ
אָדער מצה, אָבער די דאָזיקע נאַכט פֿון פסח, עסן מיר נאָר מצה?

(2) די צווייטע קשיא איז: שבכל הלילות אנו אוכלין שאר ירקות,
הלילה הזה מרור? אַלע נעכט פֿון אַ גאַנץ יאָר עסן מיר אַלערליי גרינסן,
אָבער די דאָזיקע נאַכט פֿון פסח, עסן מיר נאָר ביטערע גרינסן?

(3) די דריטע קשיא איז: שבכל הלילות אין אנו מטבילין אפילו פעם אחת,
הלילה הזה שתי פעמים? אַלע נעכט פֿון אַ גאַנץ יאָר טונקען מיר נישט אײַן
אַפֿילו איין מאָל, אָבער די דאָזיקע נאַכט פֿון פסח, טונקען מיר אײַן צוויי
מאָל – איין מאָל כרפס אין זאַלץ וואַסער, און איין מאָל מרור אין חרוסת?

(4) די פֿערטע קשיא איז: שבכל הלילות אנו אוכלין בין יושבין
ובין מסובין, הלילה הזה כולנו מסובין? אַלע נעכט פֿון אַ
גאַנץ יאָר עסן מיר סײַ זיצענדיק און סײַ אָנגעשפּאַרט, אָבער
די דאָזיקע נאַכט פֿון פסח, עסן מיר נאָר אָנגעשפּאַרט?

מײַן ליבער טאַטע, איך האָב בײַ דיר געפֿרעגט די
פֿיר קשיות, יעצט גיב מיר אַ תירוץ.

Di Fir Kashes

Tate lebn, ikh vil bay dir fregn di fir kashes:

Ma nishtano halaylo haze mikol haleyloys? Farvos is di dozike nakht fun
Peysekh andersh fun ale nekht fun a gants yor?

(1) Di ershte kashe iz,
Shebkhol haleyloys onu oykhlin khomets u'matse, halaylo haze kuloy
matse? Ale nekht fun a gants yor esn mir khomets oder matse, ober di
dozike nakht fun Peysekh, esn mir nor matse?

(2) Di tsveyte kashe iz,
Shebkhol haleyloys onu oykhlin sh'ar yerokoys, halaylo haze morer? Ale
nekht fun a gants yor esn mir alerley grinsen, ober di dozike nakht fun
Peysekh, esn mir nor bitere grinsen?

(3) Di drite kashe iz,
Shebkhol haleyloys eyn onu matbilin afile pam ekhos, halaylo haze shtey
p'omim? Ale nekht fun a gants yor tunkn mir nisht ayn afile eyn mol,
ober di dozike nakht fun Peysekh, tunkn mir ayn tsvey mol — eyn mol
karpas in zaltz vasser, un eyn mol morer in khroyses?

(4) Di ferte kashe iz,
Shebkhol haleyloys onu oykhlin beyn yoyshvin uveyn mesubin, halaylo
haze kulanu mesubin? Ale nekht fun a gants yor esn mir say zitsndik
un say ongeshpart, ober di dozike nakht fun Peysekh, esn mir nor
ongeshpart?

Mayn liber tate, ikh hob bay dir gefrekt di fir kashes, yetst gib mir a terets.

MAH NISHTANAH IN LADINO

קוֹאַנְטוֹ פוּאֵי דֵימוּדַאדַה לַה נוֹגֵ׳י לַה אֵיסטַה
מַאס קֵי טוֹדַאס לַאס נוֹגֵ׳יס?

(1) קֵי אֵין טוֹדַאס לַאס נוֹגֵ׳יס נוֹן מוֹס אֵינטִינְיֵנְטֵיס אַפִ׳יל
וֵ בֵ׳יס אוּנַה; אִי לַה נוֹגֵ׳י לַה אֵיסטַה דוֹס בֵ׳יזֵיס?

(2) קֵי אֵין טוֹדַאס לַאס נוֹגֵ׳יס מוֹס קוֹמְיֵינְטֵיס חַמֵץ א
וֹ מַצַה; אִי לַה נוֹגֵ׳י לַה אֵיסטַה טוֹדוּ אֵיל מַצַה?

(3) קֵי אֵין טוֹדַאס לַאס נוֹגֵ׳יס מוֹס קוֹמְיֵינְטֵיס רֵיסטוֹ
וֹ דֵי וֵידְרוּרַאס; אִי לַה נוֹגֵ׳י לַה אֵיסטַה לִיגֵ׳וּגַה?

(4) קֵי אֵין טוֹדַאס לַאס נוֹגֵ׳יס מוֹס קוֹמְיֵינְטֵיס אִי בִּיבֵ׳יֵנְטֵיס קֵין אַסֵינְטַאדוֹס
אִי קֵין אַרֵיסקוֹבֵ׳׳דַאדוֹס; אִי לַה נוֹגֵ׳י לַה אֵיסטַה טוֹדוֹס מוֹס אַרֵיסקוֹבֵ׳׳דַאדוֹס?

Kuanto fue demudada

Kuanto fue demudada la noche la esta mas ke todas las noches?

(1) Ke en todas las noches non mos entinyentes afilu vez una; y la noche la esta dos vezes?

(2) Ke en todas las noches mos komientes hametz o matza; y la noche la esta todo el matza?

(3) Ke en todas las noches mos komientes resto de vedruras; y la noche la esta lichuga?

(4) Ke en todas las noches mos komientes y bvientes ken asentados y ken areskovdados; y la noche la esta todos mos areskovdados?

الأسئلة الأربعة لعيد الفصح اليهودي

بماذا تختلف هذه الليلة عن كل الليالي الأخرى؟

(١ف)في كل الليالي الأخرى، نأكل الخبز المخمّر أو الخبز الفطير، في هذه الليلة فقط نأكلأن
الخبز الفطير.(1)

(٢ف)في كل الليالي الأخرى، نأكل جميع أنواع الخضراء، في هذه الليلة فقط نأكلأن
التواب بالمرّة.(2)

(٣ف)في كل الليالي الأخرى، لا نغمّس التواب حتى للمرة واحدة، في هذه الليلة نغمّس التواب
مرتين.(3)

(٤ف)في كل الليالي الأخرى، نأكل جالسين منتصبين أو متّكئين، في هذه الليلة نأكلأن
متّكئين.(4)

Al-Asila al-arba' li'eid al-Fesach al-Yehudi

Bimadha tachtalif hadhahi alleila 'an kul al-layali al-uchra?

(1) Fi kul al-layali al-uchra naakul alchubZ al-chamar ow al-chubs al-fateer, fi hadhahi al-leila naakul al-chubz al-fateer faqat?

(2) Fi kul al-layali al-uchra naakul jamia' anwa' at-tawabil al-khudra, fi hadhahi al-leila naakul faqt at-tawabil al-mara?

(3) Fi kul al-layali al-uchra la naghmus at-tawabil hata limara wahida, fi hadhahi al-leila naghmus at-tawabil maratein?

(4) Fi kul al-layali al-uchra, naakul jaliseen muntasibeen ow mutkain, fi hadhahi al-leila naakul mutkain?

MAH NISHTANAH IN RUSSIAN

Чем отличается эта ночь от других ночей?

Чем отличается эта ночь от других ночей?

(1) Почему во все ночи мы можем есть и хамец, и мацу, а в эту ночь только мацу?

(2) Почему во все ночи мы едим разную зелень, а в эту ночь – горькую зелень?

(3) Почему во все ночи мы не обмакиваем еду, а в эту ночь обмакиваем дважды (карпас в соленую воду и марор в харосет)?

(4) Почему во все другие ночи мы можем есть и сидя прямо, и облокотившись, а в эту ночь все мы (едим и пьем) облокотившись?

Chem otlichaetsja eta noch' ot drugih nochej?

Chem otlichaetsja eta noch' ot drugih nochej?

(1) Pochemu vo vse nochi my mozhem est' i hametz, i matzu, a v etu noch' tol'ko matzu?

(2) Pochemu vo vse nochi my edim raznuju zelen', a v etu noch' – gor'kuju zelen'?

(3) Pochemu vo vse nochi my ne obmakivaem edu, a v etu noch' obmakivaem dvazhdy (karpas v solenuju vodu i maror v haroset)?

(4) Pochemu vo vse drugie nochi my mozhem est' i sidja prjamo, i oblokotivshis', a v etu noch' vse my (edim i p'em) oblokotivshis'?

MAH NISHTANAH IN FRENCH

Pourquoi cette nuit se différencie-t-elle ?

Pourquoi cette nuit se différencie-t-elle de toutes les autres nuits ?

(1) Toutes les nuits, nous ne sommes pas tenus de tremper même une seule fois; cette nuit nous le faisons deux fois !

(2) Toutes les nuits, nous mangeons du 'hametz ou de la matzah; cette nuit, seulement de la matzah !

(3) Toutes les nuits, nous mangeons n'importe quel sorte de légumes; cette nuit, du Maror !

(4) Toutes les nuits, nous mangeons assis ou accoudés; cette nuit, nous sommes tous accoudés !

MAH NISHTANAH IN SPANISH

¿Qué hace diferente a esta noche?

¿Qué hace diferente a esta noche de todas las [demás] noches? ¿Ma nishtaná haláila hazé micól haleilót…

(1) En todas las noches no precisamos sumergir ni siquiera una vez, ¡y en esta noche lo hacemos dos veces! …shebejól haleilót éin ánu matbilín afílu paám eját, haláila hazé shtéi peamím?

(2) En todas las noches comemos jametz o matzá, ¡en esta noche solamente matzá! … shebejól haleilót ánu ojlín jamétz umatzá, haláila hazé kuló matzá?

(3) En todas las noches comemos cualquier clase de verdura, ¡esta noche maror! … shebejól haleilót ánu ojlín sheár ieracót, haláila hazé marór?

(4) En todas las noches comemos sentados erguidos o reclinados, ¡esta noche todos nos reclinamos!

Avadim Hayinu

There is an interesting debate in the Talmud as to the composition of our answer to the four questions of the Mah Nishtanah. According to Rabbi Samuel, our answer to the questions posed should begin with the phrase "we were Pharaoh's slaves." According to another Talmudic sage, Rav, we should begin with the phrase "in the beginning our fathers were idolaters." This difference of opinion is based on the Mishnah's requirement that our reply begin with humiliation and end with glory. In practice, we begin with Samuel's "we were slaves" and then we incorporate Rav's version after we read about the four children.

At this point, the leader in the Seder provides for the child and assembled the answer to the four questions. The telling of the Passover story is a mitzvah directed to all Jewish children and adults. Uncover the matzot and say:

Avadim hayinu l'faroh	עֲבָדִים הָיִינוּ לְפַרְעֹה
b'Mitzrayim. Vayotzi-einu Adonai	בְּמִצְרָיִם. וַיּוֹצִיאֵנוּ יְיָ
Eloheinu misham, b'yad chazakah	אֱלֹהֵינוּ מִשָּׁם, בְּיָד חֲזָקָה
uvizroa n'tuyah, v'ilu lo	וּבִזְרֹעַ נְטוּיָה, וְאִלּוּ לֹא
hotzi Hakadosh Baruch Hu	הוֹצִיא הַקָּדוֹשׁ בָּרוּךְ הוּא
et avoteinu mi-Mitzrayim,	אֶת־אֲבוֹתֵינוּ מִמִּצְרָיִם,
harei anu uvaneinu uv'nei vaneinu,	הֲרֵי אָנוּ וּבָנֵינוּ וּבְנֵי בָנֵינוּ,
m'shubadim hayinu l'faroh	מְשֻׁעְבָּדִים הָיִינוּ לְפַרְעֹה
b'Mitzrayim. Va-afilu kulanu	בְּמִצְרָיִם. וַאֲפִילוּ כֻּלָּנוּ
chachamim, kulanu n'vonim, kulanu	חֲכָמִים, כֻּלָּנוּ נְבוֹנִים,
z'keinim, kulanu yod'im	כֻּלָּנוּ זְקֵנִים, כֻּלָּנוּ יוֹדְעִים
et ha-Torah, mitzvah aleinu	אֶת־הַתּוֹרָה, מִצְוָה עָלֵינוּ
l'sapeir bitzi-at Mitzrayim.	לְסַפֵּר בִּיצִיאַת מִצְרָיִם.
V'chol hamarbeh l'sapeir bitzi-at	וְכָל הַמַּרְבֶּה לְסַפֵּר בִּיצִיאַת
Mitzrayim, harei zeh m'shubach.	מִצְרָיִם, הֲרֵי זֶה מְשֻׁבָּח:

We were Pharaoh's slaves in Egypt, and Adonai, our God, took us out of there with a strong hand and outstretched arm. If the Blessed Holy One had not taken our ancestors out of Egypt, we, our children, and our children's children would still be enslaved to Pharaoh in Egypt. And even if all of us were wise, even if all of us were clever, even if all of us were sages, even if all of us knew the Torah – we would still be duty bound to talk about the Exodus from Egypt. And the more you elaborate on the story of the Exodus from Egypt, the more praiseworthy you are.

See pp. 215–16 for songs "Go Down, Moses," "Hi-Ho, I Will Not Let Them Go,"

"Zippedee Do Da – Frogs on His Nose,"

"Yesterday," Hamilton parody "You'll Be Slaves"

QUESTIONS FOR DISCUSSION

Rabbi Joseph B. Soloveitchik teaches us that our slavery in Egypt implanted in us, almost as a part of our DNA, attributes of kindness and mercy, which makes it second nature for us to care for strangers, as we were strangers in Egypt.[52]

For the modern State of Israel, that question has come into stark play when people seek asylum within its borders. How can Israel balance compassion for the stranger with the concern of being overrun by asylum seekers? What kind of national policy can be formulated to balance security and national needs with ingrained Jewish compassion and ethical sensitivity? How should countries around the world balance homeland security with opening their borders to refugees fleeing oppression?

REFLECTION

A vivid depiction of Jewish slavery can be seen at the Arch of Titus in Rome. The bas-relief dioramas depict the Jews being forced into exile after the destruction of the Second Temple in the year 70 CE. A number of years ago, some American Jewish tourists who visited the Arch of Titus saw the following graffiti painted in Hebrew beneath the carved relief: "*Am Yisrael chai* – the Jewish people lives!"

Ma-aseh B'Rabi Eliezer

The story is told of the rabbis sitting in Bnei Brak talking throughout the night about the liberation from Egypt.

Ma-aseh b'Rabi Eli-ezer, v'Rabi

Y'hoshua, v'Rabi Elazar ben

Azaryah, v'Rabi Akiva, v'Rabi

Tarfon, she-hayu m'subin bi-Vnei

Vrak, v'hayu m'sap'rim bitzi-at

Mitzrayim, kol oto halaylah,

ad sheba-u talmideihem v'am'ru

lahem. Raboteinu, higi-a z'man

K'ri-at Sh'ma, shel Shacharit.

מַעֲשֶׂה בְּרַבִּי אֱלִיעֶזֶר, וְרַבִּי

יְהוֹשֻׁעַ, וְרַבִּי אֶלְעָזָר בֶּן

עֲזַרְיָה, וְרַבִּי עֲקִיבָא, וְרַבִּי

טַרְפוֹן, שֶׁהָיוּ מְסֻבִּין בִּבְנֵי־

בְרַק, וְהָיוּ מְסַפְּרִים בִּיצִיאַת

מִצְרַיִם, כָּל־אוֹתוֹ הַלַּיְלָה,

עַד שֶׁבָּאוּ תַלְמִידֵיהֶם וְאָמְרוּ

לָהֶם: רַבּוֹתֵינוּ, הִגִּיעַ זְמַן

קְרִיאַת שְׁמַע, שֶׁל שַׁחֲרִית:

It is told about Rabbi Eliezer, Rabbi Yehoshua, Rabbi Elazar son of Azaryah, Rabbi Akiva, and Rabbi Tarfon: One Passover night they were reclining together in Bnei Brak talking about the Exodus from Egypt. This went on all night, until their disciples came and said to them, "Masters, it is time to recite the morning Shema."

REFLECTION

One theory for this passage is that these scholars, who lived around 132–135 CE, were not engaged in study but rather in planning a revolt (what came to be known as the Bar Kochba revolt) against their Roman oppressors. Rabbi Akiva was a devoted disciple of Bar Kochba. One of the students standing guard outside the cave could have been reciting the Shema as a code to announce that the Romans were coming. We see a proof text for this in the Torah in Deuteronomy. The Torah dictates that this special Kohen, the Kohen Mashuach Milchamah, was anointed with *shemen hamishchah* (oil of anointment) and that this Kohen approached the soldiers at the onset of battle, saying Shema Yisrael and telling them, "Do not be afraid, for Hashem will be with you."[53]

What does this story about an all-nighter come to teach us? This is a prime example not only of the importance of prolonging the telling of the story of the Exodus from Egypt, but also of the fact that even knowledgeable people can learn new aspects related to *yetziat Mitzrayim* (going out of Egypt). No matter how wise we may be, there is always some new insight that can inspire us about the Exodus.

The rabbis in the Talmud ask what has greater virtue, studying or action. The answer? Study, because study leads to action. Do you agree?

Amar Rabi Elazar ben Azaryah

Amar Rabi Elazar ben Azaryah.	אָמַר רַבִּי אֶלְעָזָר בֶּן־עֲזַרְיָה.
Harei ani k'ven shivim shanah, v'lo	הֲרֵי אֲנִי כְּבֶן שִׁבְעִים שָׁנָה, וְלֹא
zachiti, shetei-ameir y'tzi-at Mitzrayim	זָכִיתִי, שֶׁתֵּאָמֵר יְצִיאַת מִצְרַיִם
baleilot. Ad shed'rashah Ben Zoma.	בַּלֵּילוֹת. עַד שֶׁדְּרָשָׁהּ בֶּן זוֹמָא.
Shene-emar: l'ma-an tizkor, et yom	שֶׁנֶּאֱמַר: לְמַעַן תִּזְכֹּר, אֶת יוֹם
tzeitcha mei-eretz Mitzrayim, kol y'mei	צֵאתְךָ מֵאֶרֶץ מִצְרַיִם, כֹּל יְמֵי
chayecha. Y'mei chayecha hayamim. Kol y'mei	חַיֶּיךָ. יְמֵי חַיֶּיךָ הַיָּמִים. כֹּל יְמֵי
chayecha haleilot. Vachachamim om'rim.	חַיֶּיךָ הַלֵּילוֹת. וַחֲכָמִים אוֹמְרִים:
Y'mei chayecha ha-olam hazeh. Kol y'mei	יְמֵי חַיֶּיךָ הָעוֹלָם הַזֶּה. כֹּל יְמֵי
chayecha l'havi limot hamashi-ach.	חַיֶּיךָ לְהָבִיא לִימוֹת הַמָּשִׁיחַ:

Rabbi Elazar son of Azaryah said: Here I am like seventy years old, yet I never understood why the story about the Exodus from Egypt should be recited at night until Ben Zoma explained it on the basis of the verse "So that you shall remember the day of your departure from Egypt all the days of your life" (Deuteronomy 16:3). If it had been written "the days of your life," it would have meant the days only; but "all the days of your life" means the nights, too. The other sages explain "all" to mean the messianic era, in addition to "the days of the present time."

REFLECTION

The Talmud teaches us that Rabbi Elazar ben Azaryah was only eighteen when he was chosen to replace Rabbi Gamliel as head of the Sanhedrin. His wife was concerned that being so young, he would not have the respect of his colleagues. But overnight, his hair turned white, and he accepted the position. That is why the text says he is "like" a man of seventy!

QUESTIONS FOR DISCUSSION

How much do appearances affect whom we respect? In contemporary times, do we disregard people's opinions and leadership if they are too young? too old?

REFLECTION

In four different places, we read in the Torah the commandment to retell the Exodus from Egypt. Why does the text reiterate that the more we talk about it, the more praiseworthy it is? This is to remind us that no matter how wise we may be, no matter how advanced our learning, all Jews are equal in the obligation to feel as though we left Egypt. And by telling the story, we should feel the experience of the Exodus from Egypt. I often wondered how to concretize that experience for people, especially children. One year, right before Passover, I took my children, who at the time were under the age of six, to an exhibit at the Schomburg Center for Research in Black Culture, located in Harlem. On display were actual artifacts from the nineteenth century – chains, bolts, and locks used on African American slaves brought to America. I can still remember the look of shock on my children's faces when they saw the tiny chains designed to shackle toddlers.

At the end of the exhibit, a glass jar held buttons that depicted the chains with a slash through them and the words "We triumphed!" When we wore the buttons at the Seder, we had in mind both ancient and modern manifestations of slavery. Another way to concretize the experience is to see if there is an "abolitionist" program in your community. For example, students at the Ramaz Middle School in New York established the Abolitionist Club. Through pizza and jewelry sales, enough money was raised to free thirty slaves in the Sudan (each slave cost $85 to redeem).

QUESTIONS FOR DISCUSSION

Many note the play on words of Mitzrayim (Egypt): the root is from the word "narrow place." What do you see as the best way to overcome those moments that constrict you and keep you from growing spiritually?

Why did the matzah quit his job? Because he didn't get a raise!
What kind of cheese do you use on Pesach? Matzarella!
Why didn't Pharaoh release the Jews? Because he was in de-Nile!

See p. 217 for song "Take Us Out of Egypt" and for Top Ten Signs the Guy Your Daughter Brought Home for the Passover Seder Isn't Going to Work Out

The Four Children

LEADER: As we are about to read about the four children, we remind ourselves that as different and as difficult as some of them may be, they each may reflect a person who is present at the Seder. The Lubavitcher Rebbe reminded us that in our day there is a fifth child – the one who is missing from our text and missing from our Seder, the child too assimilated, too alienated to even join with his or her brothers and sisters for a meal. We dedicate this reading to the task of reaching out to the missing children, to seeing what we can do to bring them back to our collective tables, homes, and Jewish community.

Baruch hamakom, baruch hu. Baruch	בָּרוּךְ הַמָּקוֹם בָּרוּךְ הוּא. בָּרוּךְ
shenatan Torah l'amo Yisra-eil,	שֶׁנָּתַן תּוֹרָה לְעַמּוֹ יִשְׂרָאֵל.
baruch hu. K'neged arba-ah	בָּרוּךְ הוּא. כְּנֶגֶד אַרְבָּעָה
vanim dib'rah Torah. Echad	בָנִים דִּבְּרָה תוֹרָה. אֶחָד
chacham, v'echad rasha, v'echad tam,	חָכָם, וְאֶחָד רָשָׁע, וְאֶחָד תָּם,
v'echad she-eino yodei-a lishol.	וְאֶחָד שֶׁאֵינוֹ יוֹדֵעַ לִשְׁאוֹל:

Blessed is the Omnipresent, blessed is God; blessed is the One Who gave the Torah to the people of Israel – may God be blessed.

The Torah has four children in mind:

the **wise** child;

the **wicked** or rebellious child;

the **simple** child;

and the child **who does**

not know how to ask.

Chacham mah hu omeir?

חָכָם מַה הוּא אוֹמֵר?

Mah ha-eidot v'hachukim

מָה הָעֵדֹת וְהַחֻקִּים

v'hamishpatim, asher tzivah

וְהַמִּשְׁפָּטִים, אֲשֶׁר צִוָּה יְיָ

Adonai Eloheinu etchem [otanu]?

אֱלֹהֵינוּ אֶתְכֶם [אוֹתָנוּ]?

V'af atah emor lo k'hilchot

וְאַף אַתָּה אֱמָר־לוֹ כְּהִלְכוֹת

ha-Pesach. Ein maftirin

הַפֶּסַח: אֵין מַפְטִירִין

achar ha-Pesach afikoman.

אַחַר הַפֶּסַח אֲפִיקוֹמָן:

Rasha mah hu omeir? Mah

רָשָׁע מַה הוּא אוֹמֵר? מָה

ha-avodah ha-zot lachem?

הָעֲבֹדָה הַזֹּאת לָכֶם?

Lachem v'lo lo. Ul'fi shehotzi et

לָכֶם וְלֹא לוֹ. וּלְפִי שֶׁהוֹצִיא

atzmo min hak'lal, kafar

אֶת־עַצְמוֹ מִן הַכְּלָל, כָּפַר

ba-ikar. V'af atah hakheih

בָּעִקָּר. וְאַף אַתָּה הַקְהֵה

et shinav, ve-emor lo. Ba-avur

אֶת־שִׁנָּיו, וֶאֱמָר־לוֹ: בַּעֲבוּר

zeh, asah Adonai li, b'tzeiti

זֶה, עָשָׂה יְיָ לִי, בְּצֵאתִי

mi-Mitzrayim, li v'lo lo. Ilu

מִמִּצְרָיִם, לִי וְלֹא־לוֹ. אִלּוּ

hayah sham, lo hayah nigal.

הָיָה שָׁם, לֹא הָיָה נִגְאָל:

Tam mah hu omeir? Mah

תָּם מַה הוּא אוֹמֵר? מַה

zot? V'amarta eilav.

זֹּאת? וְאָמַרְתָּ אֵלָיו:

B'chozek yad hotzi-anu Adonai

בְּחֹזֶק יָד הוֹצִיאָנוּ יְיָ

mi-Mitzrayim mibeit avadim.

מִמִּצְרָיִם מִבֵּית עֲבָדִים:

V'she-eino yodei-a lishol,

וְשֶׁאֵינוֹ יוֹדֵעַ לִשְׁאוֹל,

at p'tach lo. Shene-emar.

אַתְּ פְּתַח לוֹ. שֶׁנֶּאֱמַר:

V'higadta l'vincha, bayom hahu

וְהִגַּדְתָּ לְבִנְךָ, בַּיּוֹם

leimor. Ba-avur zeh asah

Adonai li, b'tzeiti mi-Mitzrayim.

הַהוּא לֵאמֹר: בַּעֲבוּר זֶה עָשָׂה

יְיָ לִי, בְּצֵאתִי מִמִּצְרָיִם:

What does the wise child say? "What is the meaning of the precepts, statutes, and laws that Adonai, our God, has commanded you [according to Maimonides and the *Mechilta*: commanded us]?" (Deuteronomy 6:20). You are to explain the rules of Passover: "It is forbidden to conclude the Passover meal by announcing: Now to the afikomen!" (Mishnah, *Pesachim* 10:8).

What does the wicked or rebellious child say? "What is this service of yours?" (Exodus 12:26). By saying "of yours," thus self-excluding from the community of Jews, the child has denied God. So you are to take the bite out of this child by saying: "This commemorates what Adonai did for me when I went out of Egypt!" (Exodus 13:8) – "for me," not for this child, who, if there, would not have been liberated.

What does the simple child say? "What is this?" (Exodus 13:14). You are to tell this child: "It was by might of hand that Adonai took us out of Egypt, out of the land of slavery" (Exodus 13:14).

As for the child who does not know how to ask – you start the child off, for it is written: "You shall tell your child that day, saying: This commemorates what Adonai did for me when I went out of Egypt" (Exodus 13:8).

BACKGROUND

The Four Children

The four children are a pedagogical tool to understand the four sources in the Torah where we are commanded to explain to children the significance of the Exodus from Egypt. The basis for the wicked or rebellious child's question is "When it shall come to pass that your children shall say to you, what does this service mean to you?" (Exodus 12:26). The basis for the child who does not know how to ask the question is "And you shall tell your son on that day, saying: It is because of what the Eternal did for me when I came out of Egypt" (Exodus 13:8). The source for the question of the simple child is "And it shall be when your child asks you in time to come, saying: What is this?" (Exodus 13:14). The source for the question of the wise child is "When your child will ask you in time to come, saying: What is the meaning of the testimonies and the statutes and the ordinances which the Eternal our God has commanded you?" (Deuteronomy 6:20). Out of respect for the wisdom of the wise child, the Haggadah begins with that child's question first.

The texts we find in the Haggadah are not solely based on the biblical texts but also have their origins in the *Mechilta* (a halachic midrash on the Book of Exodus) and the

Jerusalem Talmud. In this Haggadah we have offered as an alternate reading the text from the *Mechilta* and the Jerusalem Talmud as well as Maimonides' Haggadah, which renders in the wise child's question the Hebrew word *otanu* (to us) and not *lachem* (to you) so as to further bring out the distinction between the wise child and wicked child.

A number of questions arise regarding the order and formulation in the Haggadah of these four archetypes: Why doesn't the Haggadah follow the order that is described in the Torah, on which these passages are based? Shouldn't the wise child be paired with the child unable to ask the question, and the simple with the wicked? Here are two responses: the Vilna Gaon answered that the Haggadah did not want to end on the note of the wicked child; the Abravanel pointed out that the Haggadah starts with the most learned child and then proceeds to the wicked child, who is the most cunning, followed by the simple child, and concluding with the child who does not even know how to ask a question.

What can we really learn from the wise child? Rabbi Nachman of Breslov says that the wise child takes to heart the meaning of the words *mah hu omer* (what does he say) to hear the underlying message when others talk. Rather than judge others, the wise person seeks to understand and to help those in need. The wise person also teaches us to listen to our own true inner voices.[54]

What makes the rebellious child so bad? The Haggadah lays out a prototype of a person who has excluded him- or herself from his or her destiny as part of the Jewish people. For Jews, peoplehood and collective responsibility is an essential part of our being. For example, during the Days of Awe of Rosh Hashanah and Yom Kippur, we pray in the plural, having in mind not just ourselves but the entire community. The concept that we are all responsible for each other is at the heart of the Jewish psyche. To deny Jewish identity as being part of a larger collective – a covenantal community – leads to being characterized as a *rasha* (wicked person). Is there another way that we can look at the juxtaposition of the wicked or rebellious child next to the wise child?

Logically, we would think that the wicked child should be listed last. The Lubavitcher Rebbe (Rabbi Menachem Mendel Schneerson) provides another perspective. No child, he says, is really wicked. The *rasha* is next to the *chacham* (wise child) because the *rasha* actually has the ability to be like the wise child, if the *rasha* only turns from the wrong path. So too, the wise child is juxtaposed with the wicked or rebellious child as a reminder that a *chacham* who doesn't continue doing good deeds can become like the *rasha*. That serves as a reminder that even "perfect" people need to work on improving themselves.

Finally, Rabbi Schneerson says that the *chacham* (wise child) is responsible for reaching out to the *rasha* (wicked/rebellious one) to help that child do *teshuvah* (change his or her ways). The *chacham* has to serve as an example. This is a reminder that we should not cut ourselves off even from those with whom we have sharp disagreements. To be a truly wise person means to be a role model for others.[55]

Rabbi Shlomo Carlebach asked whether it would have been better symmetry to compare a tzaddik (righteous person) to the *rasha* rather than a *chacham*. Isn't it righteousness rather than wisdom that contrasts with wickedness? Rabbi Carlebach explained that it is one thing to have a lot of book knowledge and be a *chacham*. But a true tzaddik would be able to influence others by example to turn from their ways. Hence the other could not be a *rasha*, because the *tzaddik* would influence a *rasha* with his or her goodness.

Another way to understand the difference between the *chacham* and the *rasha* is that the *chacham* is asking a question. As challenging as a question may be, we welcome an inquisitive mind even if we do not have an answer. The *rasha*, on the other hand, is not asking a question but rather making a statement.

How should we treat the *rasha*? The text seems to endorse violence, but the sixteenth-century mystic the Alshich has a clever way of understanding the conflict through gematria (Jewish numerology). The Alshich explained that if we take the numerical value of the word *rasha* (570) and subtract the value of *shinav* (teeth, 366), we end up with 204, which equals tzaddik (righteous one). If we can figure out a way to "knock" some sense into those who seem the most alienated, they too can end up as righteous people. Our challenge is to figure out the best way to positively influence those who are negative – not through the fist but through extending a hand to those around us.

SUGGESTION

Some have suggested to have an empty chair set up to represent the "missing child," the guest yet to arrive, for whom there is always a seat at the table.

Another idea is to go around the room and ask for guests to read each of the passages about the four children "in character."

QUESTIONS FOR DISCUSSION

The *chacham* (wise child). What makes the wise child wise? What is the difference between the wise and the wicked children's questions if both ask what the observance is "to you"?

The *rasha* (wicked/rebellious child). What makes this child so bad?

The *tam* (simple child). How do you characterize a "simple" child? Although this is

usually translated as "the simple child," here it would seem that the Hag-gadah is talking about someone who possesses a certain naïveté or inno-cence – a person who is not attuned to the cruel edge of the world we live in, but needs to have his or her eyes opened. Is that (pure naïveté or innocence) a trait that we should try to emulate?

The *eino yode'a lishol* (the child who doesn't know how to ask). The rabbis ask, why is *at*, the feminine form of "you," used in the answer to this ques-tion? They answer that it implies that the particular obligation to open up and educate children rests primarily with women.[56]

Those who are not present. There are so many Jews who are not even present at a Seder table. What do you think is the best way to reach out to them?

New categories. If you were adding additional categories of types of chil-dren to this segment, what would you include?

HUMOR CORNER

How can we understand the difference between the wise child saying, "What is the meaning of these commandments to you?" and the wicked/rebellious child who also asks it similarly (if you read the text for both the wise and wicked children as *lachem*)? An old Yiddish joke shows us that it depends on the *niggun* – the intonation and the way you ask the question. A man was brought before a *beit din* (Jewish court of law) charged with slandering someone by calling him a thief. After listening to both sides, the rabbinic judge turned to the defendant and told him to apologize to the plaintiff by declaring, "*Chaim Yonkel iz nisht a gonif*" (he is not a thief). To comply with the *beit din*, the man turned to the judge and declared, "*Chaim Yonkel iz* nisht *a gonif?!*" (he is *not* a thief?!). The moral: it is all in the *niggun* – the tone you use!

Yachol Meirosh Chodesh

Yachol meirosh chodesh, talmud

lomar bayom hahu. Iy bayom hahu,

yachol mib'od yom. Talmud

lomar ba-avur zeh. Ba-avur zeh

lo amarti, ela b'sha-ah sheyeish

matzah u-maror munachim l'fanecha.

יָכוֹל מֵרֹאשׁ חֹדֶשׁ, תַּלְמוּד

לוֹמַר בַּיּוֹם הַהוּא. אִי בַּיּוֹם

הַהוּא. יָכוֹל מִבְּעוֹד יוֹם. תַּלְמוּד

לוֹמַר, בַּעֲבוּר זֶה. בַּעֲבוּר זֶה

לֹא אָמַרְתִּי, אֶלָּא בְּשָׁעָה שֶׁיֵּשׁ

מַצָּה וּמָרוֹר מֻנָּחִים לְפָנֶיךָ:

Why should the telling not begin on the first day of the month of Nissan in which the deliverance took place? Because the verse stresses "on that day," the day on which it began. In that case, should not the telling begin during the day? No, because the text stresses "this commemorates," and you cannot say "this" except when the matzah and bitter herbs are set before you.

Mit'chilah ov'dei avodah zarah hayu

avoteinu. V'achshav keir'vanu hamakom

la-avodato. Shene-emar: Vayomer

Y'hoshua el kol ha-am. Koh amar

Adonai Elohei Yisra-eil, b'eiver hanahar

yash'vu avoteichem mei-olam, Terach

avi Avraham va-avi Nachor. Vaya-avdu

Elohim acheirim. Va-ekach et avichem

et Avraham mei-eiver ha-nahar, va-

oleich oto b'chol eretz k'na-an. Va-arbeh

et zaro, va-eten lo et Yitzchak. Va-etein

l'Yitzchak et Ya-akov v'et Eisav. Va-etein

מִתְּחִלָּה עוֹבְדֵי עֲבוֹדָה זָרָה הָיוּ

אֲבוֹתֵינוּ. וְעַכְשָׁו קֵרְבָנוּ הַמָּקוֹם

לַעֲבוֹדָתוֹ. שֶׁנֶּאֱמַר: וַיֹּאמֶר

יְהוֹשֻׁעַ אֶל־כָּל־הָעָם. כֹּה אָמַר

יְיָ אֱלֹהֵי יִשְׂרָאֵל, בְּעֵבֶר הַנָּהָר

יָשְׁבוּ אֲבוֹתֵיכֶם מֵעוֹלָם, תֶּרַח

אֲבִי אַבְרָהָם וַאֲבִי נָחוֹר. וַיַּעַבְדוּ

אֱלֹהִים אֲחֵרִים: וָאֶקַּח אֶת־אֲבִיכֶם

אֶת־אַבְרָהָם מֵעֵבֶר הַנָּהָר, וָאוֹלֵךְ

אוֹתוֹ בְּכָל־אֶרֶץ כְּנָעַן. וָאַרְבֶּה אֶת־

זַרְעוֹ, וָאֶתֶּן לוֹ אֶת־יִצְחָק: וָאֶתֵּן

לְיִצְחָק אֶת־יַעֲקֹב וְאֶת־עֵשָׂו. וָאֶתֵּן

l'Eisav et har sei-ir,	לְעֵשָׂו אֶת־הַר שֵׂעִיר,
lareshet oto. V'Ya-akov	לָרֶשֶׁת אוֹתוֹ. וְיַעֲקֹב
uva-nav yar'du Mitzrayim.	וּבָנָיו יָרְדוּ מִצְרָיִם:

Originally, our ancestors were idolaters, but now the Omnipresent has drawn us to God's service, as it is said: "Joshua then said to the entire people: This is the word of Adonai, the God of Israel: Long ago your ancestors lived beyond the river [Euphrates] – Terach, Abraham's father and Nachor's father – and they worshiped other gods. But I took your father Abraham from beyond the river and led him though the whole land of Canaan, and I gave him many descendants. I gave him Isaac, and to Isaac I gave Jacob and Esau. Then I gave Esau the hill country of Seir to possess, while Jacob and his children went down to Egypt" (Joshua 24:2–4).

REFLECTION

What is particularly fascinating about the line "Originally, our ancestors were idolaters" is that we do not whitewash our history but rather acknowledge our shortcomings.

Baruch shomeir havtachato	בָּרוּךְ שׁוֹמֵר הַבְטָחָתוֹ
l'Yisra-eil. Baruch hu.	לְיִשְׂרָאֵל. בָּרוּךְ הוּא.
She-Hakadosh Baruch Hu	שֶׁהַקָּדוֹשׁ בָּרוּךְ הוּא חִשַּׁב
chishav et hakeitz, la-asot k'mah	אֶת־הַקֵּץ, לַעֲשׂוֹת כְּמָה
she-amar l'Avraham Avinu	שֶׁאָמַר לְאַבְרָהָם אָבִינוּ
bi-Vrit bein ha-B'tarim.	בִּבְרִית בֵּין הַבְּתָרִים,
Shene-emar: vayomer l'Avram	שֶׁנֶּאֱמַר: וַיֹּאמֶר לְאַבְרָם
yadoa teida, ki geir yihyeh	יָדֹעַ תֵּדַע, כִּי־גֵר יִהְיֶה
zaracha, b'eretz lo lahem,	זַרְעֲךָ, בְּאֶרֶץ לֹא לָהֶם,
va-avadum v'inu otam	וַעֲבָדוּם וְעִנּוּ אֹתָם
arba meiot shanah. V'gam	אַרְבַּע מֵאוֹת שָׁנָה: וְגַם

We do not whitewash our history but rather acknowledge our short-comings.

In every generation they rise up to annihilate us, but the Blessed Holy One saves us from them.

et hagoy asher ya-avodu dan anochi.

אֶת־הַגּוֹי אֲשֶׁר יַעֲבֹדוּ דָּן אָנֹכִי.

V'acharei chein yeitz'u, birchush gadol.

וְאַחֲרֵי כֵן יֵצְאוּ, בִּרְכֻשׁ גָּדוֹל:

Blessed be the One Who keeps promises to Israel, blessed be God. For the Blessed Holy One predestined the end [of the Egyptian bondage], doing what was promised to our father Abraham in the Covenant between the Sections, as it is said: "And God said to Avram: Know for certain that your descendants will be strangers in a land not theirs, and they [the host people] will enslave and oppress them [the Jews] for four hundred years. But I will also judge the nation they will serve, and in the end they will leave with great wealth" (Genesis 15:13–14).

V'hi She-am'dah

LEADER: We continue at this point with a review of Jewish history, the suffering imposed upon the Israelites, the plagues inflicted on the Egyptians, and the miracles God performed to redeem the Jewish people. As "people of the book," we should embrace being "people of the story," who never forget our history. When others rise to deny our memory, twist or forget our past, we are here to tell and retell our collective story. May this step of the Seder remind us to inspire and reinspire others by retelling the difficult moments of our history and our eventual redemption from slavery.

Cover the matzot and raise the wine cups.

V'hi she-am'dah la-avoteinu v'lanu.

וְהִיא שֶׁעָמְדָה לַאֲבוֹתֵינוּ וְלָנוּ.

Shelo echad bilvad, amad aleinu

שֶׁלֹּא אֶחָד בִּלְבָד, עָמַד עָלֵינוּ

l'chaloteinu. Ela sheb'chol dor vador,

לְכַלּוֹתֵנוּ. אֶלָּא שֶׁבְּכָל דּוֹר וָדוֹר,

om'dim aleinu l'chaloteinu, v'Hakadosh

עוֹמְדִים עָלֵינוּ לְכַלּוֹתֵנוּ. וְהַקָּדוֹשׁ

Baruch Hu matzileinu mi-yadam.

בָּרוּךְ הוּא מַצִּילֵנוּ מִיָּדָם:

And it is this which has stood by our ancestors and us. For not just one has risen up to annihilate us; in every generation they rise up to annihilate us, but the Blessed Holy One saves us from them.

REFLECTION

One commentary teaches us to read this passage as *she'lo echad, bi'lvad, amad aleinu l'chaloteinu* (if we are not one, then we are alone, and only then can our enemies seek to annihilate us).[57] This concept of Jewish unity is a core Jewish belief, reminding us that whatever the external crisis, our first priority is to stand as one in the face of external threat. This calls to mind the scenario described in the Torah when the Jewish people, on the way out of Egypt, were attacked by the Amalekites. We are taught that when the Jewish people held up Moshe's hands, they prevailed. The commentators tell us that this was an example of standing united.

QUESTIONS FOR DISCUSSION

The only difference between the words *united* and *untied* is where you place the *I*. How should dissent in our community be handled so it doesn't devolve into disunity? How do we construct communal policy that provides space for a variety of views without it fracturing our community? What type of boundaries should or should not be drawn?

Tzei U'lmad/Arami Oveid Avi

Here the Haggadah begins a historical narrative going back to Laban. According to the Mishnah, this portion of the Seder constitutes the core of the Haggadah.

Put down the cup of wine and uncover the matzot.

Tzei ul'mad, mah bikeish lavan	צֵא וּלְמַד, מַה בִּקֵּשׁ לָבָן
ha-arami la-asot l'Ya-akov	הָאֲרַמִּי לַעֲשׂוֹת לְיַעֲקֹב אָבִינוּ.
avinu. She-paroh lo gazar ela al	שֶׁפַּרְעֹה לֹא גָזַר אֶלָּא עַל
haz'charim, v'lavan bikeish la-akor	הַזְּכָרִים, וְלָבָן בִּקֵּשׁ לַעֲקֹר
et hakol, shenemar: Arami oveid	אֶת־הַכֹּל, שֶׁנֶּאֱמַר: אֲרַמִּי
avi, vayeired Mitzraymah,	אֹבֵד אָבִי, וַיֵּרֶד מִצְרַיְמָה,
vayagor sham bimtei m'at. Vay'hi	וַיָּגָר שָׁם בִּמְתֵי מְעָט. וַיְהִי
sham l'goy gadol, atzum varav.	שָׁם לְגוֹי גָּדוֹל, עָצוּם וָרָב:

Go and learn what Lavan the Aramean intended to do to our father Yaakov: Pharaoh decreed death only on the males, whereas Lavan wanted to eradicate all, as it is said: "The Aramean wanted to destroy my father. But he went down to Egypt and sojourned there – few in number. There he became a great, powerful, and populous nation" (Deuteronomy 26:5).

REFLECTION

The Lubavitcher Rebbe interpreted *tzei u'lmad* (go and learn) as a call for those who truly wanted to learn to leave behind them their preconceived notions and accepted ways of thinking.[58]

BACKGROUND

Why the Focus on Lavan?

Why do we have this reference to Laban in the Haggadah? On the surface, this passage serves to remind us how far back we have experienced hatred from those who sought to destroy us. (This passage comprised part of the confession that was made on Shavuot when the *bikkurim* [first fruits] were brought to the Temple.) The phrase *"arami oved avi"* is interpreted according to the midrashic commentary on Deuteronomy 26:5–8, that "Laban the wandering Aramean [or Syrian] sought to destroy my father [and is considered worse than Pharaoh]." Yet if we look at the plain meaning of the text in the Torah, we translate this verse as "my father was a wandering Aramean [or Syrian]," which is a reference to our ancestor Jacob's flight from his home (fearful of being killed by Esau for taking his birthright) to Syria, where he worked for his uncle Laban.

We do not know precisely when and why the Laban interpretation was authored. Some have suggested that the author of the Laban interpretation wanted to avoid tying the origins of the Jewish people to the Arameans; the interpretation was probably authored at a time and locale when such a connection would have been thought of as disparaging.[59]

Jewish tradition identifies Laban not merely as an ultimate trickster but as someone worse than Pharaoh. Why? While Pharaoh wanted to kill the firstborn, the Haggadah tells us that Laban sought "la'akor et hakol" (to uproot everything). Laban tricked Jacob into marrying Leah by switching her with her younger sister Rachel. By doing this, he was not merely creating dissension among a few individuals but rather desired to create machloket (infighting, disagreement, conflict) among the entire family that would have far-reaching implications for generations to come.

From the Midrash, we learn that Jacob anticipated Laban's deceit and gave Rachel secret signs so he would be able to identify her in the darkness of their wedding night. Yet Rachel did not want to embarrass her older sister by marrying first, so she shared the secret signs with Leah (hoping that Jacob would understand her motives were pure). The way that Rachel and Leah behaved toward each other provides the antidote to the dissension Laban sought to cause. This then becomes the paradigm example not only of sisterly love but of taking the needs of others into account, even to the point of self-sacrifice. For us in the modern world, this is a cautionary example to those who, like Laban, seek to cause discord and infighting within our own ranks, and a sterling example of the lengths to which we should go to create a sense of achdut (unity).[60]

The way that Rachel and Leah behaved toward each other provides the antidote to the dissension Laban sought to cause.

Vayeired Mitzraymah

Vayeired Mitzraymah, onus	וַיֵּרֶד מִצְרַיְמָה, אָנוּס
al pi hadibbur. **Vayagor sham**.	עַל פִּי הַדִּבּוּר. וַיָּגָר שָׁם.
M'lameid shelo yarad Ya-akov	מְלַמֵּד שֶׁלֹּא יָרַד יַעֲקֹב
avinu l'hishtakei-a b'Mitzrayim,	אָבִינוּ לְהִשְׁתַּקֵּעַ בְּמִצְרַיִם,
ela lagur sham, shene-emar:	אֶלָּא לָגוּר שָׁם, שֶׁנֶּאֱמַר:
vayomru el paroh, lagur	וַיֹּאמְרוּ אֶל־פַּרְעֹה, לָגוּר
ba-aretz banu, ki ein	בָּאָרֶץ בָּאנוּ, כִּי אֵין

mireh latzon asher la-a-vadecha, ki

chaveid hara-av b'eretz k'na-an. V'Atah,

yeish'vu na avadecha b'eretz goshen.

Bimtei m'at. K'mah shene-emar:

b'shivim nefesh, yar'du avotecha

Mitzray'mah. V'Atah, sam'cha Adonai

Elohecha, k'choch'vei hashamayim larov.

Vay'hi sham l'goy. M'lameid shehayu

Yisra-eil m'tzuyanim sham.

Gadol atzum. K'mah shene-emar:

uv'nei Yisra-eil, paru vayishr'tzu,

vayirbu vaya-atzmu, bimod m'od,

vatimalei ha-aretz otam.

Varav. K'mah shene-emar: R'vavah

k'tzemach ha-sadeh n'tatich, vatirbi, vatigd'li,

vatavo-i ba-adi adayim. Shadayim nachonu,

us'areich tzimei-ach, v'at eirom v'eryah.

Va-e-evor alayich va-ereich mitboseset

b'damayich va-omar lach b'damayich chayi

va-omar lach b'damayich chayi.

מִרְעֶה לַצֹּאן אֲשֶׁר לַעֲבָדֶיךָ, כִּי

כָבֵד הָרָעָב בְּאֶרֶץ כְּנָעַן. וְעַתָּה,

יֵשְׁבוּ־נָא עֲבָדֶיךָ בְּאֶרֶץ גֹּשֶׁן:

בִּמְתֵי מְעָט. כְּמָה שֶׁנֶּאֱמַר:

בְּשִׁבְעִים נֶפֶשׁ, יָרְדוּ אֲבֹתֶיךָ

מִצְרָיְמָה. וְעַתָּה, שָׂמְךָ יְיָ

אֱלֹהֶיךָ, כְּכוֹכְבֵי הַשָּׁמַיִם לָרֹב.

וַיְהִי שָׁם לְגוֹי. מְלַמֵּד שֶׁהָיוּ

יִשְׂרָאֵל מְצֻיָּנִים שָׁם:

גָּדוֹל עָצוּם. כְּמָה שֶׁנֶּאֱמַר:

וּבְנֵי יִשְׂרָאֵל, פָּרוּ וַיִּשְׁרְצוּ,

וַיִּרְבּוּ וַיַּעַצְמוּ, בִּמְאֹד מְאֹד,

וַתִּמָּלֵא הָאָרֶץ אֹתָם:

וָרָב. כְּמָה שֶׁנֶּאֱמַר: רְבָבָה כְּצֶמַח

הַשָּׂדֶה נְתַתִּיךְ, וַתִּרְבִּי, וַתִּגְדְּלִי,

וַתָּבֹאִי בַּעֲדִי עֲדָיִים: שָׁדַיִם

נָכֹנוּ, וּשְׂעָרֵךְ צִמֵּחַ, וְאַתְּ עֵרֹם

וְעֶרְיָה: וָאֶעֱבֹר עָלַיִךְ וָאֶרְאֵךְ

מִתְבּוֹסֶסֶת בְּדָמָיִךְ וָאֹמַר לָךְ

בְּדָמַיִךְ חֲיִי וָאֹמַר לָךְ בְּדָמַיִךְ חֲיִי.

"He went down to Egypt" – compelled to do so by the word of God.

"And he sojourned there" – this teaches us that he did not go to settle in Egypt but only
to sojourn there, as it is said: "And they said to Pharaoh: We have come to sojourn in the

land, as there is no pasture for your servants' sheep, for the famine is severe in the land of Canaan. Pray, then, let your servants stay in the Goshen region" (Bereishit 47:4).

"Few in number" – as it is said: "Just seventy your ancestors numbered when they went down to Egypt; but now Adonai your God, has made you as numerous as the stars in the sky" (Bereishit 47:4).

"There he became a great nation" – as it is said: "But the Children of Israel were fertile and prolific: they increased and became very numerous and the land was full of them" (Exodus 1:7).

"Mighty and populous" – as it is said: "I caused you to increase like wildflowers, and you throve and grew, and you came to full womanhood, your breasts fully fashioned, your hair grown – but you were still naked and exposed. Then I came by and saw you writhing helplessly in your own blood, and I said to you: In spite of your blood – live! And I said to you: In spite of your blood – live!" (Yechezkel 16:7, 6).

REFLECTION

The text describes Jacob's sojourn in Egypt and the settling of his sons, the resulting enslavement and finally redemption of the Jewish people. When the Jewish people left Egypt, they wanted to fulfill the promise that Joseph's bones be taken to Israel for burial. How did they know where to locate the bones? According to the Midrash (*Pirkei de-Rabi Eliezer*), it was Serach bat Asher, granddaughter of Jacob, who told Moshe where to find the bones of Joseph that the Egyptians had buried at sea.

How was she still alive? The Midrash tells us Serach had been the one who told her grandfather Jacob the news, through song, that Joseph was still alive. By slowly breaking to him this news, she was responsible for restoring Jacob's "life" and thus received from him a blessing for long life. Like Elijah, Serach is viewed as returning to aid the Jewish people at different times, not having died but rather ascended to heaven while still alive![61]

REFLECTION

Jacob went down to Egypt *onus al pi hadibbur*, compelled by the word of God, by divine decree. An alternate way to understand this is that what compelled Jacob to have to go back to Egypt was the *dibbur* – the words. The negative words that Joseph had spoken about his brothers years before to his father, coupled with the brothers' words conspiring against Joseph, remind us that it was their actions that caused Joseph and the brothers to end up in Egypt. This serves as a reminder of the terrible cost of *lashon hara* (speaking negatively about others).

HUMOR CORNER

A modern-day manifestation of being "compelled by divine decree": When Rabbi Yaakov Orenstein of Poland was serving in his first rabbinic post, in the late eighteenth century, some of his congregants asked him whether the prayer Av Harachamim should be said or omitted on the Sabbath when the blessing is recited for the new months of Iyar and Sivan. This blessing takes note of the suffering of Jews and is normally omitted on happy occasions, such as blessing the new month, yet the new months of Iyar and Sivan fall during the period of *sefirah* (when the Omer is counted), which is a time of mourning. Rabbi Orenstein did not know the answer offhand and suggested that they consult the Jewish *luach* (calendar), which contains all the answers to questions regarding customs of this kind.

The leaders in his congregation were very upset that he, as their rabbi, did not know this answer right off the bat, and so he was dismissed. Many years later, one of the leaders in this congregation was visiting the city of Lemberg and decided to pray at the main synagogue. He was very impressed by how the congregation honored their rabbi, the chief rabbi of Lemberg, and at the conclusion of the services came over to greet this eminent Torah scholar. As he came closer, he stopped in his tracks. He was shocked to see that he was the very same rabbi whom he had been instrumental in firing years earlier! Almost without thinking, he blurted out to the rabbi, "How did you get here?" Without a moment's hesitation, the chief rabbi answered, smiling, "The Av Harachamim [the most merciful Father in heaven] brought me here."[62]

QUESTIONS FOR DISCUSSION

Have you ever been in a situation where you felt you were guided by divine intervention? How have you coped in moments of crisis and despair? Have you been helped to get through a difficult situation by the support of family and friends? By your faith?

REFLECTION

The Hebrew text says that with seventy souls your father went down to Egypt. However, the Hebrew text renders the word *nefesh* (soul) in the singular, not the plural, as would be expected. It is explained that when the Jewish people became a nation, they were viewed as one unified spirit. This is evocative of the giving of the Torah to the Jewish people at Sinai, where we are told that we all stood there as one people with one heart.

KIDS' CORNER

This section of the Haggadah is an opportunity to ask children at the Seder to act out Jewish history. Assign someone ahead of time to prepare skits. Provide to the children an overview of the areas covered and tell them to let their imaginations run wild! They can play Passover charades or have a talent show. Pass around passports to show the journeys of family members seeking physical and religious freedom. Go around the table and have guests share a special Seder memory. Have each child sing a Passover song before a panel of judges. After Motzi, the winner gets a chocolate-covered matzah!

Vayarei-u Otanu Ha-Mitzrim

Vayarei-u otanu ha-Mitzrim vay'anunu,	וַיָּרֵעוּ אֹתָנוּ הַמִּצְרִים וַיְעַנּוּנוּ,
Vayit'nu aleinu avodah kashah.	וַיִּתְּנוּ עָלֵינוּ עֲבֹדָה קָשָׁה:
Vayarei-u otanu ha-Mitzrim. K'mah	וַיָּרֵעוּ אֹתָנוּ הַמִּצְרִים. כְּמָה
shene-emar: havah nitchak'mah lo, pen	שֶׁנֶּאֱמַר: הָבָה נִתְחַכְּמָה לוֹ. פֶּן
yirbeh, v'hayah ki tikrenah milchamah,	יִרְבֶּה, וְהָיָה כִּי־תִקְרֶאנָה מִלְחָמָה,
v'nosaf gam hu al soneinu,	וְנוֹסַף גַּם הוּא עַל־שֹׂנְאֵינוּ,
v'nilcham banu v'alah min ha-aretz.	וְנִלְחַם־בָּנוּ וְעָלָה מִן־הָאָרֶץ:
Vay'anunu. K'mah shene-emar: vayasimu	וַיְעַנּוּנוּ. כְּמָה שֶׁנֶּאֱמַר: וַיָּשִׂימוּ
alav sarei misim, l'ma-an anoto	עָלָיו שָׂרֵי מִסִּים, לְמַעַן עַנֹּתוֹ
b'sivlotam, va-yiven arei misk'not	בְּסִבְלֹתָם: וַיִּבֶן עָרֵי מִסְכְּנוֹת
l'faroh, et Pitom v'et Raamseis.	לְפַרְעֹה, אֶת־פִּתֹם וְאֶת־רַעַמְסֵס:
Vayit'nu aleinu avodah kashah.	וַיִּתְּנוּ עָלֵינוּ עֲבֹדָה קָשָׁה.
K'mah shene-emar: vaya-avidu Mitzrayim	כְּמָה שֶׁנֶּאֱמַר: וַיַּעֲבִדוּ מִצְרַיִם
et B'nei Yisra-eil b'farech. Vanitzak	אֶת־בְּנֵי יִשְׂרָאֵל בְּפָרֶךְ: וַנִּצְעַק
el Adonai Elohei avoteinu, vayishma	אֶל־יְיָ אֱלֹהֵי אֲבֹתֵינוּ, וַיִּשְׁמַע יְיָ
Adonai et koleinu, vayar et on'yeinu, v'et	אֶת־קֹלֵנוּ, וַיַּרְא אֶת־עָנְיֵנוּ, וְאֶת־

amaleinu, v'et lachatzeinu.

עֲמָלֵנוּ, וְאֶת לַחֲצֵנוּ:

Vanitzak el Adonai Elohei

וַנִּצְעַק אֶל־יְיָ אֱלֹהֵי

avoteinu. K'mah shene-emar:

אֲבֹתֵינוּ. כְּמָה שֶׁנֶּאֱמַר:

vay'hi va-yamim harabim ha-heim,

וַיְהִי בַיָּמִים הָרַבִּים הָהֵם,

va-yamot melech Mitzrayim, va-yei-

וַיָּמָת מֶלֶךְ מִצְרַיִם, וַיֵּאָנְחוּ

an'chu V'nei Yisra-eil min ha-avodah

בְנֵי־יִשְׂרָאֵל מִן־הָעֲבֹדָה

vayizaku. Vata-al shavatam el

וַיִּזְעָקוּ. וַתַּעַל שַׁוְעָתָם אֶל־

ha-Elohim min ha-avodah.

הָאֱלֹהִים מִן־הָעֲבֹדָה:

Vayishma Adonai et koleinu. K'mah

וַיִּשְׁמַע יְיָ אֶת־קֹלֵנוּ. כְּמָה

shene-emar: vayishma Elohim et

שֶׁנֶּאֱמַר: וַיִּשְׁמַע אֱלֹהִים

na-akatam, vayizkor Elohim

אֶת־נַאֲקָתָם, וַיִּזְכֹּר אֱלֹהִים

et b'rito, et Avraham,

אֶת־בְּרִיתוֹ, אֶת־אַבְרָהָם,

et Yitzchak, v'et Ya-akov.

אֶת־יִצְחָק, וְאֶת יַעֲקֹב:

Vayar et on'yeinu. Zo p'rishut

וַיַּרְא אֶת־עָנְיֵנוּ. זוֹ פְּרִישׁוּת

derech eretz. K'mah shene-emar:

דֶּרֶךְ אֶרֶץ, כְּמָה שֶׁנֶּאֱמַר:

vayar Elohim et B'nei

וַיַּרְא אֱלֹהִים אֶת־בְּנֵי

Yisra-eil. Vayeida Elohim.

יִשְׂרָאֵל. וַיֵּדַע אֱלֹהִים:

V'et amaleinu. Eilu ha-banim.

וְאֶת־עֲמָלֵנוּ. אֵלּוּ הַבָּנִים,

Kmah shene-emar: kol habein

כְּמָה שֶׁנֶּאֱמַר: כָּל־הַבֵּן

hayilod hay'orah tashlichu-hu,

הַיִּלּוֹד הַיְאֹרָה תַּשְׁלִיכֻהוּ,

v'chol-habat t'chayun.

וְכָל־הַבַּת תְּחַיּוּן:

V'et lachatzeinu. Zeh had'chak.

וְאֶת לַחֲצֵנוּ. זֶה הַדְּחַק,

K'mah shene-emar: v'gam ra-iti et

ha-lachatz, asher Mitzrayim lochatzim

כְּמָה שֶׁנֶּאֱמַר: וְגַם־רָאִיתִי אֶת־

הַלַּחַץ, אֲשֶׁר מִצְרַיִם לֹחֲצִים אֹתָם:

"And the Egyptians dealt cruelly with us and oppressed us, and they imposed hard labor on us" (Deuteronomy 26:6).

"And the Egyptians did evil to us" – as it is said: "Let us deal shrewdly with them and prevent them from increasing further, lest – if war breaks out – they join our enemies and fight against us, and take over the country" (Exodus 1:10).

"Oppressed us" – as it is said: "So they set taskmasters over them in order to oppress them with hard labor. And they built store-cities for Pharaoh: Pitom and Raamses" (Exodus 1:11).

"And they imposed hard labor on us" – as it is said: "And the Egyptians worked the Children of Israel ruthlessly" (Exodus 1:13).

"Then we cried out to Adonai, the God of our ancestors, and Adonai heard our voice and saw our oppression, our hardship, and our distress" (Deuteronomy 26:7).

"Then we cried out to Adonai, the God of our ancestors" – as it is said: "Long after that, the king of Egypt died. But the Children of Israel were still in grinding slavery, and they cried out, and their outcry about their slavery reached God" (Exodus 2:23).

"Adonai heard our voice" – as it is said: "And God heard their groaning, and God remembered God's covenant with Abraham, with Isaac, and with Jacob" (Exodus 2:24).

"And God saw our oppression" – this was a forced separation of husbands from their wives, as it is said: "And God saw the Children of Israel, and God knew" (Exodus 2:25).

"Our hardship" – this means the sons, as it is said: "Every newborn boy you shall throw into the Nile, but let every girl live" (Exodus 1:22).

"And our distress – refers to the brutality, as it is said: "I have also seen the brutality with which the Egyptians are oppressing them" (Exodus 3:9).

REFLECTION

Why doesn't the Torah just state that the Egyptians made us suffer? Why does it need to also include the word *vay'anunu*, which can be interpreted to mean "the Egyptians invented evil about us"? Rabbi Mordechai Gifter, the head of the Telshe Yeshiva, pointed out that Pharaoh was concerned public opinion might not be with him when he began oppressing the Jewish people. After all, the Jews were the Egyptians' neighbors and coworkers who lived peacefully in their midst. So Pharaoh had to spread outright falsehoods – for example, that the Jews would be a disloyal fifth column. This tactic worked; we see two verses later that the Egyptian people began to abhor the Jews.[63] This is also an example of the first case of "media bias" against the Jewish people. It wasn't anything that the Jews did but rather the public image of Jews that was manipulated to attribute to these accusations a perception of truth.[64]

QUESTIONS FOR DISCUSSION

When you see disinformation against the Jewish community or Israel, what do you think is the best way to confront it? What do you see as an effective way to respond to the Boycott Divestment Sanctions movement? To anti-Semitic statements? To hate speech and violence against others?

This section concludes with the concept that God heard our moans, suffering, and travail and then redeemed us. Many of us, as well as our family and friends, have waited for miracles that never happened. How should we respond when we see human suffering? When bad things happen to good people? What are theological and practical responses that we hope for? When it appears that God has not intervened, does our relationship to God change? How do we maintain our *emunah* (faith) in the face of such challenges?

How should we respond when we see human suffering? When bad things happen to good people?

REFLECTION

Elie Wiesel told the story of how one night in Auschwitz three rabbis decided to put God on trial for allowing His children to be murdered. As night was about to descend, the rabbi pronounced the verdict – guilty – and then announced, "Fellow Jews, it is now time to daven Maariv [the evening prayer]..."[65]

REFLECTION

We read that the Jewish people cried out to God, and God saw the Jewish people's affliction, including the destruction of the male children. The text reads, "Every son that is born shall be cast into the river and every

daughter shall stay alive." One commentary notes that the text does not say *tichyeh*, that the girls shall live, but rather *tichayun*, "you shall show them how to live." According to this interpretation, Pharaoh instructed his people to educate the girls in Egyptian culture and values. While the boys were doomed to a physical death, the girls were doomed to assimilation.[66]

Vayotzi-einu Hashem Mi-Mitzrayim

Vayotzi-einu Adonai mi-Mitzrayim, b'yad chazakah, uvizroa n'tuyah, uv'mora gadol uv'otot uv'mof'tim.

וַיּוֹצִאֵנוּ יְיָ מִמִּצְרַיִם, בְּיָד חֲזָקָה, וּבִזְרֹעַ נְטוּיָה, וּבְמֹרָא גָּדוֹל וּבְאֹתוֹת וּבְמוֹפְתִים:

Vayotzi-einu Adonai mi-Mitzrayim. Lo al y'dei malach, v'lo al y'dei saraf. V'lo al y'dei shali-ach. Ela Hakadosh Baruch Hu bichvodo uv'atzmo.

וַיּוֹצִאֵנוּ יְיָ מִמִּצְרַיִם. לֹא עַל־יְדֵי מַלְאָךְ, וְלֹא עַל־יְדֵי שָׂרָף. וְלֹא עַל־יְדֵי שָׁלִיחַ. אֶלָּא הַקָּדוֹשׁ בָּרוּךְ הוּא בִּכְבוֹדוֹ וּבְעַצְמוֹ.

Shene-emar: v'avarti v'eretz Mitzrayim ba-laylah hazeh, v'hikeiti chol b'chor b'eretz Mitzrayim, mei-adam v'ad b'heimah, uv'chol elohei Mitzrayim e-eseh sh'fatim ani Adonai.

שֶׁנֶּאֱמַר: וְעָבַרְתִּי בְאֶרֶץ מִצְרַיִם בַּלַּיְלָה הַזֶּה, וְהִכֵּיתִי כָל־בְּכוֹר בְּאֶרֶץ מִצְרַיִם, מֵאָדָם וְעַד בְּהֵמָה, וּבְכָל־אֱלֹהֵי מִצְרַיִם אֶעֱשֶׂה שְׁפָטִים אֲנִי יְיָ:

V'avarti v'eretz Mitzrayim balaylah hazeh, ani v'lo malach. V'hikeiti chol b'chor b'eretz Mitzrayim. ani v'lo saraf. Uv'chol elohei Mitzrayim e-eseh sh'fatim, ani v'lo hashali-ach. Ani Adonai. Ani hu v'lo acheir.

וְעָבַרְתִּי בְאֶרֶץ־מִצְרַיִם בַּלַּיְלָה הַזֶּה, אֲנִי וְלֹא מַלְאָךְ. וְהִכֵּיתִי כָל בְּכוֹר בְּאֶרֶץ־מִצְרַיִם. אֲנִי וְלֹא שָׂרָף. וּבְכָל־אֱלֹהֵי מִצְרַיִם אֶעֱשֶׂה שְׁפָטִים, אֲנִי וְלֹא הַשָּׁלִיחַ. אֲנִי יְיָ. אֲנִי הוּא וְלֹא אַחֵר:

B'yad chazakah. Zo ha-dever. בְּיָד חֲזָקָה. זוֹ הַדֶּבֶר, כְּמָה

K'mah shene-emar: hineih yad שֶׁנֶּאֱמַר: הִנֵּה יַד־יְיָ הוֹיָה,

Adonai hoyah, b'mikn'cha asher בְּמִקְנְךָ אֲשֶׁר בַּשָּׂדֶה, בַּסּוּסִים

basadeh, basusim bachamorim בַּחֲמֹרִים בַּגְּמַלִּים, בַּבָּקָר

bag'malim, babakar uvatzon, dever וּבַצֹּאן, דֶּבֶר כָּבֵד מְאֹד:

kaveid m'od. Uvizroa n'tuyah. Zo וּבִזְרֹעַ נְטוּיָה. זוֹ הַחֶרֶב,

ha-cherev. K'mah shene-emar: כְּמָה שֶׁנֶּאֱמַר: וְחַרְבּוֹ שְׁלוּפָה

v'charbo sh'lufah b'yado, n'tuyah al בְּיָדוֹ, נְטוּיָה עַל־יְרוּשָׁלָיִם:

Y'rushalayim. Uv'mora gadol. Zeh וּבְמוֹרָא גָדוֹל. זֶה גִּלּוּי שְׁכִינָה,

giluy Sh'chinah. K'mah shene-emar: כְּמָה שֶׁנֶּאֱמַר: אוֹ הֲנִסָּה

o hanisah Elohim, lavo lakachat אֱלֹהִים, לָבוֹא לָקַחַת לוֹ גוֹי

lo goy mikerev goy, b'masot מִקֶּרֶב גּוֹי, בְּמַסֹּת בְּאֹתֹת

b'otot uv'mof'tim uv'milchamah, וּבְמוֹפְתִים וּבְמִלְחָמָה, וּבְיָד

uv'yad chazakah uvizroa n'tuyah, חֲזָקָה וּבִזְרוֹעַ נְטוּיָה, וּבְמוֹרָאִים

uv'moraim g'dolim. K'chol asher גְּדֹלִים. כְּכֹל אֲשֶׁר־עָשָׂה לָכֶם

asah lachem Adonai Eloheichem יְיָ אֱלֹהֵיכֶם בְּמִצְרָיִם, לְעֵינֶיךָ:

b'Mitzrayim, l'einecha. Uv'otot. Zeh וּבְאֹתוֹת. זֶה הַמַּטֶּה, כְּמָה

hamateh, k'mah shene-emar: v'et שֶׁנֶּאֱמַר: וְאֶת הַמַּטֶּה

hamateh hazeh tikach b'yadecha, הַזֶּה תִּקַּח בְּיָדֶךָ. אֲשֶׁר

asher ta-aseh bo et ha-otot. תַּעֲשֶׂה־בּוֹ אֶת־הָאֹתֹת:

Uv'mof'tim. Zeh hadam. k'mah וּבְמוֹפְתִים. זֶה הַדָּם, כְּמָה

shene-emar: v'natati mof'tim, שֶׁנֶּאֱמַר: וְנָתַתִּי מוֹפְתִים,

bashamayim uva-aretz. בַּשָּׁמַיִם וּבָאָרֶץ.

And God brought us out of Egypt with a strong hand and an outstretched arm and with terrifying deeds, and with signs and with omens.

"And Adonai brought us out of Egypt with a strong hand and an outstretched arm and with terrifying deeds, and with signs and with omens" (Deuteronomy 26:8).

"And Adonai brought us out of Egypt" – not through an angel, and not through a seraph, and not through a messenger, but the Blessed Holy One personally, as it is said: "On that night I will pass through the land of Egypt and I will kill every firstborn in the land of Egypt, human and beast; on all the gods of Egypt I will execute judgment – I, God" (Exodus 12:2). "On that night I will pass through the land of Egypt" – I, not an angel. "And I will kill every firstborn in the land of Egypt" – I, not a seraph. "On all the gods of Egypt I will execute judgment" – I, not a messenger. I, Adonai – I am the One; nobody else.

"With a strong hand" – this is the pestilence, as it is said: "Then God's hand will strike your grazing herds – and the horses, the asses, the camels, the cattle, and the sheep – with a very severe pestilence" (Exodus 9:3).

"And an outstretched arm" – this is the sword, as it is said: "…with his sword drawn in his hand outstretched over Jerusalem" (I Chronicles 21:16).

"And with terrifying deeds" – this is the appearance of the Divine Presence, as it is said: "Has a god ever ventured to come and take a nation from within another nation by miracles, by signs and wonders, and by war, by a mighty hand and an outstretched arm and by great deeds of terror as Adonai, your God, did for you in Egypt before your very eyes?" (Deuteronomy 4:34).

"By signs" – this is the rod, as it is said: "And take along this rod with which you shall perform the signs" (Exodus 4:17).

"And with omens" – this is the blood, as it is said: "I will show wonders in the sky and on earth" (Joel 3:3).

REFLECTION

The Lubavitcher Rebbe taught that the same way that God was willing to descend to Egypt to redeem Jews, we should follow the example to leave no stone unturned to reach out to all Jews – wherever they may be and regardless of their present situations – and bring Judaism into their lives.[67] Today all over the world, even in communities with very minimal Jewish populations, we can find Chabad centers reaching out to all Jews.

QUESTIONS FOR DISCUSSION

In situations of limited communal resources, to whom should the priority for help go? To Jews who are involved in the community but need financial help, or to those Jews who are not yet connected or who are intermarried, and for whom we have to spend extra resources to reach out to them?

QUESTIONS FOR DISCUSSION

"And God took us out with an outstretched arm." How do you respond to anthropomorphic descriptions of God? Does it create a view of God as an elderly man in the sky? Are gender-neutral texts an effective vehicle to undo these types of images? Is a vital part of Jewish tradition lost if we take out reference to God as King, Lord, and Father?

HUMOR CORNER

Who is behind Pharaoh's evil empire? Darth Seder.[68]

Dam Va-eish V'tim'rot Ashan

LEADER: As we are about to spill wine from our cups to recall the plagues inflicted on the Egyptians, we follow rabbinic teaching that we are bidden not to rejoice even at the downfall of those who sought to kill us. The angels were barred from singing because of human suffering. When we are threatened, we must do all that we can to defend ourselves, but even at our most vulnerable moments, we have in mind the losses of our enemies.

*As each of the following words are said, a small amount of wine
is spilled from the cup.*

Dam	**Va-eish**	**V'tim'rot ashan**	דָּם. וָאֵשׁ. וְתִימְרוֹת עָשָׁן:

"Blood and fire and pillars of smoke" (Joel 3:3).

Davar acheir. B'yad chazakah
sh'tayim. Uvizroa n'tuyah sh'tayim.
Uv'mora gadol sh'tayim. Uv'otot
sh'tayim. Uv'mof'tim sh'tayim.

דָּבָר אַחֵר: בְּיָד חֲזָקָה שְׁתַּיִם.
וּבִזְרֹעַ נְטוּיָה שְׁתַּיִם. וּבְמוֹרָא
גָּדוֹל שְׁתַּיִם. וּבְאֹתוֹת
שְׁתַּיִם. וּבְמֹפְתִים שְׁתַּיִם:

Another explanation:

"By a mighty hand" – two [words or plagues]

"and an outstretched arm" – two [words or plagues]

"and by great deeds of terror" – two [words or plagues]

"by signs" – two [words or plagues]

"and wonders" – two [words or plagues].

REFLECTION

A midrash teaches us that after the incident at the Sea of Reeds, Pharaoh reemerged in history as the King of Nineveh. In the story of Jonah, which we read on the afternoon of Yom Kippur, Jonah is commanded to speak to the people of Nineveh to inspire them to repent. Led by their king, the people of Nineveh do *teshuvah* (turn from their evil ways). This midrash should instill hope in us that even the most wicked among us have the potential to turn away from evil and toward good.[69]

The Ten Plagues

Eilu eser makot sheheivi	אֵלּוּ עֶשֶׂר מַכּוֹת שֶׁהֵבִיא
Hakadosh Baruch Hu al	הַקָּדוֹשׁ בָּרוּךְ הוּא עַל־
ha-Mitzrim b'Mitzrayim, v'eilu hein:	הַמִּצְרִים בְּמִצְרַיִם, וְאֵלּוּ הֵן:

These are ten plagues which the Blessed Holy One brought on the Egyptians in Egypt:

As we recite each plague, we pour out a drop of wine. The same is done when reciting the abbreviated listing of Rabbi Yehudah that follows.

Dam. Tz'fardei-a. Kinim	דָּם. צְפַרְדֵּעַ. כִּנִּים.
Arov. Dever. Sh'chin.	עָרוֹב. דֶּבֶר. שְׁחִין.
Barad. Arbeh. Choshech.	בָּרָד. אַרְבֶּה. חֹשֶׁךְ.
Makat b'chorot.	מַכַּת בְּכוֹרוֹת:

Blood	Frogs	Lice
Wild Beasts	Pestilence	Boils
Hail	Locusts	Darkness
	Death of Firstborn	

Even the most wicked among us have the potential to turn away from evil and toward good.

As we recite each plague, we pour out a drop of wine.

Rabi Y'hudah hayah notein bahem simanim. רַבִּי יְהוּדָה הָיָה נוֹתֵן בָּהֶם סִמָּנִים:

D'tza"ch   Ada"sh   B'acha"v   דְּצַ"ךְ   עַדַ"שׁ   בְּאַחַ"ב:

Rabbi Yehudah made a mnemonic of them:

DeTZaKh   ADaSH   BeACHaV

BACKGROUND

Can We See the Plagues through Scientific Eyes?

Can the plagues be explained scientifically? Live Science provides fascinating ways to understand how each plague could have created a ripple effect leading to other plagues.[70] (This is reminiscent of the themes we see in the "Chad Gadya" song: one event brings on the next.)

Blood. Can the Nile looking like blood be attributed to toxic red algae bloom? This "red tide" occurs when the algae multiplies in huge numbers. The algae could have developed from a very large rainfall, giving the Nile a bloody appearance, and would have killed the fish.

Frogs. According to a CBS news report , the sight of "raining frogs" has occurred throughout history, most recently in May 2010 in Greece. Thousands of frogs, in search of food, came out of a lake and held up traffic for days. The high bacteria in the Nile due to the red algae count could have caused massive numbers of fish to die, which would have caused frogs to swarm onshore by the thousands.

Lice. The presence of the toxic algae and the dead fish and frogs could lead to swarms of insects. Scientists explain that frogs usually eat insects. If they were not around to do so, the fly population would rise precipitously and help spread diseases, including the later bubonic plague.

Wild beasts. According to a 1996 article in the scientific journal *Caduceus*, rather than being wild beasts, this plague could also have been a swarm of flies, which would have led to the latter plague of boils.

Diseased livestock. Scientists have said this is similar to Rinderpest, a virus that has killed hundreds of millions of cattle over the last five thousand years. The journal *Science* reported that Rinderpest killed 5.2 million cattle in Africa, causing a third of the Ethiopian population to die of starvation. The virus was last seen in Kenya in 2001 but was completed eradicated as of 2010.

Boils. Scientists believe this could have been an outbreak of Smallpox. In fact, the Center for Disease Control and Prevention has identified smallpox scars on mummies.

Hail. 3500 years ago a volcano exploded on an island north of Crete in the Aegean Sea. The Institute for Atmospheric Physics in Germany said the hail could have resulted from volcanic ash from that volcano, mixing with thunderstorms over Egypt.

Locusts. the volcano could have created ripe conditions for locusts. Dr. Suri Trevisanato, a Canadian molecular biologist, explains that the ash causes weather conditions that lead to higher humidity and precipitations which leads to locusts.

Darkness. this could have been an eclipse. Scientists have identified one occurring on March 5, 1223 BCE. The miracle was that the Jewish people were not affected by this eclipse!

Death of the firstborn. in 2003, the Clinical Microbiology Review explained that the algae bloom could have released toxins that can cause harm to humans. Firstborn could have been the first ones to pick the grain and therefore, first to be contaminated and they would have fallen victim to it.

Traditionally, though, we understand the plagues as being without a "scientific" or "natural" cause. As Professor Nahum Sarna explains, the tenth plague is a judgment by God to the Egyptian people. They remained silent as their Jewish neighbors were enslaved. The plagues that resulted then were the result of their abdicating their moral responsibility and acquiescing in the face of horrific actions against the Jewish people.[71]

QUESTIONS FOR DISCUSSION

Can you name ten plagues that afflict us today? Poverty? Hatred? Indifference? One writer, Shanna Silva, has identified some contemporary plagues to include pollution, modern terrorism such as ISIS and Hamas, and ugly prejudice.[72] What would you add to the list?

HUMOR CORNER

What do you call a stupid frog? A dumb *tzfarde'ah*! (*Dam tzfarde'ah* in Hebrew means "blood, frog" –the first two plagues.)

See pp. 217–18 for songs "Let Us Go" and "Leaving on a Desert Plane"

REFLECTION

Rabbinic teaching reminds us that Moshe instructed Aaron to extend his rod over the Nile to turn it into blood. Moses himself did not extend his hand over the Nile, because the Nile had saved his life, and he did not want to show ingratitude.

Can you name ten plagues that afflict us today?

The rabbis viewed each plague as a middah k'neged middah, designed to recall something that happened to the Israelites in slavery.

The Chidushei Harim, the nineteenth-century Gerrer Rebbe, wrote that there is no greater darkness than when we do not see each other, when we don't pay attention to the needs of our fellow human, when we ignore the suffering of those around us. When this happens, we don't rise from our place and can't hope to move forward. In modern times, social scientists Bibb Latané and John Darley identified a version of this psychological reaction as the bystander effect, which occurs when the presence of others discourages an individual from intervening in an emergency situation. They identified it as a "diffusion of responsibility."[73] Contrast this with Moshe's actions. When he saw an Israelite being beaten by an Egyptian, he stepped in to save him. Have you ever thought what you would do if you saw someone in trouble?

REFLECTION

The mnemonic *d'tzach, adash, b'achav* is a helpful means to remember each plague. The rabbis viewed each plague as a *middah k'neged middah*, designed to recall something that happened to the Israelites in slavery. For example, the turning of the Nile to blood was to remind the Egyptians of their indifference to the blood of the Jews who died while enslaved. Rabbi Samson Raphael Hirsch explained that the plagues, which did terrible damage to persons and property, turned the Egyptians into slaves in their own land. The final plague stands alone in the deep pain it caused.[74]

Rabbi Yosei Hag'lili Omer

Rabi Yosei Hag'lili omeir. Minayin atah omeir, shelaku ha-Mitzrim b'Mitzrayim eser makot, v'al hayam, laku chamishim makot? B'Mitzrayim mah hu omeir. Vayomru hachartumim el Paroh, etzba Elohim hi. V'al hayam mah hu omeir? Vayar Yisra-eil et hayad hag'dolah, asher asah Adonai b'Mitzrayim, vayir'u ha-am et Adonai. Vaya-aminu b'Adonai, uv'mosheh avdo. Kamah laku b'etzba, eser makot. Emor

רַבִּי יוֹסֵי הַגְּלִילִי אוֹמֵר: מִנַּיִן אַתָּה אוֹמֵר, שֶׁלָּקוּ הַמִּצְרִים בְּמִצְרַיִם עֶשֶׂר מַכּוֹת, וְעַל הַיָּם, לָקוּ חֲמִשִּׁים מַכּוֹת? בְּמִצְרַיִם מָה הוּא אוֹמֵר: וַיֹּאמְרוּ הַחַרְטֻמִּם אֶל-פַּרְעֹה, אֶצְבַּע אֱלֹהִים הוּא. וְעַל הַיָּם מָה הוּא אוֹמֵר? וַיַּרְא יִשְׂרָאֵל אֶת-הַיָּד הַגְּדֹלָה, אֲשֶׁר עָשָׂה יְיָ בְּמִצְרַיִם, וַיִּירְאוּ הָעָם אֶת-יְיָ. וַיַּאֲמִינוּ בַּיָי, וּבְמֹשֶׁה עַבְדּוֹ. כַּמָּה לָקוּ בְּאֶצְבַּע, עֶשֶׂר מַכּוֹת: אֱמוֹר מֵעַתָּה, בְּמִצְרַיִם

mei-atah, b'Mitzrayim laku

eser makot, v'al hayam,

laku chamishim makot.

Rabi Eliezer omeir:

Minayin shekol makah umakah,

sheheivi Hakadosh Baruch Hu al

ha-Mitzrim b'Mitzrayim,

hay'tah shel arba makot?

Shene-emar: y'shalach bam charon

apo, evrah vaza-am v'tzarah,

mishlachat malachei ra-im.

Evrah achat. Vaza-am sh'tayim.

V'tzarah shalosh. Mishlachat

malachei rai-im arba.

Emor mei-atah, b'Mitzrayim

laku arba-im makot, v'al

hayam laku matayim makot.

Rabi Akiva omeir: Minayin

shekol makah u-makah, sheheivi

Hakadosh Baruch Hu al

ha-Mitzrim b'Mitzrayim, hay'tah

shel chameish makot? Shene-emar:

y'shalach bam charon apo, evrah

לָקוּ עֶשֶׂר מַכּוֹת, וְעַל־

הַיָּם, לָקוּ חֲמִשִּׁים מַכּוֹת:

רַבִּי אֱלִיעֶזֶר אוֹמֵר:

מִנַּיִן שֶׁכָּל־מַכָּה וּמַכָּה,

שֶׁהֵבִיא הַקָּדוֹשׁ בָּרוּךְ הוּא

עַל הַמִּצְרִים בְּמִצְרַיִם,

הָיְתָה שֶׁל אַרְבַּע מַכּוֹת?

שֶׁנֶּאֱמַר: יְשַׁלַּח־בָּם חֲרוֹן

אַפּוֹ, עֶבְרָה וָזַעַם וְצָרָה.

מִשְׁלַחַת מַלְאֲכֵי רָעִים.

עֶבְרָה אַחַת. וָזַעַם שְׁתַּיִם.

וְצָרָה שָׁלֹשׁ. מִשְׁלַחַת

מַלְאֲכֵי רָעִים אַרְבַּע:

אֱמוֹר מֵעַתָּה, בְּמִצְרַיִם

לָקוּ אַרְבָּעִים מַכּוֹת, וְעַל

הַיָּם לָקוּ מָאתַיִם מַכּוֹת:

רַבִּי עֲקִיבָא אוֹמֵר: מִנַּיִן

שֶׁכָּל־מַכָּה וּמַכָּה, שֶׁהֵבִיא

הַקָּדוֹשׁ בָּרוּךְ הוּא עַל

הַמִּצְרִים בְּמִצְרַיִם,

הָיְתָה שֶׁל חָמֵשׁ מַכּוֹת?

שֶׁנֶּאֱמַר: יְשַׁלַּח־בָּם

חֲרוֹן אַפּוֹ, עֶבְרָה וָזַעַם

vaza-am v'tzarah. Mishlachat malachei וְצָרָה. מִשְׁלַחַת מַלְאֲכֵי רָעִים.

ra-im. Charon apo achat. Evrah sh'tayim. חֲרוֹן אַפּוֹ אַחַת. עֶבְרָה שְׁתַּיִם.

Vaza-am shalosh. V'tzarah arba. Mishlachat וָזַעַם שָׁלֹשׁ. וְצָרָה אַרְבַּע. מִשְׁלַחַת

malachei rai-im chameish. Emor mei-atah, מַלְאֲכֵי רָעִים חָמֵשׁ : אֱמוֹר מֵעַתָּה,

b'Mitzrayim laku chamishim makot, v'al בְּמִצְרַיִם לָקוּ חֲמִשִּׁים מַכּוֹת, וְעַל

hayam laku chamishim u-matayim makot. הַיָּם לָקוּ חֲמִשִּׁים וּמָאתַיִם מַכּוֹת:

Rabbi Yossé the Galilean says: How do you calculate that the Egyptians were smitten with ten plagues in Egypt and with fifty plagues on the sea? Concerning Egypt, what does it say? "And the magicians said to Pharaoh: This is the finger of God!" (Exodus 8:15). And concerning the sea what does it say? "And Israel saw the wondrous hand that God had wielded against the Egyptians, and the people feared Adonai, and they put their trust in Adonai and in God's servant Moses" (Exodus 14:31). With how many plagues were they smitten with a finger? Ten plagues. Hence, in Egypt they were smitten with ten plagues, and on the sea they were smitten with fifty plagues.

Rabbi Eliezer says: How do we know that each plague that the Blessed Holy One brought on the Egyptians in Egypt consisted of four plagues? For it is said: "God loosed upon them burning anger: wrath, and fury, and rage, a legation of evil messengers" (Psalms 78:49).

"Wrath" – one.

"And fury" – one.

"And rage" – one.

"A legation of evil messengers" – one.

Hence, in Egypt they were smitten with forty plagues, and on the sea they were smitten with two hundred plagues.

Rabbi Akiva says: How do we know that each plague that the Blessed Holy One brought on the Egyptians in Egypt consisted of five plagues? For it is said: "God loosed upon them burning anger, wrath, and fury, and rage, a legation of evil messengers" (Psalms 78:49).

"God's burning anger" – one.

"Wrath" – two.

"And fury" – three.

"And rage" – four.

"A legation of evil messengers" – five.

Hence, in Egypt they were smitten with fifty plagues, and on the sea they were smitten with 250 plagues.

REFLECTION

We are taught that the Haggadah omits any reference to or discussion of Moses in connection with the Exodus to show that it was God Who freed the Jews, lest there be any worship of Moses. In fact, Moses' name is mentioned once, in this paragraph (which cites Exodus 14:31), but even here Moses is identified as the servant of God. In Maimonides' Haggadah, this reference is omitted.

Dayeinu

LEADER: As we sing Dayeinu collectively, let us reflect on new ways that we can express our gratitude to God for all that we have in our lives.

Sing all together:

Kamah ma-alot tovot	כַּמָּה מַעֲלוֹת טוֹבוֹת
lamakom aleinu.	לַמָּקוֹם עָלֵינוּ:
Ilu hotzi-anu mi-Mitzrayim,	אִלּוּ הוֹצִיאָנוּ מִמִּצְרַיִם,
v'lo asah vahem sh'fatim, dayeinu.	וְלֹא עָשָׂה בָהֶם שְׁפָטִים, דַּיֵּנוּ:
IIu asah vahem sh'fatim,	אִלּוּ עָשָׂה בָהֶם שְׁפָטִים,
v'lo asah veiloheihem, dayeinu.	וְלֹא עָשָׂה בֵאלֹהֵיהֶם, דַּיֵּנוּ:
Ilu asah veiloheihem,	אִלּוּ עָשָׂה בֵאלֹהֵיהֶם,
v'lo harag et b'choreihem, dayeinu.	וְלֹא הָרַג אֶת־בְּכוֹרֵיהֶם, דַּיֵּנוּ:
Ilu harag et b'choreihem,	אִלּוּ הָרַג אֶת־בְּכוֹרֵיהֶם,
v'lo natan lanu et mamonam, dayeinu.	וְלֹא נָתַן לָנוּ אֶת־מָמוֹנָם, דַּיֵּנוּ:
Ilu natan lanu et mamonam,	אִלּוּ נָתַן לָנוּ אֶת־מָמוֹנָם,
v'lo kara lanu et hayam, dayeinu.	וְלֹא קָרַע לָנוּ אֶת־הַיָּם, דַּיֵּנוּ:
Ilu kara lanu et hayam,	אִלּוּ קָרַע לָנוּ אֶת־הַיָּם,
v'lo he-eviranu v'tocho	וְלֹא הֶעֱבִירָנוּ בְתוֹכוֹ
vecharavah, dayeinu.	בֶּחָרָבָה, דַּיֵּנוּ:
Ilu he-eviranu v'tocho vecharavah,	אִלּוּ הֶעֱבִירָנוּ בְתוֹכוֹ בֶּחָרָבָה,
v'lo shika tzareinu b'tocho, dayeinu.	וְלֹא שִׁקַּע צָרֵינוּ בְּתוֹכוֹ, דַּיֵּנוּ:
Ilu shika tzareinu b'tocho,	אִלּוּ שִׁקַּע צָרֵינוּ בְּתוֹכוֹ,
v'lo sipeik tzor'keinu bamidbar	וְלֹא סִפֵּק צָרְכֵּנוּ בַּמִּדְבָּר

arba-im shanah, dayeinu.	אַרְבָּעִים שָׁנָה, דַּיֵּנוּ:
Ilu sipeik tzor'keinu bamidbar	אִלּוּ סִפֵּק צָרְכֵּנוּ בַּמִּדְבָּר
arba-im shanah, v'lo	אַרְבָּעִים שָׁנָה, וְלֹא
he-echilanu et ha-man, dayeinu.	הֶאֱכִילָנוּ אֶת־הַמָּן, דַּיֵּנוּ:
Ilu he-echilanu et ha-man,	אִלּוּ הֶאֱכִילָנוּ אֶת־הַמָּן,
v'lo natan lanu et ha-Shabat,	וְלֹא נָתַן לָנוּ אֶת־הַשַּׁבָּת,
dayeinu.	דַּיֵּנוּ:
Ilu natan lanu et ha-Shabat,	אִלּוּ נָתַן לָנוּ אֶת־הַשַּׁבָּת,
v'lo keir'vanu lifnei	וְלֹא קֵרְבָנוּ לִפְנֵי
Har Sinai, dayeinu.	הַר סִינַי, דַּיֵּנוּ:
Ilu keir'vanu lifnei Har Sinai, v'lo	אִלּוּ קֵרְבָנוּ לִפְנֵי הַר סִינַי,
natan lanu et ha-Torah, dayeinu.	וְלֹא נָתַן לָנוּ אֶת־הַתּוֹרָה, דַּיֵּנוּ:
Ilu natan lanu et ha-Torah,	אִלּוּ נָתַן לָנוּ אֶת־הַתּוֹרָה,
v'lo hichnisanu l'Eretz	וְלֹא הִכְנִיסָנוּ לְאֶרֶץ
Yisra-eil, dayeinu.	יִשְׂרָאֵל, דַּיֵּנוּ:
Ilu hichnisanu l'Eretz Yisra-eil,	אִלּוּ הִכְנִיסָנוּ לְאֶרֶץ יִשְׂרָאֵל,
v'lo vanah lanu et Beit	וְלֹא בָנָה לָנוּ אֶת־בֵּית
Hab'chirah, dayeinu.	הַבְּחִירָה, דַּיֵּנוּ:

So many are the favors for which we must thank the Omnipresent One!

If God had taken us out of Egypt but not given them their punishments

That would have been good enough!

If God had given them their punishments but not taken it out on their gods

That would have been good enough!

If God had taken it out on their gods but not killed their firstborn

That would have been good enough!

If God had killed their firstborn but not handed us their wealth

That would have been good enough!

If God had handed us their wealth but not parted the sea for us

That would have been good enough!

If God had parted the sea for us but not brought us through it dry

That would have been good enough!

If God had brought us through it dry but not sunk our enemies in it

That would have been good enough!

If God had sunk our enemies in it but not provided for us in the wilderness for forty years

That would have been good enough!

If God had provided for us in the wilderness for forty years but not fed us manna

That would have been good enough!

If God had fed us the manna but not given us the Sabbath

That would have been good enough!

If God had given us the Sabbath but not drawn us near to God at Mount Sinai

That would have been good enough!

If God had drawn us near at Mount Sinai but not given us the Torah

That would have been good enough!

If God had given us the Torah but not brought us into the Land of Israel

That would have been good enough!

If God had brought us into the Land of Israel but not built us the House of God's Choosing

That would have been good enough!

Al achat kamah v'chamah tovah	עַל אַחַת כַּמָּה וְכַמָּה טוֹבָה
ch'fulah um'chupelet lamakom	כְּפוּלָה וּמְכֻפֶּלֶת לַמָּקוֹם עָלֵינוּ:
aleinu. She-hotzi-anu	שֶׁהוֹצִיאָנוּ מִמִּצְרַיִם,
mi-Mitzrayim, v'asah vahem	וְעָשָׂה בָהֶם שְׁפָטִים,
sh'fatim, v'asah vei-loheihem,	וְעָשָׂה בֵאלֹהֵיהֶם,
v'harag et b'choreihem,	וְהָרַג אֶת־בְּכוֹרֵיהֶם,
v'natan lanu et mamonam,	וְנָתַן לָנוּ אֶת־מָמוֹנָם,
v'kara lanu et hayam,	וְקָרַע לָנוּ אֶת־הַיָּם,
v'he-eviranu v'tocho vecharavah,	וְהֶעֱבִירָנוּ בְּתוֹכוֹ בֶּחָרָבָה,
v'shika tzareinu b'tocho,	וְשִׁקַּע צָרֵינוּ בְּתוֹכוֹ,
v'sipeik tzor'keinu bamidbar	וְסִפֵּק צָרְכֵּנוּ בַּמִּדְבָּר
arba-im shanah,	אַרְבָּעִים שָׁנָה,
v'he-echilanu et ha-man,	וְהֶאֱכִילָנוּ אֶת־הַמָּן,
v'natan lanu et ha-Shabat,	וְנָתַן לָנוּ אֶת־הַשַּׁבָּת,
v'keir'vanu lifnei Har Sinai,	וְקֵרְבָנוּ לִפְנֵי הַר סִינַי,
v'natan lanu et ha-Torah,	וְנָתַן לָנוּ אֶת־הַתּוֹרָה,
v'hichnisanu l'Eretz Yisra-eil,	וְהִכְנִיסָנוּ לְאֶרֶץ יִשְׂרָאֵל,
u'vanah lanu et Beit Hab'chirah,	וּבָנָה לָנוּ אֶת־בֵּית הַבְּחִירָה,
l'chapeir al kol avonoteinu.	לְכַפֵּר עַל־כָּל־עֲוֹנוֹתֵינוּ.

How many times more, then, do we owe thanks to the Omnipresent for taking us out of Egypt, and giving them their just deserts, and taking it out on their gods, and killing their firstborn, and handing us their wealth, and splitting the sea for us, and bringing us through it dry, and sinking out oppressors in it, and providing for us in the wilderness for forty years, and

feeding us manna, and giving us the Sabbath, and drawing us near at Mount Sinai, and giving us the Torah, and bringing us into the Land of Israel, and building us the House of God's Choosing for the expiation of all our sins.

See p. 219 for Dayeinu to the tune of "The Wheels of the Bus"

QUESTIONS FOR DISCUSSION

If you had to delineate categories of what you are grateful for, what would they be? Are there things in life about which you would say, "*Lo dayeinu*" (It is not enough for us)?

REFLECTION

Cultivating Gratitude

Just let this baby be born healthy and whole. That's all I ask.

I said this over and over when I was pregnant with my first child, as if I didn't know how briefly I would savor the relief when the time came, God willing, as if I didn't know how quickly and greedily I would begin to come up with new anxieties, new requests, new demands.

How easy it is to live in constant anticipation, promising God and ourselves that we will be satisfied and grateful, if only...but there is always something else. This is part of what makes us human.

When we say *Dayeinu*, on one level we are lying. We say, "It would have been enough." But we know that this is not true. No single step of our journey out of slavery would have been sufficient.

Yet, we tell this lie in order to cultivate our capacity for gratitude. We exercise our thanking muscles, trying at least for a moment to appreciate each and every small gift as if we really believed it was enough.

Of course we want more. We have hopes and dreams for ourselves and for our children. But for their sakes, and for our own, we must also be able to stop and say *Dayeinu*: "This is enough for us, thank God." For a moment, to feel that we have everything we need. That is what it means to say *Dayeinu*.

— Rabbi Sharon Cohen Anisfeld[75]

Pesach, Matzah, U-maror

The text of Pesach, Matzah, and Maror is written in a question-and-answer style, fulfilling the requirement found in the Mishnah that this be a night of questions and answers.

We do not raise the shank bone from the Seder plate during the following declaration, as it recalls the paschal sacrifice; the rabbis were sensitive that it not appear – in the absence of the Temple and sacrificial system – as though we are eating sacrifices outside the Temple.

Raban Gamli-eil hayah omeir:	רַבָּן גַּמְלִיאֵל הָיָה אוֹמֵר:
Kol shelo amar sh'loshah	כָּל שֶׁלֹּא אָמַר שְׁלֹשָׁה
d'varim eilu ba-Pesach,	דְּבָרִים אֵלּוּ בַּפֶּסַח,
lo yatza y'dei chovato, v'eilu hein:	לֹא יָצָא יְדֵי חוֹבָתוֹ, וְאֵלּוּ הֵן:
Pesach, matzah, u-maror	פֶּסַח, מַצָּה, וּמָרוֹר:

Rabban Gamliel used to say: Whoever has not mentioned these three things on Passover has not fulfilled the obligation:

the Passover offering, matzah, bitter herbs

Pesach she-hayu avoteinu och'lim,	פֶּסַח שֶׁהָיוּ אֲבוֹתֵינוּ אוֹכְלִים,
bizman shebeit hamikdash hayah	בִּזְמַן שֶׁבֵּית הַמִּקְדָּשׁ הָיָה
kayam, al shum mah? Al shum	קַיָּם, עַל שׁוּם מָה? עַל שׁוּם
she-pasach Hakadosh Baruch Hu, al	שֶׁפָּסַח הַקָּדוֹשׁ בָּרוּךְ הוּא,
batei avoteinu b'Mitzrayim, shene-	עַל בָּתֵּי אֲבוֹתֵינוּ בְּמִצְרַיִם,
emar: va-amartem zevach Pesach	שֶׁנֶּאֱמַר: וַאֲמַרְתֶּם זֶבַח פֶּסַח
hu l'Adonai, asher pasach al batei	הוּא לַייָ, אֲשֶׁר פָּסַח עַל
V'nei Yisra-eil b'Mitzrayim, b'nag'po	בָּתֵּי בְנֵי יִשְׂרָאֵל בְּמִצְרַיִם,
et Mitzrayim v'et bateinu hitzil,	בְּנָגְפּוֹ אֶת־מִצְרַיִם וְאֶת־בָּתֵּינוּ
vayikod ha-am vayishtachavu.	הִצִּיל, וַיִּקֹּד הָעָם וַיִּשְׁתַּחֲווּ.

The Passover offering that our ancestors ate when the Temple was standing – what was the reason for it? Because the Blessed Holy One passed over our ancestors' houses in Egypt, as it is said: "You shall say: It is a Passover sacrifice to Adonai, because God passed over the Houses of the Children of Israel in Egypt when smiting the Egyptians but spared our houses. And the people bowed down and prostrated themselves" (Exodus 12:27).

Hold up the broken middle matzah and say:

Matzah zo she-anu och'lim, al shum	מַצָּה זוֹ שֶׁאָנוּ אוֹכְלִים, עַל שׁוּם
mah? Al shum shelo hispik	מָה? עַל שׁוּם שֶׁלֹא הִסְפִּיק
b'tzeikam shel avoteinu l'hachamitz,	בְּצֵקָם שֶׁל אֲבוֹתֵינוּ לְהַחֲמִיץ,
ad sheniglah aleihem melech malchei	עַד שֶׁנִּגְלָה עֲלֵיהֶם מֶלֶךְ מַלְכֵי
ham'lachim, Hakadosh Baruch Hu,	הַמְּלָכִים, הַקָּדוֹשׁ בָּרוּךְ הוּא,
ug'alam, shene-emar: vayofu et	וּגְאָלָם, שֶׁנֶּאֱמַר: וַיֹּאפוּ אֶת־
habatzeik, asher hotzi-u mi-Mitzrayim,	הַבָּצֵק, אֲשֶׁר הוֹצִיאוּ מִמִּצְרָיִם,
ugot matzot, ki lo chameitz ki gor'shu	עֻגֹת מַצּוֹת, כִּי לֹא חָמֵץ: כִּי גֹרְשׁוּ
mi-Mitzrayim, v'lo yach'lu l'hitmahmeiha,	מִמִּצְרָיִם, וְלֹא יָכְלוּ לְהִתְמַהְמֵהַּ,
v'gam tzeidah lo asu lahem.	וְגַם צֵדָה לֹא עָשׂוּ לָהֶם.

This matzah that we eat – what is the reason for it? Because the dough of our ancestors had not yet risen when the Ruler of Rulers, the Blessed Holy One, became known to them and redeemed them, as it is said: "And the dough they had brought along out of Egypt they baked into unleavened cakes, for there was no leaven, because they had been driven out of Egypt and had had no time to tarry; they had not even prepared any provision for themselves" (Exodus 12:39).

Hold up the bitter herbs and say:

Maror zeh she-anu och'lim, al shum	מָרוֹר זֶה שֶׁאָנוּ אוֹכְלִים, עַל שׁוּם מָה?
mah? al shum shemeir'ru ha-Mitzrim	עַל שׁוּם שֶׁמֵּרְרוּ הַמִּצְרִים אֶת־חַיֵּי
et chayei avoteinu b'Mitzrayim, shene-	אֲבוֹתֵינוּ בְּמִצְרָיִם, שֶׁנֶּאֱמַר: וַיְמָרְרוּ

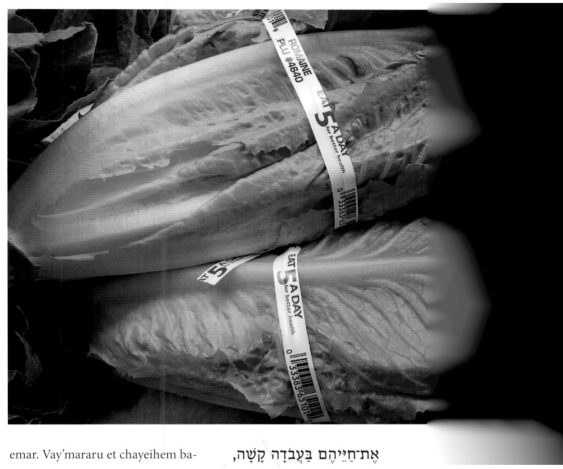

emar. Vay'mararu et chayeihem ba-
avodah kashah, b'chomer uvilveinim,
uv'chol avodah basadeh, eit kol
avodatam, asher av'du vahem b'farech.

אֶת־חַיֵּיהֶם בַּעֲבֹדָה קָשָׁה,
בְּחֹמֶר וּבִלְבֵנִים, וּבְכָל־עֲבֹדָה
בַּשָּׂדֶה: אֵת כָּל־עֲבֹדָתָם,
אֲשֶׁר עָבְדוּ בָהֶם בְּפָרֶךְ.

This bitter herb that we eat – what is the reason for it? Because the Egyptians embittered the lives of our ancestors in Egypt, as it is said: "They embittered their lives with hard labor at clay and brick-making, and all sorts of work in the fields – with all the tasks at which they ruthlessly worked them" (Exodus 1:14).

See p. 219 for kids' song "The Three Symbols"

QUESTIONS FOR DISCUSSION

Rabban Gamliel lays out the three central mitzvot of this night: recalling Korban Pesach, matzah, and maror. He says that whoever does not mention these three things at the Seder has not done his or her duty. This section constitutes the most direct response to the questions posed at the Seder. (There are different customs that people follow. Some point to all three symbols. Some only point to the Seder plate. Some raise the matzah.)

How does the mere discussion of these points fulfill the act, when normally just discussing something does not fulfill an obligation?

Do you think many of us merely go through the ritual motions? When it comes to religious ritual, how do we balance the requirement of the fixed nature of prayer and ritual with the desire for *kavanah* (spiritual feelings)? Do you feel that you go through the motions when praying? When engaging in religious ritual? How can we make the liturgical text come alive and feel more inspirational if we find our minds wandering?

QUESTIONS FOR DISCUSSION

Why was Rabban Gamliel so insistent on the recitation of these three items? Perhaps he was seeking a way to ensure that the basics of the Seder be followed, as described in the Torah. Another explanation is that he was concerned that these three symbols were being expropriated by early Christians. Does this hypothesis have any contemporary relevance for us today? When we engage in interfaith dialogue, how do we deal with the potential for religious syncretism? How should we respond to groups who seek to blur the differences between Jews and Christians?

REFLECTION

If the four cups are said to remind us of the Matriarchs/Imahot, Sarah, Rebecca, Rachel, and Leah, the three matzot are to remind us of the Patriarchs/Avot, Abraham, Isaac and Jacob.

REFLECTION

Why does merely discussing these points mean one has fulfilled one's obligation? Perhaps we can understand it from a well-known Chasidic tale. The Baal Shem Tov, the founder of Chasidism, would go into the forest, when he wanted to petition God, light a fire, and pray that a miracle would happen and misfortune would be averted. And his prayers would be answered. In each succeeding generation, his disciples would attempt to follow their master, and their prayers would be answered, despite in each succeeding generation experiencing diminishment. The Maggid of Mezeritzch no longer knew

how to light the fire, Rabbi Moshe Leib of Sassov did not know how to light the fire nor what prayer to say, and finally when it came to Rabbi Israel of Rizhin, when he spoke to God, he said he didn't know how to light the fire, say the prayer, or even find the right place in the forest. All he could do was to tell the story, and that would have to be enough to avert misfortune. And as the Chasidic tale concludes, it was![76]

Rabbi Jeffrey Cohen adds a modern twist to this Chasidic story. During the attempted coup in Russia before the final fall of Communism in the early 1990s, a young man named Ilya Krichefsky was fatally shot by a soldier. At his funeral, the Kaddish prayer was recited for the first time at an official Soviet event over the loudspeaker heard throughout Moscow. When the man's father, Marat Krichefsky, was asked how he felt to hear the Kaddish prayer broadcast, he said that given his enforced secular upbringing, Kaddish meant nothing to him, but that "it was important for the nation to know that our son was a Jew who died for Russia."[77] As Rabbi Cohen points out, a new category has been added: there are those who can't light the fire, no longer know the prayers, no longer know that special place in the forest, and no longer know how to tell the story. Yet even if they do not know the story, they know that it is an important one that must be told.

QUESTIONS FOR DISCUSSION

How can we better convey the Jewish story? Why are so many Jews disconnected from the community? What can we do to better reach those who are disconnected from Judaism and the Jewish community? What is the best Jewish "story" to tell?

At the summer 2004 Athens Olympics, Israeli windsurfer Gal Fridman won Israel's first Olympic gold medal. After he returned to Israel, his first stop was to the Tel Aviv memorial, dedicated to the memory of the eleven Israeli athletes and coaches murdered at the 1972 Munich Olympics by the PLO. Although Mr. Fridman was born after the Munich Massacre, he went to the memorial, like all high-level Israeli athletes who are brought to the site, to commemorate, honor, and remember those who were murdered.[78]

How can we better convey the Jewish story?

In every generation, every person is to experience having personally come out of Egypt.

B'chol Dor Vador

If children made a paper chain for the Seder, extend it now to all the guests and have everyone hold on to it.

LEADER: As we are about to join in reciting *b'chol dor vador*, we are reminded that each of us, through telling this story, must feel as though we left Egypt. In the words of the great Jewish philosopher Martin Buber, our Seder is transformed into a "history feast."

B'chol dor vador chayav adam lirot	בְּכָל־דּוֹר וָדוֹר חַיָּב אָדָם לִרְאוֹת
et atzmo, k'ilu hu yatza	אֶת־עַצְמוֹ, כְּאִלּוּ הוּא יָצָא
mi-Mitzrayim, shene-emar: v'higadta	מִמִּצְרַיִם, שֶׁנֶּאֱמַר: וְהִגַּדְתָּ לְבִנְךָ
l'vincha bayom hahu leimor: ba-avur zeh	בַּיּוֹם הַהוּא לֵאמֹר: בַּעֲבוּר זֶה
asah Adonai li, b'tzeiti mi-Mitzrayim. Lo	עָשָׂה יְיָ לִי, בְּצֵאתִי מִמִּצְרָיִם. לֹא
et avoteinu bilvad, ga-al Hakadosh	אֶת־אֲבוֹתֵינוּ בִּלְבָד, גָּאַל הַקָּדוֹשׁ
Baruch Hu, ela af otanu ga-al	בָּרוּךְ הוּא, אֶלָּא אַף אוֹתָנוּ גָּאַל
imahem, shene-emar: v'otanu hotzi	עִמָּהֶם, שֶׁנֶּאֱמַר: וְאוֹתָנוּ הוֹצִיא
misham, l'ma-an havi otanu, latet lanu	מִשָּׁם, לְמַעַן הָבִיא אֹתָנוּ, לָתֶת לָנוּ
et ha-aretz asher nishba la-avoteinu.	אֶת־הָאָרֶץ אֲשֶׁר נִשְׁבַּע לַאֲבֹתֵינוּ.

In every generation, every person is to experience having personally come out of Egypt, as it is said: "And you shall tell your child on that day, saying: This commemorates what Adonai did for me when I went out of Egypt" (Exodus 13:8). For the Blessed Holy One did not redeem our ancestors alone, but also redeemed us along with them, as it is said: "And God brought us out of there, in order to take us to give us the land concerning which God had made a vow to our ancestors" (Deuteronomy 6:23).

Raise the cup of wine, cover the matzot, and say:

L'fichach anachnu chayavim l'hodot,	לְפִיכָךְ אֲנַחְנוּ חַיָּבִים לְהוֹדוֹת, לְהַלֵּל,
l'haleil, l'shabei-ach, l'fa-eir, l'romeim,	לְשַׁבֵּחַ, לְפָאֵר, לְרוֹמֵם, לְהַדֵּר, לְבָרֵךְ,
l'hadeir, l'vareich, l'aleih ul'kaleis, l'mi	לְעַלֵּה וּלְקַלֵּס, לְמִי שֶׁעָשָׂה לַאֲבוֹתֵינוּ

she-asah la-avoteinu v'lanu et kol וְלָנוּ אֶת־כָּל־הַנִּסִים הָאֵלּוּ.

hanisim ha-eilu. Hotzi-anu mei- הוֹצִיאָנוּ מֵעַבְדוּת לְחֵרוּת,

avdut l'cheirut, mi-yagon l'simchah, מִיָּגוֹן לְשִׂמְחָה, וּמֵאֵבֶל לְיוֹם

umei-eivel l'yom tov, umei-afeilah l'or טוֹב, וּמֵאֲפֵלָה לְאוֹר גָּדוֹל,

gadol, umishibud ligulah. V'nomar וּמִשִּׁעְבּוּד לִגְאֻלָּה. וְנֹאמַר

l'fanav shirah chadashah. Hal'luyah. לְפָנָיו שִׁירָה חֲדָשָׁה. הַלְלוּיָהּ:

That is why we are duty bound to thank, praise, laud, glorify, exalt, extol, bless, acclaim, and adore God Who performed all these wonders for our ancestors and us: brought us from slavery to freedom, from sorrow to joy, from mourning to holiday, from darkness to great light, and from bondage to redemption. So let us declaim a new song to God. Hallelujah.

Put down the cup and uncover the matzot.

REFLECTION

David Ben-Gurion, first prime minister of the State of Israel, described the importance of the memories preserved on Pesach as he argued for the right to a Jewish state:

> More than 300 years ago a ship by the name of the Mayflower left Plymouth for the New World. It was a great event in American and English history. I wonder how many Englishmen or how many Americans know exactly the date when that ship left Plymouth, how many people were on the ship, and what was the kind of bread that people ate when they left Plymouth.
>
> Well, more than 3,300 years ago, the Jews left Egypt. It was more than 3,000 years ago and every Jew in the world knows exactly the date when we left. It was on the 15th of Nisan. The bread they ate was matzoth. Up to date all the Jews throughout the world on the 15th of Nisan eat the same matzoth, in America, in Russia, and tell the story of the [exodus] from Egypt and tell what happened, all the sufferings that happened to the Jews since they went into exile. They finish by these two sentences: "This

We are part of a chain, the chain of Jewish history.

year we are slaves; next year we will be free. This year we are here; next year we will be in Zion, in the land of Israel." Jews are like that.[79]

We are part of a chain, the chain of Jewish history. This is a chain that should not be seen as a shackle but rather as a joyous link from one generation to another, keeping the memories alive and the hope ever present.

SUGGESTION

Growing up we always sang *b'chol dor va'dor* to the melody of the "Song of the Partisans."

SUGGESTION

According to the Rambam (Maimonides), we should actually not read this as *lir'ot* (to see) but rather *liharot* (to demonstrate) – to really feel as if we left Egypt. Each person is obligated to demonstrate having left Egypt. Use this as an opportunity to ask those present: What was it like when you left Egypt in such a hurry? Who did you walk with? What did you take with you? What did you leave behind? Why?

QUESTIONS FOR DISCUSSION

In recent years young Israelis have taken to tattooing on their arms the number that was seared on their grandparents' flesh when they were imprisoned in Auschwitz.[80] They have said that this is their way to never forget what their grandparents went through.

A Jewish nurse in Florida chose to have the word *zachor* (remember) tattooed on her arm in honor of the survivors she took care of.[81] Is this an appropriate way to concretize the words of the Seder? Or is this a suggestion that leaves you horrified?

One Orthodox Israeli woman wanted to tattoo her mother's number on her finger so as to never forget her mother's travails, but her husband objected. Instead, her mother and children gave her for her birthday a gold bracelet with her mother's number, held together by leather straps reminiscent of tefillin straps, a reminder of her late father, who was also a Holocaust survivor. What is your opinion of this alternative form of memorial?

HUMOR CORNER

A little girl comes home from school and excitedly tells her mom what she learned in Hebrew school: "When the Jewish people stood at the Sea of Reeds, they were being chased by the Egyptians. All of a sudden a huge tractor rolled out along with another machine and sucked the water out. Then another machine came and laid down a moving sidewalk that allowed the Jewish people to cross." The little girl's mother looked shocked

and said, "They taught you what?!" The little girl replied, "Mommy, if I told you what they really taught me, you would never believe it!"

Hallel – Hal'luyah

LEADER: As we begin our recitation of Hallel tonight, which expresses our praise and gratitude to God for redeeming us from Egypt, let us try to live our lives like the song we sing. Hallel can serve as a leitmotif: to be ever grateful for all our blessings – grateful to God and to our family and friends for how they enrich our lives and community. May we always merit to share happy times together and be ever thankful for God's blessings upon us.

Hal'luyah, hal'lu avdei Adonai,	הַלְלוּיָהּ. הַלְלוּ עַבְדֵי יְיָ.
hal'lu et sheim Adonai. Y'hi sheim	הַלְלוּ אֶת־שֵׁם יְיָ. יְהִי שֵׁם
Adonai m'vorach, mei-atah v'ad olam.	יְיָ מְבֹרָךְ מֵעַתָּה וְעַד עוֹלָם:
Mimizrach shemesh ad m'vo-o,	מִמִּזְרַח שֶׁמֶשׁ עַד מְבוֹאוֹ.
m'hulal sheim Adonai. Ram al kol	מְהֻלָּל שֵׁם יְיָ. רָם עַל־כָּל־
goyim Adonai, al hashamayim k'vodo.	גּוֹיִם יְיָ. עַל הַשָּׁמַיִם כְּבוֹדוֹ:
Mi k'Adonai Eloheinu, hamagbihi	מִי כַּיְיָ אֱלֹהֵינוּ. הַמַּגְבִּיהִי
lashavet. Hamashpili lirot,	לָשָׁבֶת: הַמַּשְׁפִּילִי לִרְאוֹת
bashamayim uva-aretz. M'kimi	בַּשָּׁמַיִם וּבָאָרֶץ: מְקִימִי
mei-afar dal, mei-ashpot yarim	מֵעָפָר דָּל. מֵאַשְׁפֹּת יָרִים
evyon. L'hoshivi im	אֶבְיוֹן: לְהוֹשִׁיבִי עִם־
n'divim, im n'divei amo.	נְדִיבִים. עִם נְדִיבֵי עַמּוֹ:
Moshivi akeret habayit, eim	מוֹשִׁיבִי עֲקֶרֶת הַבַּיִת אֵם
habanim s'meichah. Hal'luyah.	הַבָּנִים שְׂמֵחָה. הַלְלוּיָהּ:

Give praise – O Adonai's servants – praise the name of Adonai. Blessed be the name of Adonai now and forever. From the sun's rising place to its setting place let the name of Adonai be praised. High above all the nations is

Hallel can serve as a leitmotif to be ever grateful for all our blessings – grateful to God and to our family and friends for how they enrich our lives and community.

Adonai, our God: enthroned so high yet deigning to look so low; raising the wretched out of the dust, lifting the poor off the dung heap, to give them a place among the high and mighty – among the high and mighty of God's people; making the barren recluse a happy mother of children. Hallelujah. (Psalms 113)

B'tzeit Yisra-eil

B'tzeit Yisra-eil mi-Mitzrayim, beit

Ya-akov mei-am loeiz. Hay'tah Y'hudah

l'kod'sho, Yisra-eil mamsh'lotav. Hayam

ra-ah vayanos, ha-Yardein yisov l'achor.

Heharim rak'du ch'eilim, g'va-ot

kivnei tzon. Mah l'cha hayam ki tanus,

ha-Yardein tisov l'achor. He-harim

tirk'du ch'eilim, g'va-ot kivnei

tzon. Milifnei adon chuli aretz,

milifnei Eloha Ya-akov. Hahof'chi hatzur

agam mayim, chalamish l'may'no mayim.

בְּצֵאת יִשְׂרָאֵל מִמִּצְרָיִם, בֵּית
יַעֲקֹב מֵעַם לֹעֵז: הָיְתָה יְהוּדָה
לְקָדְשׁוֹ. יִשְׂרָאֵל מַמְשְׁלוֹתָיו: הַיָּם
רָאָה וַיָּנֹס, הַיַּרְדֵּן יִסֹּב לְאָחוֹר:
הֶהָרִים רָקְדוּ כְאֵילִים. גְּבָעוֹת
כִּבְנֵי־צֹאן: מַה־לְּךָ הַיָּם כִּי תָנוּס.
הַיַּרְדֵּן תִּסֹּב לְאָחוֹר: הֶהָרִים
תִּרְקְדוּ כְאֵילִים. גְּבָעוֹת כִּבְנֵי־
צֹאן: מִלִּפְנֵי אָדוֹן חוּלִי אָרֶץ.
מִלִּפְנֵי אֱלוֹהַּ יַעֲקֹב: הַהֹפְכִי הַצּוּר
אֲגַם־מָיִם. חַלָּמִישׁ לְמַעְיְנוֹ־מָיִם.

When Israel came out of Egypt,

the House of Yaakov from a strange-languaged people –

Judah became God's sanctuary,

Israel God's dominion.

The sea saw and fled;

the Jordan turned back.

The mountains skipped liked rams,

the hills like young sheep.

What is it, sea; why do you run?

Jordan – why do you turn back?

Why, mountains,

do you skip like rams,

you hills like young sheep?

Dance, earth, when the Lord appears,

when Yaakov's God shows

Who turned the rock into a pool of water,

the flint-rock into a gushing fountain! (Psalms 114)

Ga-al Yisra-eil

All the participants lift their cups of wine and say:

Baruch Atah Adonai, Eloheinu Melech	בָּרוּךְ אַתָּה יְיָ, אֱלֹהֵינוּ מֶלֶךְ
ha-olam, asher g'alanu v'ga-al	הָעוֹלָם, אֲשֶׁר גְּאָלָנוּ וְגָאַל
et avoteinu mi-Mitzrayim,	אֶת־אֲבוֹתֵינוּ מִמִּצְרַיִם,
v'higi-anu l'lalaylah hazeh, le-echol	וְהִגִּיעָנוּ לַלַּיְלָה הַזֶּה, לֶאֱכָל־
bo matzah u-maror. Kein, Adonai	בּוֹ מַצָּה וּמָרוֹר. כֵּן, יְיָ
Eloheinu veilohei avoteinu,	אֱלֹהֵינוּ וֵאלֹהֵי אֲבוֹתֵינוּ,
yagi-einu l'moadim v'lirgalim	יַגִּיעֵנוּ לְמוֹעֲדִים וְלִרְגָלִים
acheirim, ha-ba-im likrateinu	אֲחֵרִים, הַבָּאִים לִקְרָאתֵנוּ
l'shalom. S'meichim b'vinyan	לְשָׁלוֹם. שְׂמֵחִים בְּבִנְיַן
irecha, v'sasim ba-avodatecha,	עִירֶךָ, וְשָׂשִׂים בַּעֲבוֹדָתֶךָ,
v'nochal sham min haz'vachim	וְנֹאכַל שָׁם מִן הַזְּבָחִים
umin hap'sachim (*On Saturday night*	וּמִן הַפְּסָחִים (במוצאי
substitute: min hap'sachim umin	שבת אומרים מן הַפְּסָחִים
haz'vachim), asher yagi-a damam, al kir	וּמִן הַזְּבָחִים), אֲשֶׁר יַגִּיעַ

mizbachacha l'ratzon, v'nodeh l'cha shir   דָּמָם, עַל קִיר מִזְבַּחֲךָ לְרָצוֹן, וְנוֹדֶה

chadash al g'ulateinu, v'al p'dut nafsheinu.   לְךָ שִׁיר חָדָשׁ עַל גְּאֻלָּתֵנוּ, וְעַל פְּדוּת

Baruch Atah Adonai, ga-al Yisra-eil.   נַפְשֵׁנוּ: בָּרוּךְ אַתָּה יְיָ, גָּאַל יִשְׂרָאֵל:

Blessed are You, Adonai, our God, Ruler of the universe, Who redeemed us and redeemed our ancestors from Egypt and enabled us to live to this night to eat matzah and bitter herbs. In the same way, Adonai, our God and God of our ancestors, let us live until the other set times and festivals approach us – let us reach them in peace, rejoicing in the rebuilding of Your service, and partaking of the sacrifices and the Passover offerings whose blood shall reach the walls of Your altar propitiously, and we will thank You with a new song for our redemption and the emancipation of our souls. Blessed are You, Adonai, Who redeemed Israel.

LEADER: As we are about to drink this second cup of wine, we have in mind that our sages ordained four cups of wine to emphasize the special nature of this evening of the Seder. In Ashkenazic custom, a separate blessing is required for each cup, despite the common custom not to repeat a blessing over a food for which there is no interruption (reciting the Haggadah is not seen as an interruption). Here we observe four different mitzvot by reciting four different *b'rachot*. May this be a symbol for us that our lives always be abundant with the chance to perform mitzvot and that we embrace our chance to do good in the world. May our cups always be overflowing!

Hineni muchan u-mezuman l'kayem mitzvat   הִנְנִי מוּכָן וּמְזוּמָן לְקַיֵּם מִצְוַת

kos sheni me'arba kosot.   כּוֹס שֵׁנִי מֵאַרְבַּע כּוֹסוֹת.

L'shem yichud kudsha brich hu   לְשֵׁם יִחוּד קוּדְשָׁא בְּרִיךְ הוּא

u-shechinteh al yedei hahu tamir   וּשְׁכִינְתֵּיהּ עַל יְדֵי הַהוּא טָמִיר

v'neelam b'shem kol Yisrael.   וְנֶעֱלָם בְּשֵׁם כָּל יִשְׂרָאֵל:

Here I am, ready and willing to fulfill the mitzvah of drinking the second of the four cups of wine, as is the will of the Holy One.

Say the following blessing and drink the second cup, reclining to the left:

Baruch Atah Adonai, Eloheinu Melech ha-olam, Borei p'ri hagafen.

בָּרוּךְ אַתָּה יְיָ, אֱלֹהֵינוּ מֶלֶךְ הָעוֹלָם, בּוֹרֵא פְּרִי הַגָּפֶן:

Blessed are You, Adonai, our God, Ruler of the universe, Creator of the fruit of the vine.

SECOND CUP

REFLECTION

We have now recited the first two chapters of Hallel, praising God for our exodus from Egypt. Later, after the meal, we will conclude the recitation of Hallel, in an unusual splitting of the prayer. Hallel is usually only recited on holidays during the day and while standing. Here at the Seder, another unusual aspect is that we chant it at night, while sitting, which symbolizes our freedom.

The first part of the Seder Hallel depicts our past experience of the Exodus, which we are commanded to recall every day and at Passover to actually relive. The second part, recited after the meal, revolves around the theme of praise to God and depicts our hope for the ultimate redemption. According to the Abarbanel, the divisions correspond to what we experience at this point in the Seder: the Exodus, crossing the Sea of Reeds, and the giving of the Torah. After the meal, we focus on our hope for the future, which is the theme of the concluding chapters of Hallel.

In the Talmud we are taught that when we say Hallel, we conclude with Birkat Hashir (the blessing of song), which many think is the concluding blessing of the Hallel. Yet it was Rabbi Hai Gaon who taught that this Hallel, unlike any other, is not merely recital of praise, rather it is fulfillment of the obligation of song.

QUESTIONS FOR DISCUSSION

Why is only half of Hallel recited at the end of Passover on the seventh day (traditionally understood as the day the Jews were at the Sea of Reeds)?

One reason given is that like our custom of pouring off some wine when recalling the Ten Plagues, we are not to rejoice even when our enemies are dying. In Proverbs 24:17–18, we read, "Do not rejoice when your enemy falls, and do not let your heart be glad when he stumbles, lest the Lord see it and be displeased." In addition, there are two midrashim that depict God's reaction to the events at the Sea of Reeds. In one midrash in *Megillah* 10b, as the Egyptians are drowning in the Sea of Reeds, God restrains the angels from singing God's praises, proclaiming to the angels:

We have now recited the first two chapters of Hallel.

"The work of My hands is being drowned, and you are chanting hymns?" In another version, God says, "My legions are drowning, and you would sing to Me?" These two versions of the midrash lead us to pose these questions. How should we react upon the suffering of our enemies? Is there a "right" way for the community to respond? In the case of our enemies, should we rejoice at their downfall? Should we feel any remorse at their deaths? How do we balance victory with compassion for our enemies?

See p. 219 for song "Through the Red Sea"

Rachtzah: Hand Washing with a Blessing

LEADER: As we prepare to ritually wash our hands with a blessing, let us dedicate this step of the Seder to the memory of two people connected to water: Bitya bat Pharaoh, the daughter of Pharaoh who took Moses out of the waters of the Nile and threw her lot in with the Jewish people, and Nachshon, who was the first person to enter the waters of the Sea of Reeds. May they inspire us to see how the actions of one person can change our world for the better and teach us not to be afraid to be risk-takers for the betterment of our world.

Pour water over each hand three times and say the following blessing:

Baruch Atah Adonai, Eloheinu	בָּרוּךְ אַתָּה יְיָ אֱלֹהֵינוּ
Melech ha-olam, asher	מֶלֶךְ הָעוֹלָם, אֲשֶׁר
kid'shanu b'mitzvotav, v'tzivanu	קִדְּשָׁנוּ בְּמִצְוֹתָיו, וְצִוָּנוּ
al n'tilat yadayim.	עַל נְטִילַת יָדָיִם:

Blessed are You, Adonai, our God, Ruler of the universe, Who sanctified us with Your commandments and commanded us concerning the washing of the hands.

REFLECTION

In the *Be'er Avraham* commentary on the Haggadah (1708), Rabbi Abraham Grate of Prague points out that several of the symbols of the Seder are interpreted to refer to Bitya, daughter of Pharaoh, who tradition teaches saved Moses. Rabbi Grate explains that this symbol of washing our hands is to commemorate Bitya's bathing in the Nile and her rescuing Moses with her hands from the water.[82]

SUGGESTION

Sing a *niggun* (a wordless melody) in between washing hands and making the blessing over the matzot.

REFLECTION

As we are about to make the blessing over matzah, we remember that this bread made by our ancestors in haste represents both the bread of affliction and the

Today there are those who still eat the bread of affliction.

We don't want to do anything to dilute the special flavor of the matzah, and thus we refrain from salting it.

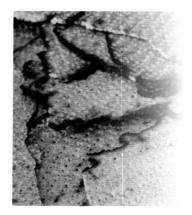

bread of freedom. Today there are those who still eat the bread of affliction, living in abject poverty, oppression, and abuse. We pray that soon they too will eat the matzah of redemption.

Motzi: Blessing for Matzah

Pick up the three matzot from the Seder tray and say the following blessing:

Baruch Atah Adonai, Eloheinu Melech

ha-olam, hamotzi lechem min ha-aretz.

בָּרוּךְ אַתָּה יְיָ, אֱלֹהֵינוּ מֶלֶךְ
הָעוֹלָם, הַמּוֹצִיא לֶחֶם מִן הָאָרֶץ:

Blessed are You, Adonai, our God, Ruler of the universe, Who brings forth bread from the earth.

Matzah: Eating Matzah

Replace the bottom matzah. Everybody gets a piece of the top and middle matzot. Say the following blessing and eat, reclining.

Baruch Atah Adonai, Eloheinu Melech

ha-olam, asher kid'shanu b'mitzvotav

v'tzivanu al achilat matzah.

בָּרוּךְ אַתָּה יְיָ, אֱלֹהֵינוּ מֶלֶךְ
הָעוֹלָם, אֲשֶׁר קִדְּשָׁנוּ בְּמִצְוֹתָיו
וְצִוָּנוּ עַל אֲכִילַת מַצָּה:

Blessed are You, Adonai, our God, Ruler of the universe, Who sanctified us with Your commandments and commanded us concerning the eating of matzah.

REFLECTION

The Maharal points out that while it is customary to salt our bread or matzah to recall the salting of sacrifices, on Seder night we don't want to do anything to dilute the special flavor of the matzah, and thus we refrain from salting the matzah prior to eating it.

REFLECTION

Only at the Seder are we commanded to eat matzah. The rest of Passover, eating matzah is optional, even though it is prohibited on all days of Passover to consume chametz.

REFLECTION

In 1944, the Jewish inmates in Bergen-Belsen had no matzah. Due to the risk of death from starvation, the rabbis in the camp decided that eating chametz would be permitted and that before eating it, one should say the following with heartfelt intention: "Our Father in heaven, behold, it is revealed and known before You that our will is to do Your will and to celebrate the Passover Festival by eating matzah and by observing the prohibition against chametz. However, our hearts are pained that our servitude prevents us, and we are in mortal danger. Behold, we are ready and prepared to fulfill Your commandment 'And you shall live by them and not die by them...' [Leviticus 18:5; *Yoma* 85b] and to 'Guard yourself and guard your soul exceedingly [i.e., keep yourself alive]' [Deuteronomy 4:9]. Therefore, our prayer to You is that You should keep us alive and sustain and redeem us speedily so that we can observe Your decrees and do Your will and serve You whole-heartedly. Amen."[83]

The "Chametz on Passover Prayer" from Bergen-Belsen Passover 1944, used by permission of the Ghetto Fighters' House Museum, Israel/Photo Archive

As we dip the bitter herbs, let us have in mind not only the bitterness and suffering of the past, but also of those who today are in pain, who are enslaved, who yearn to be free.

REFLECTION

Rabbi Binny Friedman tells a true story of a group of ultra-Orthodox residents from Bnei Brak who in summer 2014 came to a field near the Gaza Strip to harvest wheat for Pesach. Every summer they search for wheat ripe enough to harvest in August – when the sun dries the wheat most intensely as part of the process of producing *shmurah matzah* (matzah made from wheat specially guarded against moisture to prevent it from rising and becoming unleavened). The wheat is then stored till its use in baking matzot in the spring.

Since a Shemittah (sabbatical) year was coming up in 5775, they would need to harvest enough for two years' worth of matzos. At Kibbutz Sufa, right next to the border with Gaza, they found a large field sown in mid-January (apparently a rare occurrence) with two thousand acres of green wheat – exactly what they needed.

With Operation Protective Edge's air campaign underway in summer 2014, they could see the pillars of smoke over Gaza and the Israeli air force hitting back against the Hamas missile launchers, but were nonetheless able to harvest the wheat and load it onto trucks for the cleaning and storage process in the plant located further north.

Two days later, in what is now a well-documented event, thirteen terrorists, armed to the teeth, emerged from a tunnel that led from the Gaza Strip and opened into the wheat fields of Kibbutz Sufa. The terrorists had been counting on emerging unnoticed amidst the tall wheat stalks, all of which had just been cut down by the Bnei Brak matzah bakers. Since the field was now in fact bare, they were immediately spotted by the Israeli army and were prevented from launching what would have been a horrendous terrorist attack intended to hit nearby homes all at once. Indeed, one could say a lot of Jewish lives were protected by the mitzvot of Shemittah in the summer of 2014.[84]

Maror: Bitter Herbs

LEADER: We come now to the section of our Seder where we will concretize for ourselves the bitterness of our ancestors' slavery in Egypt by eating maror, bitter herbs. As we dip the bitter herbs, let us have in mind not only the bitterness and suffering of the past, but also of those who today are in pain, who are enslaved, who yearn to be free. May their bitterness be healed, may their suffering be eased as our ancestors' maror of bitterness was eventually transformed into the taste of freedom.

We now have the second dipping of the evening. We dip the maror and chazeret in the charoset and recite the following blessing. Since the maror is reminiscent of our enslavement, we do not recline when eating it.

Baruch Atah Adonai, Eloheinu Melech ha-olam, asher kid'shanu b'mitzvotav v'tzivanu al achilat maror.

בָּרוּךְ אַתָּה יְיָ אֱלֹהֵינוּ מֶלֶךְ הָעוֹלָם, אֲשֶׁר קִדְּשָׁנוּ בְּמִצְוֹתָיו וְצִוָּנוּ עַל אֲכִילַת מָרוֹר:

Blessed are You, Adonai, our God, Ruler of the universe, Who sanctified us with Your commandments and commanded us concerning the eating of maror.

REFLECTION

Rabbi Nachman of Breslov tells the story of two beggars, one Jewish and one Gentile, who were hungry and looking for a meal. The Jewish beggar told his non-Jewish friend to join him the next night at the synagogue; with the arrival of Passover, they would both get invited to a meal. He followed his friend's advice, and they both found places to eat. Later that night they met up, and the non-Jew was furious. The Jewish beggar couldn't understand why until he heard his friend's tale of woe. The non-Jew was not familiar with the Seder. Shortly after he arrived, he was given a whole cup of wine to drink. He started to feel woozy, but smelling food, he figured he would soon have a chance to eat. Eventually they gave him some food, but it was just a small piece of parsley that did nothing to satiate him. He wondered when he would finally get something to fill him up. Soon he received a piece of matzah, which tasted like cardboard. Finally, they gave him a larger vegetable, and being so famished, he took a double portion, but it turned out to be horseradish. The horrible burning in his mouth led him to flee from the table and his hosts. His Jewish friend said to him that if he had only hung on for a few minutes more, he would have been rewarded with a huge holiday meal. Rabbi Nachman analogizes this story to our situation: after all the bitterness of our suffering, we are on the cusp of being redeemed. We only need to hold on, to have some more patience as we await the redemption![85]

REFLECTION

Charoset, made from a mixture of nuts, fruits, and wine, is designed to invoke the mortar paste that our forefathers and foremothers used to keep the bricks together.

In the Talmud (*Pesachim* 116a), we find a reference explaining why we are required to eat charoset. Rabbi Elazar ben Zadok says: Charoset is a religious requirement. Why is it a religious requirement (even though it is not mentioned in the Torah)? Rabbi Levi said: In memory of the apple tree under which the Jewish women in Egypt gave birth to their children so they would not be seen by the Egyptians.

See page 220 for songs "A Spoonful of Charoset" and "Disco Deliverance: We Will Survive"

Korech: Sandwich

Using the bottom matzah from the tray, everybody makes a maror sandwich, says the following passages, and eats reclining to the left.

Zeicher l'mikdash k'hileil. Kein asah

זֵכֶר לְמִקְדָּשׁ כְּהִלֵּל: כֵּן עָשָׂה

Hileil bizman she-Beit ha-Mikdash hayah

הִלֵּל בִּזְמַן שֶׁבֵּית הַמִּקְדָּשׁ הָיָה

kayam. Hayah koreich Pesach, matzah,

קַיָּם. הָיָה כּוֹרֵךְ פֶּסַח מַצָּה וּמָרוֹר

u-maror v'ocheil b'yachad. L'kayeim mah

וְאוֹכֵל בְּיַחַד. לְקַיֵּם מַה שֶׁנֶּאֱמַר:

shene-emar. Al matzot um'rorim yochlu-hu.

עַל־מַצּוֹת וּמְרוֹרִים יֹאכְלֻהוּ:

In remembrance of the Temple, according to Hillel the Elder. This is what Hillel did when the Temple was standing: he would wrap together the portion of the Passover offering, the matzah and the maror and eat them together, in order to do what is said: "On matzot and bitter herbs they shall eat it" (Numbers 9:11).

REFLECTION

How were the paschal sacrifice, matzah, and maror to be eaten? Separately or together? The rabbis differed and thus retained in the Seder Hillel's tradition to create a "sandwich" effect.

The Earl of Sandwich might have it named after him, but this is the earliest source we can find for a sandwich!

QUESTIONS FOR DISCUSSION

Many people today find themselves part of the sandwich generation – taking care of both young children and elderly parents. For the Jewish community, there also is the phenomenon of being caught between having to take care of our local communal needs as well as those in Israel and overseas. How do we balance communal needs with the needs of Jews in Israel and overseas? Jewish causes with general societal charity and social justice needs? Which should have greater priority? How should we allocate limited resources?

Shulchan Orech: The Meal

LEADER: In Jerusalem, at the time of the Temple, thousands of people converged on the city and yet, the rabbis teach us, there was enough room to accommodate everybody. Let this be an inspiration to us to be ever hospitable and open our doors not only at Pesach but all throughout the year.

Remove the Seder plate from the table and eat the festival meal.

Some have the custom of beginning the Seder meal with hard-boiled eggs dipped in salt water; others may have consumed this earlier in the Seder.

HUMOR CORNER

The Twitter version of Jewish history: They came to kill us. We won. Let's eat!

The fifth question of the Seder: When do we eat? (Answer: Now!)

REFLECTION

Another custom many have is to begin the Passover meal with boiled eggs dipped in salt water. Why eggs? This is a food traditionally eaten by mourners, and thus we recall even at the Seder the destruction of the Temple by

eating boiled eggs. Another reason is that with many types of food, the longer you cook it, the softer it gets. Yet with an egg, the longer it cooks, the harder it gets. The rabbis said that eggs should remind us of our ancestors in Egypt. The more the Jewish people were oppressed, the firmer their resolve became.

Tzafun: Eating the Afikomen

LEADER: As we complete the meal with the afikomen, we pray that our lives should always be filled not only with finding the material needs that we require but the spiritual sustenance as well. The afikomen represents the Korban Pesach, the paschal sacrifice, that we are taught was to be eaten to satiation. May this afikomen, as the last food that we will eat tonight, satiate us with the spiritual hope it represents – a sense of completeness and belief in a new spiritual awakening and redemption.

Put the Seder plate back on the table, give everybody a piece of matzah from the large section put away for the afikomen, returned by the children who searched for it, say the following passage, and eat reclining to the left.

Zecher l'korban Pesach hanechal

al ha-sovah.

זֵכֶר לְקָרְבַּן פֶּסַח הַנֶּאֱכָל

עַל הַשּׂוֹבַע:

In remembrance of the Passover offering, eaten after satiation.

REFLECTION

Tzafun means that which is hidden. The afikomen was hidden away earlier in the evening, and the children searched for it. Only now that it has been found can we continue with the Seder by eating it and savoring the flavor for the rest of the night. It was the Chatam Sofer who taught us to interconnect the signs of the Seder. Here, Tzafun is juxtaposed to Barech (Blessing). An insight we can glean from this is that often in order to discover God's blessings in our lives, it is up to us to search for them and bring them out in the open.

REFLECTION

A strange dichotomy exists regarding the institution of the afikomen. The Mishnah text states that after eating from the Passover offering, we should not end the meal with the afikomen. The root of the word *afikomen* comes from the Greek *epikomon* (revelry). Among the Greeks it became the custom after a symposium to go from one group of people to the next and engage in revelry, i.e., a bacchanal. Hence the rabbis were opposed to this concept of an afikomen. They structured the Seder version of the

afikomen to take the place of the Passover offering; that is why we should consume it before midnight, just as the Passover offering had to be. This portion of the middle matzah is to be as our afikomen, which we translate as dessert, with nothing coming afterwards, save for the cups of wine to follow (*Pesachim* 119b).[86]

Thus the last taste of the Seder would be the afikomen. In fact the way that we understand the words of the Mishnah is that we don't eat anything else after the afikomen, leaving us all with the same flavor in our mouths, whether rich or poor. This serves as the reminder to us of the Korban Pesach, which was eaten last.

SUGGESTION

Some have the custom of putting aside a piece of the afikomen to eat on Pesach Sheni, one month later.

A song of ascents: When God returned the captives of Zion, we were like dreamers.

Barech: Grace after Meals

Some have the custom to pass around water, *mayim achronim* (after-water), to pour over their fingers before Birkat Hamazon. However, on Seder night we do not use *mayim achronim*, as tonight is Leil Shimurim, a night of special protection when we don't have to fear.[87]

Fill the third cup.

Shir Hama-alot

Shir hama-alot b'shuv Adonai et shivat
tzion hayinu k'chol'mim. Az yimalei
s'chok pinu ul'shoneinu rinah az
yomru vagoyim higdil Adonai la-asot im
eileh. Higdil Adonai la-asot
imanu hayinu s'meichim. Shuvah Adonai
et sh'viteinu ka-afikim banegev.
Hazor'im b'dimah b'rinah yiktzoru.
Haloch yeileich uvachoh nosei meshech
hazara bo yavo v'rinah nosei alumotav.

שִׁיר הַמַּעֲלוֹת בְּשׁוּב יְיָ אֶת שִׁיבַת
צִיּוֹן הָיִינוּ כְּחֹלְמִים: אָז יִמָּלֵא
שְׂחוֹק פִּינוּ וּלְשׁוֹנֵנוּ רִנָּה אָז
יֹאמְרוּ בַגּוֹיִם הִגְדִּיל יְיָ לַעֲשׂוֹת
עִם אֵלֶּה: הִגְדִּיל יְיָ לַעֲשׂוֹת
עִמָּנוּ הָיִינוּ שְׂמֵחִים: שׁוּבָה יְיָ
אֶת שְׁבִיתֵנוּ כַּאֲפִיקִים בַּנֶּגֶב:
הַזֹּרְעִים בְּדִמְעָה בְּרִנָּה יִקְצֹרוּ:
הָלוֹךְ יֵלֵךְ וּבָכֹה נֹשֵׂא מֶשֶׁךְ הַזָּרַע
בֹּא יָבֹא בְרִנָּה נֹשֵׂא אֲלֻמֹּתָיו:

A song of ascents: When Adonai returned the captives of Zion, we were like dreamers. Then was our mouth filled with laughter, and our tongue with exultation: then said they among the nations, Adonai has done great things for them. Adonai has done great things for us; so we rejoiced! Bring back our captives, O Adonai, as the streams in the south. They that sow in tears shall reap in joy. The one who walks along tearfully carrying the bag of seed shall come back with joy, carrying sheaves of grain. (Psalms 126)

Some add:

T'hilat Adonai y'daber pi, vivareich kol
basar sheim kodsho l'olam va-ed.

תְּהִלַּת יְיָ יְדַבֶּר פִּי, וִיבָרֵךְ כָּל בָּשָׂר
שֵׁם קָדְשׁוֹ לְעוֹלָם וָעֶד. וַאֲנַחְנוּ נְבָרֵךְ יָהּ

Va-anachnu n'vareich Yah mei·atah	מֵעַתָּה וְעַד עוֹלָם הַלְלוּיָהּ.
v'ad olam hal'luyah. Hodu l'Adonai	הוֹדוּ לַיי כִּי טוֹב, כִּי לְעוֹלָם
ki tov, ki l'olam chasdo, mi y'maleil	חַסְדּוֹ. מִי יְמַלֵּל גְּבוּרוֹת יְיָ
g'vurot Adonai yashmia kol t'hilato.	יַשְׁמִיעַ כָּל תְּהִלָּתוֹ.

My mouth will speak Adonai's praise, every creature will bless Your holy Name forever and ever. And we will bless God from now until forever. Halleluyah. Give thanks to Adonai for God is good, for God's kindness is forever. Who can express Adonai's mighty acts, who can declare all God's praise? (Psalms 115:1)

Some say:

Hin'ni muchan u-m'zuman	הִנְנִי מוּכָן וּמְזֻמָּן
l'kayeim mitzvat asei	לְקַיֵּם מִצְוַת עֲשֵׂה
shel Birkat Hamazon, shene-emar:	שֶׁל בִּרְכַּת הַמָּזוֹן, שֶׁנֶּאֱמַר.
v'achalta, v'savata u-veirachta	וְאָכַלְתָּ וְשָׂבָעְתָּ וּבֵרַכְתָּ
et Adonai Elohecha,	אֶת־יְיָ אֱלֹהֶיךָ
al ha-aretz ha-tovah	עַל־הָאָרֶץ הַטֹּבָה
asher natan lach.	אֲשֶׁר נָתַן־לָךְ.

I am prepared and ready to perform the mitzvah of Blessing after the Meal, as it is said, "And you shall eat and you shall be satisfied and you shall bless Adonai, your God, for the good land which God gave you" (Deuteronomy 8:10).

Zimmun

If at least three men above bar mitzvah age are present, a male who is conducting the Seder or or a man appointed by the leader lifts his cup of wine and leads the saying of Grace after Meals. If there are three or more women above the age of bat mitzvah present and fewer than three men, a woman may lead the zimmun and the men should answer (she should

substitute "G'virotai [v'rabotai]"). If more than ten men are present, add in the word "Eloheinu." (Some may substitute in Yiddish: "Rabbosai, mir velen bentshen" [for women: "G'virosai, mir velen bentshen").

Leader: Rabotai [u-g'virotai] n'vareich.

המזמן: רַבּוֹתַי [וּגְבִיוֹתַי] נְבָרֵךְ!

The others respond: Y'hi sheim Adonai m'vorach mei-atah v'ad olam.

המסובין: יְהִי שֵׁם יְיָ מְבֹרָךְ מֵעַתָּה וְעַד עוֹלָם.

Leader: Y'hi sheim Adonai m'vorach mei-atah v'ad olam. Birshut maranan v'rabanan v'rabotai [u-g'virotai], n'vareich (Eloheinu) she-achalnu mishelo.

המזמן: יְהִי שֵׁם יְיָ מְבֹרָךְ מֵעַתָּה וְעַד עוֹלָם. בִּרְשׁוּת מָרָנָן וְרַבָּנָן וְרַבּוֹתַי [וּגְבִירוֹתַי], נְבָרֵךְ (אֱלֹהֵינוּ) שֶׁאָכַלְנוּ מִשֶּׁלּוֹ.

Others: Baruch (Eloheinu) she-achalnu mishelo uv'tuvo chayinu.

המסובין: בָּרוּךְ (אֱלֹהֵינוּ) שֶׁאָכַלְנוּ מִשֶּׁלּוֹ וּבְטוּבוֹ חָיִינוּ.

Leader: Baruch (Eloheinu) she-achalnu mishelo uv'tuvo chayinu.

המזמן: בָּרוּךְ (אֱלֹהֵינוּ) שֶׁאָכַלְנוּ מִשֶּׁלּוֹ וּבְטוּבוֹ חָיִינוּ.

All: Baruch hu uvaruch sh'mo.)

בָּרוּךְ הוּא וּבָרוּךְ שְׁמוֹ:

Leader: Gentlemen [and ladies], let us offer a blessing.

Others: May Adonai's name be blessed now and forever.

Leader: May Adonai's name be blessed now and forever. By permission of our masters and teachers and gentlemen [and ladies], let us bless God (*if ten men past bar mitzvah are present, say "our God" instead of "God"*) of Whose food we have eaten.

Others: Blessed be God (*or, if ten men are present, "our God"*) of Whose food we have eaten and through Whose goodness we live.

Leader: Blessed be God (*or, if ten adult males are present, "our God"*) of Whose food we we have eaten and through Whose goodness we live.

All: Blessed is God and blessed is the Name.

All begin the Grace after Meals:

Hazan et Hakol

Baruch Atah Adonai, Eloheinu Melech   בָּרוּךְ אַתָּה יְיָ, אֱלֹהֵינוּ מֶלֶךְ

ha-olam, hazan et ha-olam kulo   הָעוֹלָם, הַזָּן אֶת הָעוֹלָם כֻּלּוֹ

b'tuvo b'chein b'chesed uv'rachamim   בְּטוּבוֹ בְּחֵן בְּחֶסֶד וּבְרַחֲמִים

hu notein lechem l'chol basar   הוּא נוֹתֵן לֶחֶם לְכָל בָּשָׂר

ki l'olam chasdo. Uv'tuvo   כִּי לְעוֹלָם חַסְדּוֹ. וּבְטוּבוֹ

hagadol tamid lo chasar lanu,   הַגָּדוֹל תָּמִיד לֹא חָסַר לָנוּ,

v'al yechsar lanu mazon l'olam   וְאַל יֶחְסַר לָנוּ מָזוֹן לְעוֹלָם

va-ed. Ba-avur sh'mo hagadol,   וָעֶד. בַּעֲבוּר שְׁמוֹ הַגָּדוֹל,

ki Hu Eil zan um'farneis lakol   כִּי הוּא אֵל זָן וּמְפַרְנֵס לַכֹּל

umeitiv lakol, umeichin mazon   וּמֵטִיב לַכֹּל, וּמֵכִין מָזוֹן

l'chol b'riotav asher bara.   לְכֹל בְּרִיּוֹתָיו אֲשֶׁר בָּרָא.

(*Some, when reciting the following, open their palms:* Ka-amur, potei-ach et yadecha u-masbia l'chol chai ratzon.)   (כָּאָמוּר, פּוֹתֵחַ אֶת יָדֶךָ, וּמַשְׂבִּיעַ לְכָל חַי רָצוֹן.)

Baruch Atah Adonai, hazan et hakol.   בָּרוּךְ אַתָּה יְיָ, הַזָּן אֶת הַכֹּל:

Blessed are You, Adonai, our God, Ruler of the universe, Who feeds the entire world from God's bounty – with grace, with loving-kindness, mercifully. God gives food to all flesh, for God's loving-kindness is eternal. And because of God's great goodness we have never lacked food, and may we never lack it. For God's great name's sake – for God feeds and provides for all, and is good to all, and prepares food for all created creatures.

(*Some, when reciting the following, open their palms:* You open Your hand and satisfy the desire of every living creature.)

Blessed are You, Adonai, Who nourishes all.

Blessed are You, God, Who nourishes all.

We thank You, God... for bringing us out from the land of Egypt.

Nodeh L'cha

Nodeh l'cha Adonai Eloheinu al shehinchalta la-avoteinu, eretz chemdah tovah ur'chavah, v'al shehotzeitanu Adonai Eloheinu mei-eretz Mitzrayim, uf'ditanu mibeit avadim, v'al b'rit'cha shechatamta bivsareinu,* v'al Torat'cha shelimad'tanu, v'al chukecha shehodatanu v'al chayim chein vachesed shechonantanu, v'al achilat mazon sha-atah zan um'farneis otanu tamid, b'chol yom uv'chol eit uv'chol sha-ah.

נוֹדֶה לְךָ יְיָ אֱלֹהֵינוּ עַל שֶׁהִנְחַלְתָּ
לַאֲבוֹתֵינוּ, אֶרֶץ חֶמְדָּה טוֹבָה
וּרְחָבָה, וְעַל שֶׁהוֹצֵאתָנוּ יְיָ
אֱלֹהֵינוּ מֵאֶרֶץ מִצְרַיִם, וּפְדִיתָנוּ,
מִבֵּית עֲבָדִים, וְעַל בְּרִיתְךָ
שֶׁחָתַמְתָּ בִּבְשָׂרֵנוּ,* וְעַל תּוֹרָתְךָ
שֶׁלִּמַּדְתָּנוּ, וְעַל חֻקֶּיךָ שֶׁהוֹדַעְתָּנוּ
וְעַל חַיִּים חֵן וָחֶסֶד שֶׁחוֹנַנְתָּנוּ,
וְעַל אֲכִילַת מָזוֹן שָׁאַתָּה זָן
וּמְפַרְנֵס אוֹתָנוּ תָּמִיד, בְּכָל
יוֹם וּבְכָל עֵת וּבְכָל שָׁעָה:

We thank You, Adonai, our God, for allotting to our ancestors a desirable, goodly, and ample land, and for bringing us out, Adonai our God, from the land of Egypt, for emancipating us from a land of slavery, for sealing Your covenant in our flesh,* for teaching us Your Torah, for making Your statutes known to us, for bestowing life, grace, and loving-kindness upon us, and for feeding us and supplying us with food continually, every day, at all times, and at every hour.

Some have in mind:

...v'al mitzvotecha

shechatamta b'libeinu...

...וְעַל מִצְווֹתֶיךָ

שֶׁחָתַמְתָּ בְּלִבֵּנוּ...

...and for Your mitzvot that You sealed in our hearts...

V'al Hakol

V'al hakol Adonai Eloheinu anachnu

modim lach, um'var'chim otach,

yitbarach shimcha b'fi kol chai

tamid l'olam va-ed. Kakatuv,

v'achalta v'savata, uveirachta et

Adonai Elohecha al ha-aretz hatovah

asher natan lach. Baruch Atah Adonai,

al ha-aretz v'al hamazon.

וְעַל הַכֹּל יְיָ אֱלֹהֵינוּ אֲנַחְנוּ

מוֹדִים לָךְ, וּמְבָרְכִים אוֹתָךְ,

יִתְבָּרַךְ שִׁמְךָ בְּפִי כָל חַי

תָּמִיד לְעוֹלָם וָעֶד. כַּכָּתוּב,

וְאָכַלְתָּ וְשָׂבָעְתָּ, וּבֵרַכְתָּ אֶת

יְיָ אֱלֹהֶיךָ עַל הָאָרֶץ הַטֹּבָה

אֲשֶׁר נָתַן לָךְ. בָּרוּךְ אַתָּה יְיָ,

עַל הָאָרֶץ וְעַל הַמָּזוֹן:

For all this, Adonai, our God, we thank You and bless You. May Your name
be blessed by every living thing always, forever. As it is written: "When you
have eaten your fill, you shall bless Adonai, your God, for the goodly land
God has given you" (Deuteronomy 8:10). Blessed are You, Adonai, for the
land and for the food.

Racheim Na

Racheim na Adonai Eloheinu,

al Yisra-eil amecha, v'al

Y'rushalayim irecha, v'al

tzion mishkan k'vodecha,

v'al malchut Beit David

m'shichecha, v'al Habayit hagadol

v'hakadosh shenikra shimcha

alav. Eloheinu, Avinu,

R'einu, zuneinu, parn'seinu,

רַחֶם נָא יְיָ אֱלֹהֵינוּ,

עַל יִשְׂרָאֵל עַמֶּךָ, וְעַל

יְרוּשָׁלַיִם עִירֶךָ, וְעַל

צִיּוֹן מִשְׁכַּן כְּבוֹדֶךָ,

וְעַל מַלְכוּת בֵּית דָּוִד

מְשִׁיחֶךָ, וְעַל הַבַּיִת הַגָּדוֹל

וְהַקָּדוֹשׁ שֶׁנִּקְרָא שִׁמְךָ

עָלָיו. אֱלֹהֵינוּ, אָבִינוּ,

רְעֵנוּ, זוּנֵנוּ, פַּרְנְסֵנוּ,

v'chalk'leinu, v'harvicheinu, v'harvach lanu	וְכַלְכְּלֵנוּ, וְהַרְוִיחֵנוּ, וְהַרְוַח לָנוּ
Adonai Eloheinu m'heirah mikol tzaroteinu,	יְיָ אֱלֹהֵינוּ מְהֵרָה מִכָּל צָרוֹתֵינוּ.
v'na, al tatzricheinu Adonai Eloheinu, lo	וְנָא, אַל תַּצְרִיכֵנוּ יְיָ אֱלֹהֵינוּ, לֹא
lidei mat'nat basar vadam, v'lo lidei	לִידֵי מַתְּנַת בָּשָׂר וָדָם, וְלֹא לִידֵי
halva-atam. Ki im l'yad'cha ham'lei-ah,	הַלְוָאָתָם. כִּי אִם לְיָדְךָ הַמְּלֵאָה,
hap'tuchah, hak'doshah v'har'chavah, shelo	הַפְּתוּחָה, הַקְּדוֹשָׁה וְהָרְחָבָה, שֶׁלֹּא
neivosh v'lo nikaleim l'olam va-ed.	נֵבוֹשׁ וְלֹא נִכָּלֵם לְעוֹלָם וָעֶד:

Have mercy, Adonai, our God, on Israel Your people, on Jerusalem Your city, on Zion the dwelling place of Your glory, on the kingdom of the House of David Your anointed one, and on the great and holy House that is called by Your name. Our God, our Parent, our Shepherd – pasture us, feed us, provide for us, and sustain us, and give us relief – and give us speedy relief, Adonai, our God, from all our troubles. Do not, we beg You, Adonai, our God, cause us to become dependent on the handouts of mortals or on their loans, but only on Your hand – full, open, bountiful and generous – so that we shall never be ashamed or be put to shame.

R'tzeih

On Shabbat, say the following passage:

R'tzeih v'hachalitzeinu Adonai Eloheinu	רְצֵה וְהַחֲלִיצֵנוּ יְיָ אֱלֹהֵינוּ בְּמִצְוֹתֶיךָ
b'mitzvotecha uv'mitzvat yom hashvi-i	וּבְמִצְוַת יוֹם הַשְּׁבִיעִי הַשַּׁבָּת
ha-Shabat hagadol v'hakadosh hazeh.	הַגָּדוֹל וְהַקָּדוֹשׁ הַזֶּה. כִּי יוֹם זֶה
Ki yom zeh gadol v'kadosh hu l'fanecha,	גָּדוֹל וְקָדוֹשׁ הוּא לְפָנֶיךָ, לִשְׁבָּת
lishbot bo v'lanuach bo b'ahavah	בּוֹ וְלָנוּחַ בּוֹ בְּאַהֲבָה כְּמִצְוַת
k'mitzvat r'tzonecha uvirtzon'cha hani-	רְצוֹנֶךָ. וּבִרְצוֹנְךָ הָנִיחַ לָנוּ יְיָ
ach lanu Adonai Eloheinu, shelo t'hei	אֱלֹהֵינוּ, שֶׁלֹּא תְהֵא צָרָה וְיָגוֹן
tzarah v'yagon va-anachah b'yom	וַאֲנָחָה בְּיוֹם מְנוּחָתֵנוּ. וְהַרְאֵנוּ יְיָ

m'nuchateinu. V'hareinu Adonai

אֱלֹהֵינוּ בְּנֶחָמַת צִיּוֹן

Eloheinu b'nechamat tzion irecha,

עִירָךְ, וּבְבִנְיַן יְרוּשָׁלַיִם

uv'vinyan Y'rushalayim ir kod'shecha,

עִיר קָדְשֶׁךָ, כִּי אַתָּה

ki Atah Hu Ba-al hayshuot

הוּא בַּעַל הַיְשׁוּעוֹת

uva-al hanechamot.

וּבַעַל הַנֶּחָמוֹת:

Let it be Your will, Adonai, our God, that we be strengthened by performing Your commandments – especially by observing this seventh day, this great and holy Sabbath, for this day is great and holy before You, to pause and rest on it lovingly as it was Your pleasure to command. And let it be your will, Adonai, our God, that there shall be no cause for trouble, sorrow, or sighing on our day of rest. And show us, Adonai, our God, Zion Your city comforted and Jerusalem Your holy city rebuilt, for You are the Giver of salvation and the Giver of consolation.

Ya-aleh V'yavo

Eloheinu veilohei avoteinu,

אֱלֹהֵינוּ וֵאלֹהֵי אֲבוֹתֵינוּ,

ya-aleh v'yavo v'yagi-a,

יַעֲלֶה וְיָבֹא וְיַגִּיעַ,

v'yei-ra-eh, v'yeiratzeh, v'yishama,

וְיֵרָאֶה, וְיֵרָצֶה, וְיִשָּׁמַע,

v'yipakeid, v'yizacheir zichroneinu

וְיִפָּקֵד, וְיִזָּכֵר זִכְרוֹנֵנוּ

ufikdoneinu, v'zichron avoteinu,

וּפִקְדוֹנֵנוּ, וְזִכְרוֹן

v'zichron mashi-ach ben david

אֲבוֹתֵינוּ, וְזִכְרוֹן מָשִׁיחַ

avdecha, v'zichron Y'rushalayim

בֶּן דָּוִד עַבְדֶּךָ, וְזִכְרוֹן

ir kod'shecha, v'zichron kol am'cha

יְרוּשָׁלַיִם עִיר קָדְשֶׁךָ,

beit Yisra-eil l'fanecha, lifleitah

וְזִכְרוֹן כָּל עַמְּךָ בֵּית

l'tovah l'chein ul'chesed ul'rachamim,

יִשְׂרָאֵל לְפָנֶיךָ, לִפְלֵיטָה

l'chayim ul'shalom b'yom Chag

לְטוֹבָה לְחֵן וּלְחֶסֶד

Hamatzot hazeh. Zoch'reinu Adonai
Eloheinu bo l'tovah. Ufok'deinu vo
livrachah. V'hoshi-einu vo l'chayim,
uvidvar y'shuah v'rachamim, chus
v'chaneinu, v'racheim aleinu v'hoshi-
einu, ki eilecha eineinu, ki Eil Melech
chanun v'rachum Atah.

וּלְרַחֲמִים, לְחַיִּים וּלְשָׁלוֹם בְּיוֹם
חַג הַמַּצּוֹת הַזֶּה. זָכְרֵנוּ יְיָ אֱלֹהֵינוּ
בּוֹ לְטוֹבָה. וּפָקְדֵנוּ בּוֹ לִבְרָכָה.
וְהוֹשִׁיעֵנוּ בּוֹ לְחַיִּים, וּבִדְבַר
יְשׁוּעָה וְרַחֲמִים, חוּס וְחָנֵּנוּ, וְרַחֵם
עָלֵינוּ וְהוֹשִׁיעֵנוּ, כִּי אֵלֶיךָ עֵינֵינוּ,
כִּי אֵל מֶלֶךְ חַנּוּן וְרַחוּם אָתָּה:

Our God and God of our ancestors: let the remembrance and mindfulness of us, the
remembrance of our ancestors, of the Messiah, annointed son of David, Your servant,
the remembrance of Jerusalem Your holy city, and the remembrance of Your entire
people the House of Israel come to You, reach You, be seen by You, be favored by You,
be heard by You, recollected by You and remembered by you to our relief, to our benefit,
for grace, for loving-kindness and for mercy, for life and for peace, on this Matzot Festival Day. On this day, Adonai, our God, remember us for good, be mindful of us on it for
blessing, and preserve us on it for a good life. And be so merciful as to grace us with the
promise of salvation and mercy, and have mercy on us and save us. For to You our eyes
are turned, for You are a gracious and merciful God Ruler.

Uv'neih Y'rushalayim

Uv'neih Y'rushalayim ir hakodesh
bimheirah v'yameinu. Baruch Atah Adonai,
Boneih b'rachamav Y'rushalayim. Amein.

וּבְנֵה יְרוּשָׁלַיִם עִיר הַקֹּדֶשׁ
בִּמְהֵרָה בְיָמֵינוּ. בָּרוּךְ אַתָּה יְיָ,
בּוֹנֵה בְּרַחֲמָיו יְרוּשָׁלָיִם. אָמֵן.

And rebuild Jerusalem the holy city speedily in our days. Blessed are You, Adonai, merciful Rebuilder of Jerusalem. Amen.

Ha-Eil Avinu

Baruch Atah Adonai, Eloheinu
Melech ha-olam, ha-Eil Avinu,
Malkeinu, Adireinu Bor'einu, Go-
aleinu, Yotz'reinu, K'dosheinu K'dosh
Ya-akov, Roeinu Roeih Yisra-eil.
Hamelech hatov, v'hameitiv lakol,
sheb'chol yom vayom Hu heitiv, Hu
meitiv, Hu yeitiv lanu. Hu g'malanu,
Hu gom'leinu, Hu yigm'leinu la-
ad l'chein ul'chesed ul'rachamim
ul'revach hatzalah v'hatzlachah

בָּרוּךְ אַתָּה יְיָ אֱלֹהֵינוּ
מֶלֶךְ הָעוֹלָם, הָאֵל אָבִינוּ,
מַלְכֵּנוּ, אַדִּירֵנוּ בּוֹרְאֵנוּ,
גּוֹאֲלֵנוּ, יוֹצְרֵנוּ, קְדוֹשֵׁנוּ
קְדוֹשׁ יַעֲקֹב, רוֹעֵנוּ רוֹעֵה
יִשְׂרָאֵל. הַמֶּלֶךְ הַטּוֹב,
וְהַמֵּטִיב לַכֹּל, שֶׁבְּכָל יוֹם
וָיוֹם הוּא הֵטִיב, הוּא
מֵטִיב, הוּא יֵיטִיב לָנוּ. הוּא
גְּמָלָנוּ, הוּא גוֹמְלֵנוּ, הוּא
יִגְמְלֵנוּ לָעַד לְחֵן וּלְחֶסֶד

b'rachah vi-shuah, nechamah,

parnasah v'chalkalah, v'rachamim,

v'chayim v'shalom, v'chol tov,

umikol tuv l'olam al y'chas'reinu.

וּלְרַחֲמִים וּלְרֶוַח הַצָּלָה וְהַצְלָחָה

בְּרָכָה וִישׁוּעָה, נֶחָמָה, פַּרְנָסָה

וְכַלְכָּלָה, וְרַחֲמִים וְחַיִּים וְשָׁלוֹם, וְכָל

טוֹב, וּמִכָּל טוּב לְעוֹלָם אַל יְחַסְּרֵנוּ:

Blessed are You, Adonai, our God, Ruler of the universe, the God Who is our Parent, our Ruler, our Mighty One, our Creator, our Redeemer, our Maker, our Holy One, the Holy One of Yaakov, our Shepherd – Israel's Shepherd – the Ruler Who is good and does good to all, Who every day did good, does good, will do good to all of us; who bestowed, bestows, and will bestow favors on us forever: grace, loving-kindness, mercy and relief, succor and prosperity, blessing and salvation, consolation, maintenance and sustenance, and life, and peace, and all that is good; and may God never let us lack for any good thing.

Harachaman

Harachaman, hu yimloch

aleinu l'olam va-ed.

Harachaman, hu yitbarach

bashamayim uva-aretz.

Harachaman, hu yishtabach l'dor

dorim, v'yitpa-ar banu la-ad ul'neitzach

n'tzachim, v'yithadar banu la-ad ul'ol'mei

olamim. Harachaman, hu y'farn'seinu

b'chavod. Harachaman, hu yishbor

uleinu mei-al tzavareinu, v'hu yolicheinu

kom'miut l'artzeinu.

Harachaman, hu yishlach lanu b'rachah

הָרַחֲמָן, הוּא יִמְלוֹךְ

עָלֵינוּ לְעוֹלָם וָעֶד.

הָרַחֲמָן, הוּא יִתְבָּרַךְ

בַּשָּׁמַיִם וּבָאָרֶץ.

הָרַחֲמָן, הוּא יִשְׁתַּבַּח לְדוֹר דּוֹרִים,

וְיִתְפָּאַר בָּנוּ לָעַד וּלְנֵצַח נְצָחִים,

וְיִתְהַדַּר בָּנוּ לָעַד וּלְעוֹלְמֵי עוֹלָמִים.

הָרַחֲמָן, הוּא יְפַרְנְסֵנוּ בְּכָבוֹד.

הָרַחֲמָן, הוּא יִשְׁבּוֹר עֻלֵּנוּ

מֵעַל צַוָּארֵנוּ וְהוּא יוֹלִיכֵנוּ

קוֹמְמִיּוּת לְאַרְצֵנוּ.

הָרַחֲמָן, הוּא יִשְׁלַח לָנוּ בְּרָכָה

m'rubah babayit hazeh, v'al

shulchan zeh she-achalnu alav.

Harachaman, hu yishlach lanu

et Eiliyahu Hanavi zachur

latov, vivaser lanu b'sorot

tovot y'shuot v'nechamot.

מְרֻבָּה בַּבַּיִת הַזֶּה, וְעַל

שֻׁלְחָן זֶה שֶׁאָכַלְנוּ עָלָיו.

הָרַחֲמָן, הוּא יִשְׁלַח לָנוּ

אֶת אֵלִיָּהוּ הַנָּבִיא זָכוּר

לַטּוֹב, וִיבַשֶּׂר לָנוּ בְּשׂוֹרוֹת

טוֹבוֹת יְשׁוּעוֹת וְנֶחָמוֹת.

Merciful One – may You reign over us forever.

Merciful One – may You be blessed in heaven and on earth.

Merciful One – may You be praised throughout all generations, and be glorified through us for all eternity, and be beautified through us forever and for all eternity.

Merciful One – may You sustain us with honor.

Merciful One – may You break the yoke from our necks and may God lead us proud and upright back to our land.

Merciful One – may You send blessings in abundance to this house and upon this table at which we have eaten.

Merciful One – may You send us the Prophet Eliyahu so fondly remembered, to bring us good tidings, salvations and consolations.

Blessing the Host

Guests at someone else's table say (adding the words in parentheses if in one's parents' home):

Harachaman, hu y'vareich et (avi

mori) ba-al habayit hazeh, v'et

(imi morati) ba-alat habayit

hazeh, otam v'et beitam v'et

zaram v'et kol asher lahem,

הָרַחֲמָן, הוּא יְבָרֵךְ אֶת (אָבִי

מוֹרִי) בַּעַל הַבַּיִת הַזֶּה, וְאֶת

(אִמִּי מוֹרָתִי) בַּעֲלַת הַבַּיִת

הַזֶּה, אוֹתָם וְאֶת בֵּיתָם וְאֶת

זַרְעָם וְאֶת כָּל אֲשֶׁר לָהֶם,

Merciful One – may You send blessings in abundance to this house and upon this table at which we have eaten.

Merciful One – may You bless (*children at their parents' table say:* my father my teacher,) the head of this household, and (*children at their parents' table say:* my mother my teacher,) the head of this household – them and their household and their children and all that is theirs,

Those eating at their own table say (adding in the words in parentheses if one is married/has children):

Harachaman, hu y'vareich oti

(v'et ishti/ishi, v'et

zari,) v'et kol asher li,

הָרַחֲמָן, הוּא יְבָרֵךְ אוֹתִי

(וְאֶת אִשְׁתִּי/אִישִׁי, וְאֶת

זַרְעִי,) וְאֶת כָּל אֲשֶׁר לִי,

Merciful One – may You bless me (and my wife/husband, and my children,) and all that is mine.

For all the guests at the table:

Harachaman hu y'vareich et

kol ham'subin kahn,

הָרַחֲמָן הוּא יְבָרֵךְ אֶת

כָּל הַמְסֻבִּין כַּאן,

Merciful One – may You bless all others seated at this table,

All continue:

otanu v'et kol asher lanu. K'mo

shenitbar'chu avoteinu, Avraham

Yitzchak v'Ya-akov* bakol, mikol, kol.

Kein y'vareich otanu kulanu yachad

bivrachah sh'leimah, v'nomar amein.

אוֹתָנוּ וְאֶת כָּל אֲשֶׁר לָנוּ. כְּמוֹ

שֶׁנִּתְבָּרְכוּ אֲבוֹתֵינוּ, אַבְרָהָם

יִצְחָק וְיַעֲקֹב:* בַּכֹּל, מִכֹּל, כֹּל.

כֵּן יְבָרֵךְ אוֹתָנוּ כֻּלָּנוּ יַחַד

בִּבְרָכָה שְׁלֵמָה, וְנֹאמַר אָמֵן:

us and all that is ours. Just as our fathers Abraham, Isaac, and Jacob* were blessed with all, of all, all, so may God bless us, all of us together, with a perfect blessing; and let us say: Amen.

* Some have in mind:

V'imoteinu Sarah, Rivkah, Racheil, v'Leiah.

וְאִמּוֹתֵינוּ שָׂרָה, רִבְקָה, רָחֵל וְלֵאָה.

And You have blessed our mothers Sarah, Rebecca, Rachel, and Leah.

Bamarom

Bamarom y'lam'du aleihem

v'aleinu z'chut, shet'hei l'mishmeret

shalom, v'nisa v'rachah mei-eit

Adonai utz'dakah mei-Elohei

yisheinu, v'nimtza chein v'seichel

tov b'einei Elohim v'adam:

בַּמָּרוֹם יְלַמְּדוּ עֲלֵיהֶם וְעָלֵינוּ

זְכוּת, שֶׁתְּהֵא לְמִשְׁמֶרֶת

שָׁלוֹם, וְנִשָּׂא בְרָכָה מֵאֵת

יְיָ וּצְדָקָה מֵאֱלֹהֵי יִשְׁעֵנוּ,

וְנִמְצָא חֵן וְשֵׂכֶל טוֹב

בְּעֵינֵי אֱלֹהִים וְאָדָם:

In the heavens, may there be invoked for them and for us such merit as will be a safeguard of peace, and so that we may carry a blessing from Adonai and justice from our Saving-God, and so that we may "win favor and approbation from God and from people" (Mishlei 3:4).

Harachaman

Say the following only on Shabbat.

Harachaman, hu yanchileinu

yom shekulo Shabat um'nuchah

l'chayei ha-olamim.

הָרַחֲמָן, הוּא יַנְחִילֵנוּ

יוֹם שֶׁכֻּלוֹ שַׁבָּת וּמְנוּחָה

לְחַיֵּי הָעוֹלָמִים.

Merciful One – may You grant us the Day-That-Is-All-Shabbat and rest, reflecting eternal life.

On all days continue as follows.

Harachaman, hu yanchileinu

yom shekulo tov.

Harachaman, hu yevareich

et Medinat Yisra-eil, reisheet

הָרַחֲמָן, הוּא יַנְחִילֵנוּ

יוֹם שֶׁכֻּלוֹ טוֹב.

הָרַחֲמָן, הוּא יְבָרֵךְ

אֶת מְדִינַת יִשְׂרָאֵל,

tz'michat g'ulateinu.   רֵאשִׁית צְמִיחַת גְּאֻלָּתֵנוּ.

Harachaman, hu yevareich et chayalei   הָרַחֲמָן, הוּא יְבָרֵךְ אֶת חַיָּלֵי

tzava hahaganah l'Yisra-eil v'chayalei   צְבָא הַהֲגָנָה לְיִשְׂרָאֵל וְחַיָּלֵי

Artzot ha-Brit v'yagein aleihem.   אַרְצוֹת הַבְּרִית וְיָגֵן עֲלֵיהֶם.

Harachaman, hu y'zakeinu limot   הָרַחֲמָן, הוּא יְזַכֵּנוּ לִימוֹת

hamashi-ach ul'chayei ha-olam haba.   הַמָּשִׁיחַ וּלְחַיֵּי הָעוֹלָם הַבָּא.

Migdol y'shuot malko, v'oseh   מִגְדּוֹל יְשׁוּעוֹת מַלְכּוֹ, וְעֹשֶׂה

chesed limshicho l'David ul'zaro ad   חֶסֶד לִמְשִׁיחוֹ לְדָוִד וּלְזַרְעוֹ עַד

olam. Oseh shalom bimromav,   עוֹלָם: עֹשֶׂה שָׁלוֹם בִּמְרוֹמָיו,

hu ya-aseh shalom, aleinu v'al   הוּא יַעֲשֶׂה שָׁלוֹם, עָלֵינוּ וְעַל

kol Yisra-eil, v'imru amein.   כָּל יִשְׂרָאֵל, וְאִמְרוּ אָמֵן:

Merciful One – may You bequeath to us a Day-That-Is-All-Good.

Merciful One – may God bless the State of Israel, the dawn of our redemption.

Merciful One – may God bless the soldiers of the Israel Defense Forces and the United States Armed Forces and protect them from harm.

Merciful One – may God judge us worthy of the messianic era and the life of the World-That-Is-to-Be.

"God is a Tower of Victory for the sovereign, Who deals graciously with God's anointed one – with David and his descendants forever" (II Samuel 22:51).

"God Who keeps God's high spheres in harmony" (Job 25:2) – may God grant harmony to us and to all Israel. Now say: Amen.

Y'ru

Y'ru et Adonai k'doshav, ki ein machsor   יְראוּ אֶת יְיָ קְדֹשָׁיו, כִּי אֵין מַחְסוֹר

lirei-av. K'firim rashu v'ra-eivu,   לִירֵאָיו: כְּפִירִים רָשׁוּ וְרָעֵבוּ, וְדוֹרְשֵׁי יְיָ

v'dor'shei Adonai lo yachs'ru chol tov.   לֹא יַחְסְרוּ כָל טוֹב: הוֹדוּ לַייָ כִּי טוֹב,

Hodu l'Adonai ki tov, ki l'olam chasdo. כִּי לְעוֹלָם חַסְדּוֹ: פּוֹתֵחַ אֶת

Potei-ach et yadecha, umasbi-a l'chol יָדֶךָ, וּמַשְׂבִּיעַ לְכָל חַי רָצוֹן:

chai ratzon. Baruch hagever asher בָּרוּךְ הַגֶּבֶר אֲשֶׁר יִבְטַח

yivtach b'Adonai, v'hayah Adonai בַּיְיָ, וְהָיָה יְיָ מִבְטַחוֹ: נַעַר

mivtacho: na-ar hayiti gam zakanti v'lo הָיִיתִי גַם זָקַנְתִּי וְלֹא רָאִיתִי

ra-iti tzadik ne-ezav, v'zaro m'vakeish צַדִּיק נֶעֱזָב, וְזַרְעוֹ מְבַקֶּשׁ

lachem. Adonai oz l'amo yitein, Adonai לָחֶם: יְיָ עֹז לְעַמּוֹ יִתֵּן, יְיָ

y'vareich et amo vashalom. יְבָרֵךְ אֶת עַמּוֹ בַשָּׁלוֹם:

"Fear Adonai, you, God's holy ones; for those who fear God want for noth-ing" (Psalms 34:10). "Lions have been reduced to starvation; but those who seek Adonai lack no good thing" (Psalms 34:11). "Give thanks to Adonai, Who is good and Whose loving-kindness endures forever" (Psalms 118:1). "You give openhandedly, filling the need of every living creature" (Psalms 145:16). "Blessed is one who trusts in Adonai and places confidence in Ado-nai" (Jeremiah 17:7). "I was a youngster and now am old, and never have I seen the righteous forsaken nor their children begging bread" (Psalms 37:35). "God will give strength to the people Israel, God will bless Israel with peace" (Psalms 29:11).

REFLECTION

Toward the end of the Grace after Meals, in the last paragraph, a quote from Psalms (37:25) is included: "I was a youngster and now am old, and never have I seen the righteous forsaken nor their children begging bread." Many Holocaust survivors I know skip this verse; some people follow a custom of reciting it in a very low tone. Rabbi Jeffrey Cohen provides an insight into this verse, tradition-ally ascribed to King David. He says not to translate the words *lo ra'iti* as "I have not seen," but rather as "I have not watched," i.e., I have not stood idly by as a spectator without intervening.[88]

Some say:

Hineni muchan u-mezuman הִנְנִי מוּכָן וּמְזוּמָן

l'kayem mitzvat kos shlishi לְקַיֵּם מִצְוַת כּוֹס שְׁלִישִׁי

me'arba kosot. L'shem yichud   מֵאַרְבַּע כּוֹסוֹת. לְשֵׁם יְחוּד

kudsha brich hu u-shechinteh   קוּדְשָׁא בְּרִיךְ הוּא וּשְׁכִינְתֵּיה

al yedei hahu tamir   עַל יְדֵי הַהוּא טָמִיר

v'neelam b'shem kol Yisrael.   וְנֶעְלָם בְּשֵׁם כָּל יִשְׂרָאֵל.

Here I am, ready and willing to fulfill the mitzvah of drinking the third of the four cups of wine, as is the will of the Holy One.

Say the following blessing and drink the third cup, reclining to the left.

Baruch Atah Adonai, Eloheinu Melech   בָּרוּךְ אַתָּה יְיָ, אֱלֹהֵינוּ מֶלֶךְ

ha-olam, Borei p'ri hagafen.   הָעוֹלָם, בּוֹרֵא פְּרִי הַגָּפֶן:

Blessed are You, Adonai, our God, Ruler of the universe, Creator of the fruit of the vine.

Kos Eliyahu: Elijah's Cup

SUGGESTION

Another custom, based on the tradition begun at the table of the eighteenth-century Chasidic master Rabbi Naftali of Ropshitz is to pass Elijah's Cup around to all the attendees and have them pour off a bit of their wine or grape juice into Elijah's Cup. This is to remind us that in order to bring the redemption we all have to be engaged in the process of improving our world.

REFLECTION

This custom of pouring a special glass of wine to honor Elijah the prophet has its roots in the rabbinic controversy over how many cups of wine we are commanded to drink. We drink one cup for each of four verses from the Torah that represent God's saving action in redeeming us from Egypt. The rabbis could not agree whether there should be a fifth cup, based on the fifth verse, "And I will bring you into the land." Thus they designated a "fifth cup" in honor of Elijah,

to whom Jewish tradition ascribes the role of announcing the final redemption from exile. In messianic times, it will be Elijah who will answer all
unsolved questions, including the question of a fifth cup.

*See pp. 221–22 for songs "Ode to Elijah," "Les Miselijah," and "Elijah!"
and Rabbi Shlomo Carlebach story "Welcoming Elijah"*

QUESTIONS FOR DISCUSSION

Rabbi Menachem Kasher has suggested that there should be a fifth cup of
wine, in honor of the establishment of the State of Israel, a modern miracle! Do you think that the creation of the State of Israel is *reishit smichat
geulateinu* (the dawn of our redemption)? Is it a religious event? Or only
secular? Should we dedicate Elijah's Cup to the State of Israel?

REFLECTION

As we open our door to welcome Elijah, we recite the Sh'foch Chamat'cha, "Pour out Your wrath upon the nations of the world." How can we balance the humanism of our Seder – welcoming all who are hungry, the hope that Elijah will come – with the passage of Sh'foch Chamat'cha, which on the surface seems vengeful, filled with revenge and retribution directed toward the nations of the world?

Sh'foch Chamat'cha dates to the period of the Crusaders when Jews were hunted down and murdered. Often a blood libel was the charge against Jews that Christian children's blood was ostensibly used to bake matzah. By opening our doors on this Leil Shimurim, we show that we are unafraid of telling the world how we really feel, because we are assured divine assistance.

Having both viewpoints represents realpolitik: there is a time for humanism and a time for self-defense.

The text of Sh'foch Chamat'cha is not indicting all the nations of the world but rather only those that have not yet recognized God. This is not an indiscriminate attack on nations of the world but a realistic assessment that there are those who still today rise to come after us. And there are those who stand in silence as others attack us, whether physically or through words.

REFLECTION

We open the door for a variety of reasons. Passover night is called Leil Shimurim, a night of watching, and opening the door is proof in our belief that the Messiah will come. It also symbolizes the concept that all are invited to the Seder, even at this concluding stage. A historical reason that Jews may have adapted this custom was to rebut any charges of a blood libel; our doors are open for all to come in and see what we are doing. That might also explain the reasoning of the Taz, who suggested that we use white wine only.

REFLECTION

An interesting addition here is Sh'foch Ahavat'cha. While many question its authenticity, one scholar believes it is from a sixteenth-century Worms Haggadah written by a descendant of Rashi. It is the exact opposite in tone and content: it refers to those nations that do recognize God and act in a just fashion toward Jews. Think of righteous Gentiles during the Holocaust who rescued Jews at peril to their own lives.

Sh'foch Chamat'cha

LEADER: Having made the blessing over the third cup of wine, we now turn to open the door for Elijah: Elijah, the harbinger of the messianic era; Elijah, who will answer all those questions to which we haven't found the answers. As we open the door to welcome him in, let it be a symbol to carry us through the whole year to be welcoming in our homes and our hearts; not to let our disputes divide us; to be open to greater commitment to Judaism, greater attempts to welcome in the strangers, the alienated, and the other; and may God's sheltering presence always envelope us and our homes and lives with peace.

Fill Elijah's Cup, open the front door, and say:

Sh'foch chamat'cha el hagoyim,	שְׁפֹךְ חֲמָתְךָ אֶל־הַגּוֹיִם,
asher lo y'dau-cha v'al	אֲשֶׁר לֹא יְדָעוּךָ וְעַל־
mamlachot asher b'shimcha	מַמְלָכוֹת אֲשֶׁר בְּשִׁמְךָ
lo kara-u. Ki achal et	לֹא קָרָאוּ: כִּי אָכַל אֶת־
Ya-akov v'et navei-hu heishamu.	יַעֲקֹב. וְאֶת־נָוֵהוּ הֵשַׁמּוּ:
Sh'foch aleihem zamecha, vacharon	שְׁפֹךְ־עֲלֵיהֶם זַעְמֶךָ, וַחֲרוֹן
ap'cha yasigeim. Tirdof b'af	אַפְּךָ יַשִּׂיגֵם: תִּרְדֹּף בְּאַף
v'tashmideim, mitachat sh'mei Adonai.	וְתַשְׁמִידֵם, מִתַּחַת שְׁמֵי יְיָ:

"Pour out Your wrath on the nations that know You not and on the kingdoms that do not invoke Your name. For they have devoured Jacob and laid waste his homestead" (Psalms 79:6–7). "Pour out Your fury on them and let Your blazing anger overtake them" (Psalms 69:25). "Pursue them in anger and exterminate them from under Adonai's skies" (Lamentations 3:66).

See p. 222 for Seder Reading of Remembrance of those murdered in the Holocaust

Sh'foch Ahavatcha

Sh'foch ahavatcha al ha-goyim asher	שְׁפֹךְ אַהֲבָתְךָ עַל הַגּוֹיִם אֲשֶׁר
yoducha, v'al mamlachot asher	יְדָעוּךָ וְעַל מַמְלָכוֹת אֲשֶׁר
b'shimcha korim b'glal chasadim	בְּשִׁמְךָ קוֹרְאִים בִּגְלַל חֲסָדִים
sheheim osim im Yaakov um'ginim	שֶׁהֵם עוֹשִׂים עִם יַעֲקֹב וּמְגִנִּים
al amcha Yisrael mipnei ochleihem.	עַל עַמְּךָ יִשְׂרָאֵל מִפְּנֵי אוֹכְלֵיהֶם.
Yizku lir'ot b'sukkat b'chirecha	יִזְכּוּ לִרְאוֹת בְּסֻכַּת בְּחִירֶךָ
v'lismoach b'simchat goyecha.	וְלִשְׂמוֹחַ בְּשִׂמְחַת גּוֹיֶיךָ.

Pour out Your love on the nations of the world who have known You and on the kingdoms who call upon Your name. For they show loving-kindness to the seed of Jacob, and they defend Your people Israel from those who would devour them alive. May they live to see the sukkah of peace spread over Your chosen ones and to participate in the joy of Your nations.

At the conclusion of the Seder after singing Eliyahu Hanavi and closing the door, some follow the Chasidic custom to take Elijah's Cup and pour it back into the wine bottle. This is to symbolize that our help is also needed to help bring our redemption. Others have the tradition of leaving the wine from Kos Eliyahu covered on the table to be used for the Kiddush on the next day at lunch.

Close the door. Fill the fourth cup.

HUMOR CORNER

Sandy Hackett, son of the late comedian/actor Buddy Hackett, related that his parents hosted many entertainers at their Seder. The young Sandy once opened the door to let Elijah in, and standing there was Gregory Peck. "He asked me if he was too late for the services and I said, 'No, go right in, Dad's expecting you.'"[89]

KIDS' CORNER

A note for parents/Seder leaders: See what happens when the children return to the table after they have opened and then closed the door for Elijah. Engage them in a discussion about whether they think the level of the wine in the cup has fallen because of Elijah's arrival. Some parents have even "helped" this discussion along by pouring off a drop from the cup while the children are busy opening the door for Elijah!

Hallel: Praising

Lo Lanu

Hallel concludes at this point as a reminder of the future redemption that still awaits us.

LEADER: As we conclude the second section of Hallel, may we be inspired by the words *"Pitchu li shaarei tzedek"* (open for me the gates of righteousness). May the gates always be open for us; may we be deemed worthy to experience the final redemption and have faith in its coming.

Lo lanu, Adonai, lo lanu, ki	לֹא לָנוּ יְיָ לֹא לָנוּ כִּי לְשִׁמְךָ
l'shimcha tein kavod, al chasd'cha al	תֵּן כָּבוֹד, עַל חַסְדְּךָ עַל
amitecha. Lamah yomru hagoyim,	אֲמִתֶּךָ. לָמָּה יֹאמְרוּ הַגּוֹיִם,
ayeih na Eloheihem. Veiloheinu	אַיֵּה נָא אֱלֹהֵיהֶם. וֵאלֹהֵינוּ
vashamayim, kol asher chafeitz	בַשָּׁמָיִם כֹּל אֲשֶׁר חָפֵץ
asah. Atzabeihem kesef v'zahav,	עָשָׂה. עֲצַבֵּיהֶם כֶּסֶף וְזָהָב,
ma-aseih y'dei adam. Peh lahem	מַעֲשֵׂה יְדֵי אָדָם. פֶּה לָהֶם
v'lo y'dabeiru, einayim lahem	וְלֹא יְדַבֵּרוּ, עֵינַיִם לָהֶם
v'lo yiru. Oz'nayim lahem v'lo	וְלֹא יִרְאוּ. אָזְנַיִם לָהֶם
yishma-u, af lahem v'lo y'richun.	וְלֹא יִשְׁמָעוּ, אַף לָהֶם וְלֹא
Y'deihem v'lo y'mishun, ragleihem	יְרִיחוּן. יְדֵיהֶם וְלֹא יְמִישׁוּן,
v'lo y'haleichu, lo yehgu bigronam.	רַגְלֵיהֶם וְלֹא יְהַלֵּכוּ, לֹא
K'mohem yihyu oseihem, kol asher	יֶהְגּוּ בִּגְרוֹנָם. כְּמוֹהֶם יִהְיוּ
botei-ach bahem. Yisra-eil b'tach	עֹשֵׂיהֶם, כֹּל אֲשֶׁר בֹּטֵחַ
b'Adonai, ezram u-maginam hu.	בָּהֶם: יִשְׂרָאֵל בְּטַח בַּיְיָ,
Beit Aharon bitchu v'Adonai, ezram	עֶזְרָם וּמָגִנָּם הוּא. בֵּית

umaginam hu. Yirei Adonai bitchu

אַהֲרֹן בָּטְחוּ בַייָ, עֶזְרָם וּמָגִנָּם הוּא.

v'Adonai, ezram u-maginam hu.

יִרְאֵי יְיָ בִּטְחוּ בַייָ, עֶזְרָם וּמָגִנָּם הוּא:

Not to us, Adonai, not to us, but to Your name bring glory, for the sake of Your loving-kindness, of Your constancy. Why should the nations say: "Where, then, is their God?" – when our God is in heaven, doing whatever God wishes. Their idols are silver and gold, the work of human hands. They have a mouth but speak not; eyes they have but they do not see. They have ears but they do not hear; nose they have but they smell not; hands – but they do not feel; feet – but they do not walk; their throat cannot utter a sound. Their makers become like them, and so do all who trust in them. Israel trusts in Adonai – God is their help and shield. The House of Aaron trusts in Adonai – God is their help and shield. The God-fearers trust in Adonai – God is their help and shield. (Psalms 115:1–11)

Zacharnu Y'vareich

Adonai z'charanu y'vareich, y'vareich et

יְיָ זְכָרָנוּ יְבָרֵךְ, יְבָרֵךְ אֶת

beit Yisra-eil, y'vareich et beit aharon.

בֵּית יִשְׂרָאֵל, יְבָרֵךְ אֶת בֵּית

Y'vareich yirei Adonai, hak'tanim im

אַהֲרֹן. יְבָרֵךְ יִרְאֵי יְיָ, הַקְּטַנִּים

hag'dolim. Yoseif Adonai aleichem,

עִם הַגְּדֹלִים. יֹסֵף יְיָ עֲלֵיכֶם,

aleichem v'al b'neichem. B'ruchim atem

עֲלֵיכֶם וְעַל בְּנֵיכֶם. בְּרוּכִים

l'Adonai, oseih shamayim va-aretz.

אַתֶּם לַייָ, עֹשֵׂה שָׁמַיִם

Hashamayim shamayim l'Adonai, v'ha-

וָאָרֶץ. הַשָּׁמַיִם שָׁמַיִם לַייָ,

aretz natan livnei adam. Lo hameitim

וְהָאָרֶץ נָתַן לִבְנֵי אָדָם. לֹא

y'hal'lu yah, v'lo kol yor'dei dumah. Va-

הַמֵּתִים יְהַלְלוּ יָהּ, וְלֹא כָּל

anachnu n'vareich yah, mei-atah v'ad olam,

יֹרְדֵי דוּמָה. וַאֲנַחְנוּ נְבָרֵךְ יָהּ,

hal'luyah.

מֵעַתָּה וְעַד עוֹלָם, הַלְלוּיָהּ:

Adonai remembers us – Adonai will bless: Adonai will bless the House of Israel. Adonai will bless the House of Aharon. Adonai will bless the God-fearers – the small and the great alike. May God give you increase – you and your children. Blessed are you of

Adonai, Maker of the heavens and earth. The heavens are Adonai's heavens, but the earth God gave to people. Not the dead praise God, not those who go down to the Realm of Silence. But we shall bless God, now and forever. Hallelujah. (Psalms 115:12–18)

Ahavti Ki Yishma

Ahavti ki yishma Adonai, et koli	אָהַבְתִּי כִּי יִשְׁמַע יְיָ, אֶת קוֹלִי
tachanunay. Ki hitah oz'no li,	תַּחֲנוּנָי. כִּי הִטָּה אָזְנוֹ לִי
uv'yamai ekra. Afafuni chevlei	וּבְיָמַי אֶקְרָא: אֲפָפוּנִי חֶבְלֵי
mavet, um'tzarei sh'ol m'tza-uni,	מָוֶת, וּמְצָרֵי שְׁאוֹל מְצָאוּנִי
tzarah v'yagon emtza. Uv'sheim	צָרָה וְיָגוֹן אֶמְצָא. וּבְשֵׁם יְיָ
Adonai ekra, anah Adonai maltah	אֶקְרָא, אָנָּה יְיָ מַלְּטָה נַפְשִׁי.
nafshi. Chanun Adonai v'tzadik,	חַנּוּן יְיָ וְצַדִּיק, וֵאלֹהֵינוּ
v'Eiloheinu m'racheim. Shomeir	מְרַחֵם. שֹׁמֵר פְּתָאִים יְיָ
p'ta-im Adonai, daloti v'li y'hoshi-a.	דַּלּוֹתִי וְלִי יְהוֹשִׁיעַ. שׁוּבִי
Shuvi nafshi limnuchay'chi, ki	נַפְשִׁי לִמְנוּחָיְכִי, כִּי יְיָ גָּמַל
Adonai gamal alay'chi. Ki chilatzta	עָלָיְכִי. כִּי חִלַּצְתָּ נַפְשִׁי מִמָּוֶת
nafshi mimavet, et eini min dimah,	אֶת עֵינִי מִן דִּמְעָה, אֶת
et ragli midechi. Et-haleich lifnei	רַגְלִי מִדֶּחִי. אֶתְהַלֵּךְ לִפְנֵי יְיָ,
Adonai, b'artzot hachayim. He-	בְּאַרְצוֹת הַחַיִּים. הֶאֱמַנְתִּי
emanti ki adabeir, ani aniti m'od.	כִּי אֲדַבֵּר, אֲנִי עָנִיתִי מְאֹד.
Ani amarti v'chof'zi,	אֲנִי אָמַרְתִּי בְחָפְזִי
kol ha-adam kozeiv.	כָּל הָאָדָם כֹּזֵב.

I yearn that Adonai should hear my supplicating voice, that God should bend an ear to me whenever in my lifetime I cry out. The coils of death are

taking me in their grip, the torments of Hell are overtaking me, trouble and anguish are my lot. So I call out in Adonai's name: "Please, Adonai, save my life!" Gracious is Adonai, and just; our God is merciful, Adonai protects the simple; when I am down and out, Adonai will save me. Rest again, my soul, for Adonai has been good to you. For You have rescued me from death, my eyes from weeping, my feet from stumbling. I will walk in Adonai's presence in the realm of the living. I trusted [in God] even when I thought I was finished, when I was at my wits' end, when in my desperation I said: "All people are untrustworthy." (Psalms 116:1–11)

Mah Ashiv

Mah ashiv l'Adonai, kol tagmulohi alay. Kos y'shuot esa, uv'sheim Adonai ekra. N'darai l'Adonai ashaleim, negdah na l'chol amo. Yakar b'einei Adonai, hamav'tah lachasidav. Anah Adonai ki ani avdecha, ani avd'cha ben amatecha, pitachta l'moseiray. L'cha ezbach zevach todah, uv'sheim Adonai ekra. N'darai l'Adonai ashaleim, negdah na l'chol amo. B'chatzrot beit Adonai, b'tocheichi Y'rushalayim, hal'luyah.

מָה אָשִׁיב לַיְיָ, כָּל תַּגְמוּלוֹהִי עָלָי. כּוֹס יְשׁוּעוֹת אֶשָּׂא, וּבְשֵׁם יְיָ אֶקְרָא. נְדָרַי לַיְיָ אֲשַׁלֵּם, נֶגְדָה נָּא לְכָל עַמּוֹ. יָקָר בְּעֵינֵי יְיָ הַמָּוְתָה לַחֲסִידָיו. אָנָּה יְיָ כִּי אֲנִי עַבְדֶּךָ אֲנִי עַבְדְּךָ, בֶּן אֲמָתֶךָ פִּתַּחְתָּ לְמוֹסֵרָי. לְךָ אֶזְבַּח זֶבַח תּוֹדָה וּבְשֵׁם יְיָ אֶקְרָא. נְדָרַי לַיְיָ אֲשַׁלֵּם נֶגְדָה נָּא לְכָל עַמּוֹ. בְּחַצְרוֹת בֵּית יְיָ בְּתוֹכֵכִי יְרוּשָׁלָיִם הַלְלוּיָהּ.

How can I repay Adonai for all the bounties granted to me? I will raise the cup of salvation and invoke Adonai's name. I will pay my vows to Adonai in the presence of all God's people. Grievous in God's eyes is the death of Adonai's faithful ones. Please, Adonai – I am indeed Your servant; I am Your servant, child of Your maidservant; You have loosed my bonds. To You, I will bring a thanksgiving offering, and I will invoke Adonai's name. I will pay my vows to God in the presence of God's entire people. In the courts of God's House in the heart of Jerusalem. Hallelujah. (Psalms 116:12–19)

Hal'lu

Hal'lu et Adonai, kol goyim,	הַלְלוּ אֶת יְיָ, כָּל גּוֹיִם,
shab'chu-hu, kol ha-umim. Ki	שַׁבְּחוּהוּ כָּל הָאֻמִּים. כִּי
gavar aleinu chasdo, ve-emet	גָבַר עָלֵינוּ חַסְדּוֹ, וֶאֱמֶת
Adonai l'olam, hal'luyah.	יְיָ לְעוֹלָם הַלְלוּיָהּ:
Hodu l'Adonai ki tov,	הוֹדוּ לַיְיָ כִּי טוֹב,
ki l'olam chasdo.	כִּי לְעוֹלָם חַסְדּוֹ:
Yomar na Yisra-eil,	יֹאמַר נָא יִשְׂרָאֵל,
ki l'olam chasdo.	כִּי לְעוֹלָם חַסְדּוֹ:
Yomru na Veit Aharon,	יֹאמְרוּ נָא בֵית אַהֲרֹן,
ki l'olam chasdo.	כִּי לְעוֹלָם חַסְדּוֹ:
Yomru na yirei Adonai,	יֹאמְרוּ נָא יִרְאֵי יְיָ,
ki l'olam chasdo.	כִּי לְעוֹלָם חַסְדּוֹ:

"Praise Adonai all you nations; laud the Almighty, all peoples. For great is God's loving-kindness toward us, and Adonai's God's constancy is everlasting. Hallelujah." (Psalms 117:1–2).

Give thanks to Adonai, for God is good	*For God's grace endures forever.*
Say it now, Israel	*For God's grace endures forever.*
Say it now, House of Aaron	*For God's grace endures forever.*
Say it now, God-fearers (Psalms 118:1–4)	*For God's grace endures forever.*

Min Hameitzar

Min hameitzar karati yah, anani	מִן הַמֵּצַר קָרָאתִי יָהּ,
vamerchav yah. Adonai li lo ira, mah	עָנָנִי בַמֶּרְחָב יָהּ. יְיָ לִי

ya-aseh li adam. Adonai li b'oz'ray,

va-ani ereh v'son'ay. Tov lachasot

b'Adonai, mib'toach ba-adam. Tov

lachasot b'Adonai, mib'toach bindivim.

Kol goyim s'vavuni, b'sheim Adonai ki

amilam. Sabuni gam s'vavuni, b'sheim

Adonai ki amilam. Sabuni chidvorim

do-achu k'eish kotzim, b'sheim Adonai

ki amilam. Dachoh d'chitani linpol,

v'Adonai azarani. Ozi v'zimrat yah,

vay'hi li lishuah. Kol rinah vishuah

b'aholei tzadikim, y'min Adonai osah

chayil. Y'min Adonai romeimah, y'min

Adonai osah chayil. Lo amut ki echyeh,

va-asapeir ma-asei yah. Yasor yis'rani

yah, v'lamavet lo n'tanani. Pitchu li

sha-arei tzedek, avo vam odeh yah. Zeh

hasha-ar l'Adonai, tzadikim yavo-u vo.

לֹא אִירָא, מַה יַּעֲשֶׂה לִי אָדָם. יְיָ

לִי בְּעֹזְרָי, וַאֲנִי אֶרְאֶה בְשֹׂנְאָי.

טוֹב לַחֲסוֹת בַּיְיָ, מִבְּטֹחַ בָּאָדָם.

טוֹב לַחֲסוֹת בַּיְיָ מִבְּטֹחַ בִּנְדִיבִים.

כָּל גּוֹיִם סְבָבוּנִי בְּשֵׁם יְיָ כִּי

אֲמִילַם. סַבּוּנִי גַם סְבָבוּנִי בְּשֵׁם

יְיָ כִּי אֲמִילַם. סַבּוּנִי כִדְבֹרִים

דֹּעֲכוּ כְּאֵשׁ קוֹצִים, בְּשֵׁם יְיָ כִּי

אֲמִילַם. דָּחֹה דְחִיתַנִי לִנְפֹּל,

וַיְיָ עֲזָרָנִי. עָזִּי וְזִמְרָת יָהּ, וַיְהִי

לִי לִישׁוּעָה. קוֹל רִנָּה וִישׁוּעָה

בְּאָהֳלֵי צַדִּיקִים, יְמִין יְיָ עֹשָׂה

חָיִל. יְמִין יְיָ רוֹמֵמָה, יְמִין יְיָ

עֹשָׂה חָיִל. לֹא אָמוּת כִּי אֶחְיֶה,

וַאֲסַפֵּר מַעֲשֵׂי יָהּ. יַסֹּר יִסְּרַנִי

יָהּ, וְלַמָּוֶת לֹא נְתָנָנִי. פִּתְחוּ לִי

שַׁעֲרֵי צֶדֶק, אָבֹא בָם אוֹדֶה יָהּ.

זֶה הַשַּׁעַר לַיְיָ, צַדִּיקִים יָבֹאוּ בוֹ.

In my distress I called on God; God answered by setting me free. God is with me; I have no fear: What can people do to me? Adonai is with me helping me, so I shall gloat over my enemies. It is better to trust in Adonai than to trust in people. It is better to trust in Adonai than to trust in the great. All the nations have beset me; but in Adonai's name I will surely rout them. They surround me on all sides; but in Adonai's name I will surely rout them. They surround me like bees at the honeycomb; they attack me like flames

at the stubble; but in Adonai's name I will surely rout them. They wanted to knock me down, but Adonai helped me. Adonai is my strength and my power, and Adonai has become my salvation. Joyous shouts of deliverance resound in the tents of the righteous: Adonai's right hand is triumphant. I shall not die – I shall live, and proclaim God's works. God chastened me severely, but God did not hand me over to death. Open the gates of victory to me: I would enter them, I would give thanks to God. This is Adonai's gate – the victors enter through it. (Psalms 118:5–20)

Od'cha Ki Anitani

Od'cha ki anitani, vat'hi li lishuah. Od'cha ki anitani, vat'hi li lishuah. Even ma-asu habonim, hay'tah l'rosh pinah. Even ma-asu habonim, hay'tah l'rosh pinah. Mei-eit Adonai hay'tah zot, hi niflat b'eineinu. Mei-eit Adonai hay'tah zot, hi niflat b'eineinu. Zeh hayom asah Adonai, nagilah v'nism'chah vo. Zeh hayom asah Adonai, nagilah v'nism'chah vo. Ana, Adonai, hoshi-ah na! Ana, Adonai, hoshi-ah na!	אוֹדְךָ כִּי עֲנִיתָנִי, וַתְּהִי לִי לִישׁוּעָה. אוֹדְךָ כִּי עֲנִיתָנִי וַתְּהִי לִי לִישׁוּעָה. אֶבֶן מָאֲסוּ הַבּוֹנִים, הָיְתָה לְרֹאשׁ פִּנָּה. אֶבֶן מָאֲסוּ הַבּוֹנִים, הָיְתָה לְרֹאשׁ פִּנָּה. מֵאֵת יְיָ הָיְתָה זֹּאת, הִיא נִפְלָאת בְּעֵינֵינוּ: מֵאֵת יְיָ הָיְתָה זֹּאת, הִיא נִפְלָאת בְּעֵינֵינוּ. זֶה הַיּוֹם עָשָׂה יְיָ, נָגִילָה וְנִשְׂמְחָה בוֹ. זֶה הַיּוֹם עָשָׂה יְיָ נָגִילָה וְנִשְׂמְחָה בוֹ. אָנָּא יְהוָה, הוֹשִׁיעָה נָּא! אָנָּא יְהוָה, הוֹשִׁיעָה נָּא!

Ana, Adonai, hatzlichah na!

אָנָּא יְהֹוָה, הַצְלִיחָה נָּא!

Ana, Adonai, hatzlichah na!

אָנָּא יְהֹוָה, הַצְלִיחָה נָּא!

I thank You for You have answered me, and You have become my salvation. I thank You for You have answered me, and You have become my salvation. The stone that the builders rejected has become the chief cornerstone. The stone that the builders rejected has become the chief cornerstone. This is Adonai's doing: it is marvelous in our eyes. This is Adonai's doing: it is marvelous in our eyes. This is the day which Adonai made: let us exult and rejoice on it. This is the day which Adonai made: let us exult and rejoice in it. (Psalms 118:21–24)

Please, Adonai, deliver us!

Please, Adonai, deliver us!

Please, Adonai, let us prosper!

Please, Adonai, let us prosper! (Psalms 118:25)

Baruch Haba

Baruch haba b'sheim Adonai, beirachnuchem mibeit Adonai. Baruch haba b'sheim Adonai, beirachnuchem mibeit Adonai. Eil Adonai vaya-er lanu, isru chag ba-avotim ad karnot hamizbei-ach. Eil Adonai vaya-er lanu, isru chag ba-avotim, ad karnot hamizbei-ach. Eili Atah v'odeka, Elohai arom'meka. Eili Atah v'odeka, Elohai arom'meka. Hodu l'Adonai ki tov, ki l'olam chasdo. Hodu l'Adonai ki tov, ki l'olam chasdo.

בָּרוּךְ הַבָּא בְּשֵׁם יְיָ, בֵּרַכְנוּכֶם מִבֵּית יְיָ. בָּרוּךְ הַבָּא בְּשֵׁם יְיָ, בֵּרַכְנוּכֶם מִבֵּית יְיָ. אֵל יְיָ וַיָּאֶר לָנוּ, אִסְרוּ חַג בַּעֲבֹתִים עַד קַרְנוֹת הַמִּזְבֵּחַ. אֵל יְיָ וַיָּאֶר לָנוּ, אִסְרוּ חַג בַּעֲבֹתִים, עַד קַרְנוֹת הַמִּזְבֵּחַ. אֵלִי אַתָּה וְאוֹדֶךָ אֱלֹהַי אֲרוֹמְמֶךָ. אֵלִי אַתָּה וְאוֹדֶךָ אֱלֹהַי אֲרוֹמְמֶךָ: הוֹדוּ לַיְיָ כִּי טוֹב, כִּי לְעוֹלָם חַסְדּוֹ: הוֹדוּ לַיְיָ כִּי טוֹב, כִּי לְעוֹלָם חַסְדּוֹ.

May all who enter be blessed in Adonai's name; we bless you from Adonai's House. May all who enter be blessed in Adonai's name; we bless you from Adonai's House. God is Adonai and God has given us light; bind the Festival Offering with branches to the altar's horns. God is God, and God has given us light; bind the Festival Offering with branches to the altar's horns. You are my God and I will thank You, my God – and I will extol You. You are my God and I will thank You, my God – and I will extol You. Give thanks to Adonai for God is good; God's grace endures forever. Give thanks to Adonai, for God is good; God's grace endures forever. (Psalms 118:126–29)

Hodu

Hodu l'Adonai ki tov, ki	הוֹדוּ לַיָי כִּי טוֹב, כִּי
l'olam chasdo. Hodu	לְעוֹלָם חַסְדּוֹ: הוֹדוּ
leilohei ha-Elohim, ki l'olam	לֵאלֹהֵי הָאֱלֹהִים, כִּי
chasdo. Hodu la-adonei	לְעוֹלָם חַסְדּוֹ: הוֹדוּ
ha-adonim, ki l'olam chasdo.	לַאֲדֹנֵי הָאֲדֹנִים, כִּי לְעוֹלָם
L'oseih nifla-ot g'dolot l'vado, ki	חַסְדּוֹ: לְעֹשֵׂה נִפְלָאוֹת
l'olam chasdo. L'oseih hashamayim	גְּדֹלוֹת לְבַדּוֹ, כִּי לְעוֹלָם
bitvunah, ki l'olam chasdo.	חַסְדּוֹ: לְעֹשֵׂה הַשָּׁמַיִם
L'roka ha-aretz al hamayim, ki l'olam	בִּתְבוּנָה, כִּי לְעוֹלָם
chasdo. L'oseih orim g'dolim, ki l'olam	חַסְדּוֹ: לְרוֹקַע הָאָרֶץ עַל
chasdo. Et hashemesh l'memshelet	הַמָּיִם, כִּי לְעוֹלָם חַסְדּוֹ:
bayom, ki l'olam chasdo.	לְעֹשֵׂה אוֹרִים גְּדֹלִים,
Et hayarei-ach v'chochavim	כִּי לְעוֹלָם חַסְדּוֹ: אֶת
l'memsh'lot balay'lah, ki l'olam	הַשֶּׁמֶשׁ לְמֶמְשֶׁלֶת בַּיוֹם,
chasdo. L'makeih Mitzrayim	כִּי לְעוֹלָם חַסְדּוֹ: אֶת
bivchoreihem, ki l'olam chasdo.	הַיָּרֵחַ וְכוֹכָבִים לְמֶמְשָׁלוֹת

May all who enter be blessed in God's name.

God's grace endures forever.

Vayotzei Yisra-eil mitocham, ki l'olam

chasdo. B'yad chazakah uvizro-a n'tuyah,

ki l'olam chasdo.

L'gozeir yam suf ligzarim, ki l'olam

chasdo. 'he-evir Yisra-eil b'tocho,

ki l'olam chasdo. V'ni-eir paroh v'cheilo

v'yam suf, ki l'olam chasdo.

L'molich amo bamidbar, ki l'olam

chasdo. L'makeih m'lachim g'dolim,

ki l'olam chasdo. Vayaharog m'lachim

adirim, ki l'olam chasdo.

L'Sichon melech ha-Emori, ki l'olam

chasdo. Ul'Og melech ha-Bashan, ki

l'olam chasdo. V'natan artzam

l'nachalah, ki l'olam chasdo.

Nachalah l'Yisra-eil avdo, ki l'olam

chasdo. Sheb'shifleinu zachar lanu, ki

l'olam chasdo. Vayifr'keinu mitzareinu,

ki l'olam chasdo. Notein lechem l'chol

basar, ki l'olam chasdo.

Hodu l'Eil hashamayim, ki l'olam chasdo.

בַּלַּיְלָה, כִּי לְעוֹלָם חַסְדּוֹ: לְמַכֵּה

מִצְרַיִם בִּבְכוֹרֵיהֶם, כִּי לְעוֹלָם

חַסְדּוֹ: וַיּוֹצֵא יִשְׂרָאֵל מִתּוֹכָם, כִּי

לְעוֹלָם חַסְדּוֹ: בְּיָד חֲזָקָה וּבִזְרוֹעַ

נְטוּיָה, כִּי לְעוֹלָם חַסְדּוֹ: לְגֹזֵר יַם

סוּף לִגְזָרִים, כִּי לְעוֹלָם חַסְדּוֹ:

וְהֶעֱבִיר יִשְׂרָאֵל בְּתוֹכוֹ, כִּי לְעוֹלָם

חַסְדּוֹ: וְנִעֵר פַּרְעֹה וְחֵילוֹ בְיַם סוּף,

כִּי לְעוֹלָם חַסְדּוֹ: לְמוֹלִיךְ עַמּוֹ

בַּמִּדְבָּר, כִּי לְעוֹלָם חַסְדּוֹ: לְמַכֵּה

מְלָכִים גְּדֹלִים, כִּי לְעוֹלָם חַסְדּוֹ:

וַיַּהֲרֹג מְלָכִים אַדִּירִים, כִּי לְעוֹלָם

חַסְדּוֹ: לְסִיחוֹן מֶלֶךְ הָאֱמֹרִי, כִּי

לְעוֹלָם חַסְדּוֹ: וּלְעוֹג מֶלֶךְ הַבָּשָׁן, כִּי

לְעוֹלָם חַסְדּוֹ: וְנָתַן אַרְצָם לְנַחֲלָה,

כִּי לְעוֹלָם חַסְדּוֹ: נַחֲלָה לְיִשְׂרָאֵל

עַבְדּוֹ, כִּי לְעוֹלָם חַסְדּוֹ: שֶׁבְּשִׁפְלֵנוּ

זָכַר לָנוּ, כִּי לְעוֹלָם חַסְדּוֹ: וַיִּפְרְקֵנוּ

מִצָּרֵינוּ, כִּי לְעוֹלָם חַסְדּוֹ: נוֹתֵן לֶחֶם

לְכָל בָּשָׂר, כִּי לְעוֹלָם חַסְדּוֹ: הוֹדוּ

לְאֵל הַשָּׁמַיִם, כִּי לְעוֹלָם חַסְדּוֹ:

Give thanks to Adonai, for God is good;

God's grace endures forever.

Give thanks to God-of-all-the-Gods;

God's grace endures forever.

Give thanks to the Sovereign-of-all-the-sovereigns;

God's grace endures forever.

To the One Who alone works great marvels;

God's grace endures forever.

To the One Who made the heavens with wisdom;

God's grace endures forever.

To the One Who laid the earth on the waters;

God's grace endures forever.

To the One Who made great lights;

God's grace endures forever.

The sun to rule by day;

God's grace endures forever.

The moon and stars to rule by night;

God's grace endures forever.

To the One Who struck Egypt through their firstborn;

God's grace endures forever.

And brought Israel out of their midst;

God's grace endures forever.

With a strong hand and an outstretched arm;

God's grace endures forever.

To the One Who split apart the Reed Sea;

God's grace endures forever.

And led Israel right through it;

God's grace endures forever.

But hurled Pharaoh and his host into the Reed Sea;

God's grace endures forever.

To the One Who led the Jewish people through the wilderness;

God's grace endures forever.

To God Who struck down mighty kings;

God's grace endures forever.

And also slew great potentates;

God's grace endures forever.

Sihon king of the Amorites;

God's grace endures forever.

And Og king of Bashan;

God's grace endures forever.

And then God bequeathed their land;

God's grace endures forever.

To God's servant Israel to have;

God's grace endures forever.

Who remembered us when we were down and out;

God's grace endures forever.

And rescued us from our enemies;

God's grace endures forever.

Who supplies food to all flesh;

God's grace endures forever.

Thank the God of all heavens;

God's grace endures forever. (Psalms 136)

REFLECTION

In the words of the great German-Jewish poet Heinrich Heine, "Since the Exodus, freedom has always spoken with a Hebrew accent."

REFLECTION

We recite the prayer Nishmat, which is normally sung in the Sabbath and festival morning liturgy. In reciting these prayers we emphasize God as the source of our life Who redeems us. Due to a dispute in the Talmud as to what was meant by the requirement to end the Seder with Hallel and Birkat Hashir, our custom is to include both.

Nishmat

Nishmat kol chai, t'vareich et	נִשְׁמַת כָּל חַי, תְּבָרֵךְ אֶת
shimcha Adonai Eloheinu,	שִׁמְךָ יְיָ אֱלֹהֵינוּ. וְרוּחַ
v'ruach kol basar t'fa-eir	כָּל בָּשָׂר, תְּפָאֵר וּתְרוֹמֵם
ut'romeim zichr'cha malkeinu	זִכְרְךָ מַלְכֵּנוּ תָּמִיד, מִן
tamid, min ha-olam v'ad ha-olam	הָעוֹלָם וְעַד הָעוֹלָם אַתָּה
Atah Eil, umibaladecha ein lanu	אֵל. וּמִבַּלְעָדֶיךָ אֵין לָנוּ
melech goeil umoshi-a, podeh	מֶלֶךְ גּוֹאֵל וּמוֹשִׁיעַ, פּוֹדֶה
umatzil um'farneis um'racheim,	וּמַצִּיל וּמְפַרְנֵס וּמְרַחֵם,
b'chol eit tzarah v'tzukah, ein	בְּכָל עֵת צָרָה וְצוּקָה. אֵין
lanu melech ela Atah. Elohei	לָנוּ מֶלֶךְ אֶלָּא אָתָּה: אֱלֹהֵי
harishonim v'ha-acharonim,	הָרִאשׁוֹנִים וְהָאַחֲרוֹנִים,
Eloha kol b'riot, adon kol toladot,	אֱלוֹהַּ כָּל בְּרִיּוֹת, אֲדוֹן
hamhulal b'rov hatishbachot,	כָּל תּוֹלָדוֹת, הַמְהֻלָּל בְּרֹב
hamnaheig olamo b'chesed,	הַתִּשְׁבָּחוֹת, הַמְנַהֵג עוֹלָמוֹ
uv'riotav b'rachamim. V'Adonai	בְּחֶסֶד, וּבְרִיּוֹתָיו בְּרַחֲמִים.
lo yanum v'lo yishan, ham'oreir	וַיְיָ לֹא יָנוּם וְלֹא יִישָׁן,
y'sheinim v'hameikitz nirdamim,	הַמְעוֹרֵר יְשֵׁנִים וְהַמֵּקִיץ

v'hameisi-ach il'mim, v'hamatir asurim, נִרְדָּמִים, וְהַמֵּשִׂיחַ אִלְּמִים, וְהַמַּתִּיר

v'hasomeich nof'lim, v'hazokeif אֲסוּרִים, וְהַסּוֹמֵךְ נוֹפְלִים, וְהַזּוֹקֵף

k'fufim, l'cha l'vad'cha anachnu modim. כְּפוּפִים, לְךָ לְבַדְּךָ אֲנַחְנוּ מוֹדִים.

The breath of every living thing blesses Your name, Adonai, our God, and the spirit of all flesh glorifies and extols the memory of You, our Ruler, always. Always and forever God You are, and besides You we have no Ruler who liberates and saves, redeeming, rescuing, providing and exercising mercy in every time of trouble and distress. We have no Ruler but You. God of first and last, God of all creatures, Ruler of all the born, Who is lauded with manifold praises, Who directs the universe with loving-kindness and the creatures with mercy. And Adonai does not slumber or sleep – the One Who awakens the sleeping and rouses the slumbering, gives speech to the mute and sets free the imprisoned, supports the falling and straightens the bent – to You alone we give thanks.

Ilu finu malei shirah kayam, ul'shoneinu אִלּוּ פִינוּ מָלֵא שִׁירָה כַּיָּם, וּלְשׁוֹנֵנוּ

rinah kahamon galav, v'siftoteinu רִנָּה כַּהֲמוֹן גַּלָּיו, וְשִׂפְתוֹתֵינוּ שֶׁבַח

shevach k'merchavei raki-a, v'eineinu כְּמֶרְחֲבֵי רָקִיעַ, וְעֵינֵינוּ מְאִירוֹת

m'irot kashemesh v'chayarei-ach, כַּשֶּׁמֶשׁ וְכַיָּרֵחַ, וְיָדֵינוּ פְרוּשׂוֹת כְּנִשְׁרֵי

v'yadeinu f'rusot k'nishrei shamayim, שָׁמַיִם, וְרַגְלֵינוּ קַלּוֹת כָּאַיָּלוֹת, אֵין

v'ragleinu kalot ka-ayalot, ein anachnu אֲנַחְנוּ מַסְפִּיקִים, לְהוֹדוֹת לְךָ יְיָ

maspikim l'hodot l'cha, Adonai אֱלֹהֵינוּ וֵאלֹהֵי אֲבוֹתֵינוּ, וּלְבָרֵךְ אֶת

Eloheinu veilohei avoteinu, ul'vareich שְׁמָךְ עַל אַחַת מֵאָלֶף אֶלֶף אַלְפֵי

et sh'mecha, al achat mei-alef elef אֲלָפִים וְרִבֵּי רְבָבוֹת פְּעָמִים, הַטּוֹבוֹת

alfei alafim v'ribei r'vavot p'amim, שֶׁעָשִׂיתָ עִם אֲבוֹתֵינוּ וְעִמָּנוּ.

hatovot she-asita im avoteinu v'imanu. מִמִּצְרַיִם גְּאַלְתָּנוּ יְיָ אֱלֹהֵינוּ, וּמִבֵּית

Mi-Mitzrayim g'altanu, Adonai עֲבָדִים פְּדִיתָנוּ, בְּרָעָב זַנְתָּנוּ, וּבְשָׂבָע

Eloheinu, umibeit avadim p'ditanu. כִּלְכַּלְתָּנוּ, מֵחֶרֶב הִצַּלְתָּנוּ, וּמִדֶּבֶר

B'ra-av zantanu, uv'sava kilkaltanu,
meicherev hitzaltanu, umidever
milat-tanu, umeicholayim ra-im
v'ne-emanim dilitanu. Ad heinah
azarunu rachamecha, v'lo azavunu
chasadecha, v'al tit'sheinu, Adonai
Eloheinu, lanetzach. Al kein eivarim
shepilagta banu, v'ruach un'shamah
shenafachta b'apeinu, v'lashon asher
samta b'finu, hein heim yodu vivar'chu
vishab'chu vifa-aru virom'mu v'ya-
aritzu v'yakdishu v'yamlichu et
shimcha malkeinu. Ki chol peh l'cha
yodeh, v'chol lashon l'cha tishava,
v'chol berech l'cha tichra, v'chol komah
l'fanecha tishtachaveh, v'chol l'vavot
yira-ucha, v'chol kerev uch'layot
y'zam'ru lishmecha, kadavar shekatuv,
kol atzmotai tomarnah, Adonai, mi
chamocha, matzil ani meichazak
mimenu, v'ani v'evyon migoz'lo.

מַלַּטְתָּנוּ, וּמֵחֲלָיִם רָעִים
וְנֶאֱמָנִים דִּלִּיתָנוּ: עַד
הֵנָּה עֲזָרוּנוּ רַחֲמֶיךָ, וְלֹא
עֲזָבוּנוּ חֲסָדֶיךָ וְאַל תִּטְּשֵׁנוּ
יְיָ אֱלֹהֵינוּ לָנֶצַח. עַל כֵּן
אֵבָרִים שֶׁפִּלַּגְתָּ בָּנוּ, וְרוּחַ
וּנְשָׁמָה שֶׁנָּפַחְתָּ בְּאַפֵּינוּ,
וְלָשׁוֹן אֲשֶׁר שַׂמְתָּ בְּפִינוּ,
הֵן הֵם יוֹדוּ וִיבָרְכוּ וִישַׁבְּחוּ
וִיפָאֲרוּ וִירוֹמְמוּ וְיַעֲרִיצוּ
וְיַקְדִּישׁוּ וְיַמְלִיכוּ אֶת
שִׁמְךָ מַלְכֵּנוּ, כִּי כָל פֶּה לְךָ
יוֹדֶה, וְכָל לָשׁוֹן לְךָ תִשָּׁבַע,
וְכָל בֶּרֶךְ לְךָ תִכְרַע, וְכָל
קוֹמָה לְפָנֶיךָ תִשְׁתַּחֲוֶה,
וְכָל לְבָבוֹת יִירָאוּךָ, וְכָל
קֶרֶב וּכְלָיוֹת יְזַמְּרוּ לִשְׁמֶךָ.
כַּדָּבָר שֶׁכָּתוּב, כָּל עַצְמוֹתַי
תֹּאמַרְנָה יְיָ מִי כָמוֹךָ.
מַצִּיל עָנִי מֵחָזָק מִמֶּנּוּ,
וְעָנִי וְאֶבְיוֹן מִגֹּזְלוֹ:

From Egypt You liberated us, God, our God, from slavery You emancipated us.

All my bones shall say, "God, who is like You!"

Even if our mouth were an ocean of song, and our tongue were rolling seas
of exultation, our lips spacious skies of praise, our eyes radiant as the sun

and the moon, our hands outspread like soaring eagles, and our feet as fleet as the hinds – with all this we would still not be able to thank You, Adonai, our God and God of our ancestors, and to bless Your name for even one-thousands-of-a-thousandth-of-a-thousandth-of-a-ten-thousandth-of-a-myriad of all the favors You granted our ancestors and us. From Egypt You liberated us, Adonai, our God, from slavery You emancipated us. In famine You fed us, providing plentifully. From the swords You saved us and from pestilence rescued us, from terrible, deadly diseases You delivered us. Till now Your mercies have succored us, Your loving-kindness has not failed us. So, Adonai, do not ever fail us. Therefore, the limbs that You have shaped in us, and the breath and spirit that You have breathed in our nostrils, and the tongue that You have placed in our mouth – they, all of them, shall give thanks and bless and praise and glorify and exalt and revere and hallow and enthrone Your name, our Ruler. Indeed, every mouth shall acknowledge You, every tongue shall swear allegiance to You, every knee shall bend to You, every erect body shall prostrate itself before You, all hearts shall fear You, all innards shall sing to Your name, as it is said: "All my bones shall say, 'Adonai, who is like You – rescuing the wretched from those stronger than them, the poor and the needy from their despoilers!'" (Psalms 35:10).

Mi yidmeh lach, umi yishveh lach, umi   מִי יִדְמֶה לָּךְ, וּמִי יִשְׁוֶה לָּךְ וּמִי יַעֲרָךְ

ya-aroch lach, ha-Eil hagadol hagibor   לָךְ: הָאֵל הַגָּדוֹל הַגִּבּוֹר וְהַנּוֹרָא,

v'hanora, Eil elyon, koneih shamayim   אֵל עֶלְיוֹן קֹנֶה שָׁמַיִם וָאָרֶץ: נְהַלֶּלְךָ

va-aretz. N'halelcha un'shabeichacha   וּנְשַׁבֵּחֲךָ וּנְפָאֶרְךָ וּנְבָרֵךְ אֶת־שֵׁם

un'fa-ercha, un'vareich et sheim kod'shecha,   קׇדְשֶׁךָ. כָּאָמוּר, לְדָוִד,

ka-amur, l'david, bar'chi nafshi et Adonai,   בָּרְכִי נַפְשִׁי אֶת יְיָ, וְכׇל

v'chol k'ravai et sheim kod'sho.   קְרׇבַי אֶת שֵׁם קׇדְשׁוֹ:

Who is like You, who can be compared to You, who can equal You – great,
mighty, and awesome God, supreme God, Creator of heaven and earth?!
We shall praise You, laud You, glorify You, and bless Your holy name, as it
is said: "Bless Adonai, O my soul; all my being – bless God's holy name!"
(Psalms 103:1)

Ha-Eil B'ta-atzumot

Ha-Eil b'ta-atzumot uzecha, hagadol   הָאֵל בְּתַעֲצֻמוֹת עֻזֶּךָ, הַגָּדוֹל

bichvod sh'mecha, hagibor lanetzach,   בִּכְבוֹד שְׁמֶךָ. הַגִּבּוֹר לָנֶצַח

v'hanora b'nor'otecha, hamelech   וְהַנּוֹרָא בְּנוֹרְאוֹתֶיךָ. הַמֶּלֶךְ

hayosheiv al kisei ram v'nisa.   הַיּוֹשֵׁב עַל כִּסֵּא רָם וְנִשָּׂא:

Shochein ad, marom v'kadosh sh'mo.   שׁוֹכֵן עַד, מָרוֹם וְקָדוֹשׁ

V'chatuv, ran'nu tzadikim b'Adonai,   שְׁמוֹ: וְכָתוּב, רַנְּנוּ צַדִּיקִים

laysharim navah t'hilah.   בַּיְיָ, לַיְשָׁרִים נָאוָה תְהִלָּה.

God in the vastness of Your power, great in the glory of Your name, mighty
forever, and awesome in Your awe-inspiring acts, Ruler enthroned in a high
and exalted seat –
Inhabiter-of-Eternity-in-a-High-and-Holy-Place is God's name. And it is
written: "Exult in Adonai, O your righteous; it befits the upright to acclaim
the Holy One" (Psalms 33:1).

B'fi y'sharim tithalal,   בְּפִי יְשָׁרִים תִּתְהַלָּל. וּבְדִבְרֵי

uv'divrei tzadikim titbarach, uvilshon   צַדִּיקִים תִּתְבָּרַךְ. וּבִלְשׁוֹן

chasidim titromam, uv'kerev   חֲסִידִים תִּתְרוֹמָם. וּבְקֶרֶב

k'doshim titkadash. Uv'makhalot   קְדוֹשִׁים תִּתְקַדָּשׁ:

riv'vot am'cha beit Yisra-eil, b'rinah

וּבְמַקְהֲלוֹת רִבְבוֹת עַמְּךָ בֵּית יִשְׂרָאֵל,

yitpa-ar shimcha malkeinu, b'chol dor

בְּרִנָּה יִתְפָּאַר שִׁמְךָ מַלְכֵּנוּ, בְּכָל דּוֹר

vador, shekein chovat kol haytzurim,

וָדוֹר. שֶׁכֵּן חוֹבַת כָּל הַיְצוּרִים,

l'fanecha Adonai Eloheinu veilohei

לְפָנֶיךָ יְיָ אֱלֹהֵינוּ, וֵאלֹהֵי אֲבוֹתֵינוּ,

avoteinu, l'hodot, l'haleil, l'shabei-ach,

לְהוֹדוֹת לְהַלֵּל לְשַׁבֵּחַ לְפָאֵר

l'fa-eir, l'romeim, l'hadeir, l'vareich, l'aleih

לְרוֹמֵם לְהַדֵּר לְבָרֵךְ לְעַלֵּה וּלְקַלֵּס,

ul'kaleis, al kol divrei shirot v'tishb'chot

עַל כָּל דִּבְרֵי שִׁירוֹת וְתִשְׁבָּחוֹת

david ben yishai avd'cha m'shichecha.

דָּוִד בֶּן יִשַׁי עַבְדְּךָ מְשִׁיחֶךָ:

By the mouth of the upright You shall be praised, and by the lips of the righteous You
shall be blessed, and by the tongues of the pious You shall be exalted, and by the innards
of the holy You shall be hallowed. And in the assemblies of the myriads of Your people
the House of Israel shall Your name, O our Ruler, be glorified in joyous song in every
generation. For it is the duty of all creatures, God, our God and God of our ancestors, to
give thanks, to praise, laud, glorify, extol, honor, bless, exalt, and adore You even beyond
all the songs and praises of David son of Jesse Your servant, Your anointed one.

Yishtabach

Yishtabach shimcha la-ad malkeinu,

יִשְׁתַּבַּח שִׁמְךָ לָעַד מַלְכֵּנוּ, הָאֵל

ha-Eil hamelech hagadol v'hakadosh

הַמֶּלֶךְ הַגָּדוֹל וְהַקָּדוֹשׁ בַּשָּׁמַיִם

bashamayim uva-aretz. Ki l'cha na-eh,

וּבָאָרֶץ. כִּי לְךָ נָאֶה, יְיָ אֱלֹהֵינוּ

Adonai Eloheinu veilohei avoteinu,

וֵאלֹהֵי אֲבוֹתֵינוּ: שִׁיר וּשְׁבָחָה,

shir ush'vachah, haleil v'zimrah, oz

הַלֵּל וְזִמְרָה, עֹז וּמֶמְשָׁלָה,

umemshalah, netzach, g'dulah ug'vurah,

נֶצַח, גְּדֻלָּה וּגְבוּרָה, תְּהִלָּה

t'hilah v'tiferet, k'dushah umalchut.

וְתִפְאֶרֶת, קְדֻשָּׁה וּמַלְכוּת. בְּרָכוֹת

B'rachot v'hoda-ot mei-atah v'ad olam.

וְהוֹדָאוֹת מֵעַתָּה וְעַד עוֹלָם.

Baruch Atah Adonai, Eil Melech gadol   בָּרוּךְ אַתָּה יְיָ, אֵל מֶלֶךְ גָּדוֹל

batishbachot, Eil hahoda-ot, Adon   בַּתִּשְׁבָּחוֹת, אֵל הַהוֹדָאוֹת,

hanifla-ot, habocheir b'shirei   אֲדוֹן הַנִּפְלָאוֹת, הַבּוֹחֵר בְּשִׁירֵי

zimrah, Melech, Eil, chei ha-olamim.   זִמְרָה, מֶלֶךְ אֵל חֵי הָעוֹלָמִים.

Forever praised in Your name, our Ruler – God, great and holy Ruler in heaven and on earth. Because You are worthy – Adonai, our God and God of our ancestors – of song and praise, hymn and psalm, power and dominion, victory, greatness and might, fame and glory, sanctity and sovereignty, blessings and thanksgiving to Your great and holy name, for You are God, now and forever.

Blessed are You, Adonai, Ruler, sublime in praises, God of thanksgiving, Lord of wonders, Who prefers songs of psalmody, Sole Ruler, God, Ever-living One.

Some say:

Hineni muchan u-mezuman l'kayem   הִנְנִי מוּכָן וּמְזוּמָן לְקַיֵּם

mitzvat kos revi'i me'arba   מִצְוַת כּוֹס רְבִיעִי מֵאַרְבַּע

kosot. L'shem yichud kudsha   כּוֹסוֹת. לְשֵׁם יְחוּד קוּדְשָׁא

brich hu u-shechinteh   בְּרִיךְ הוּא וּשְׁכִינְתֵּיה

al yedei hahu tamir   עַל יְדֵי הַהוּא טָמִיר

v'neelam b'shem kol Yisrael.   וְנֶעֱלָם בְּשֵׁם כָּל יִשְׂרָאֵל.

Here I am, ready and willing to fulfill the mitzvah of drinking the fourth of the four cups of wine, as is the will of the Holy One.

Lift the cup of wine, say the following blessing, and drink the fourth cup, reclining to the left.

Baruch Atah Adonai, Eloheinu   בָּרוּךְ אַתָּה יְיָ, אֱלֹהֵינוּ מֶלֶךְ

Melech ha-olam, Borei p'ri hagafen.   הָעוֹלָם, בּוֹרֵא פְּרִי הַגָּפֶן:

Blessed are You, Adonai, our God, Ruler of the universe, Creator of the fruit of the vine.

Forever praised in Your name, our Ruler – God, great and holy Ruler in heaven and on earth.

FOURTH CUP

Brachah Achronah

Say the concluding blessing after wine:

Baruch Atah Adonai, Eloheinu Melech ha-olam, al hagefen v'al p'ri hagefen. V'al t'nuvat hasadeh, v'al eretz chemdah tovah ur'chavah, sheratzita v'hinchalta la-avoteinu, le-echol mipiryah v'lisboa mituvah. Rachem na, Adonai Eloheinu, al Yisra-eil amecha, v'al Y'rushalayim irecha, v'al tzion mishkan k'vodecha, v'al mizb'checha, v'al heicholecha. Uv'neih Y'rushalayim ir hakodesh bimheirah v'yameinu, v'ha-aleinu l'tochah, v'sam'cheinu b'vinyanah, v'nochol mipiryah v'nisba mituvah, un'varechcha aleha bikdushah uv'tahorah. (*On Shabbat, add*: ur'tzeih v'hachalitzeinu b'yom ha-Shabat hazeh.) V'sam'cheinu b'yom chag hamatzot hazeh. Ki Atah Adonai tov umeitiv lakol, v'nodeh l'cha al ha-aretz v'al p'ri hagafen. Baruch Atah Adonai, al ha-aretz v'al p'ri hagafen.

בָּרוּךְ אַתָּה יְיָ אֱלֹהֵינוּ מֶלֶךְ הָעוֹלָם עַל הַגֶּפֶן וְעַל פְּרִי הַגֶּפֶן. וְעַל תְּנוּבַת הַשָּׂדֶה, וְעַל אֶרֶץ חֶמְדָּה טוֹבָה וּרְחָבָה, שֶׁרָצִיתָ וְהִנְחַלְתָּ לַאֲבוֹתֵינוּ, לֶאֱכוֹל מִפִּרְיָהּ וְלִשְׂבּוֹעַ מִטּוּבָהּ. רַחֶם נָא יְיָ אֱלֹהֵינוּ עַל יִשְׂרָאֵל עַמֶּךָ, וְעַל יְרוּשָׁלַיִם עִירֶךָ, וְעַל צִיּוֹן מִשְׁכַּן כְּבוֹדֶךָ, וְעַל מִזְבְּחֶךָ וְעַל הֵיכָלֶךָ. וּבְנֵה יְרוּשָׁלַיִם עִיר הַקֹּדֶשׁ בִּמְהֵרָה בְיָמֵינוּ, וְהַעֲלֵנוּ לְתוֹכָהּ, וְשַׂמְּחֵנוּ בְּבִנְיָנָהּ וְנֹאכַל מִפִּרְיָהּ וְנִשְׂבַּע מִטּוּבָהּ, וּנְבָרֶכְךָ עָלֶיהָ בִּקְדֻשָּׁה וּבְטָהֳרָה (וּרְצֵה וְהַחֲלִיצֵנוּ בְּיוֹם הַשַּׁבָּת הַזֶּה.) וְשַׂמְּחֵנוּ בְּיוֹם חַג מַצּוֹת הַזֶּה. כִּי אַתָּה יְיָ טוֹב וּמֵטִיב לַכֹּל, וְנוֹדֶה לְּךָ עַל הָאָרֶץ וְעַל פְּרִי הַגֶּפֶן. בָּרוּךְ אַתָּה יְיָ, עַל הָאָרֶץ וְעַל פְּרִי הַגֶּפֶן:

Blessed are You, Adonai, our God, Ruler of the universe, for the vine and the fruit of the vine, and for the yield of the field, and for the land so lovely, so good and so spacious that You saw fit to bequeath to our ancestors to eat of its produce and sate ourselves on its bounty. Have mercy, Adonai, our God, on Israel Your people and on Jerusalem Your city and on Zion the abode of Your glory, on Your altar and on Your shrine. Rebuild Jerusalem the holy city speedily in our days. And bring us back up to it and let us rejoice in its upbuilding, let us eat of its fruit and sate ourselves on its bounty, and we will bless You for it in holiness and purity. (*On the Sabbath, say:* And may it please You to strengthen us on this Sabbath day.) And grant us joy on this Matzot Festival Day, for You, Adonai, are good and You do good to all. We thank You for the Land and for the fruit of its vine. Blessed are You, Adonai, for the Land and for the fruit of the vine.

Counting the Omer

Second night only – if you didn't count in the synagogue.

Baruch ata Adonai Eloheinu	בָּרוּךְ אַתָּה יְיָ אֱלֹהֵינוּ מֶלֶךְ
Melech Haolam asher kidishanu	הָעוֹלָם, אֲשֶׁר קִדְּשָׁנוּ בְּמִצְוֹתָיו
bimitzvotav vizivanu al Sefirat	וְצִוָּנוּ עַל סְפִירַת הָעֹמֶר.
ha-Omer. Hayom yom echad	הַיּוֹם יוֹם אֶחָד לָעֹמֶר/
la-Omer/Hayom yom echad ba-	הַיּוֹם יוֹם אֶחָד בָּעֹמֶר.
Omer. Harachaman Hu yachzir	הָרַחֲמָן הוּא יַחֲזִיר לָנוּ
lanu avodat Beit Hamikdash	עֲבוֹדַת בֵּית הַמִּקְדָּשׁ
limkomah, bimheirah b'yameinu,	לִמְקוֹמָהּ, בִּמְהֵרָה
amein selah.	בְיָמֵינוּ, אָמֵן סֶלָה.

Blessed are You Adonai, our God, Ruler of the universe, who has sanctified us with Your commandments and commanded us concerning the counting of the Omer.

Today is the first day from the Omer/Today is the first day of the Omer.

May the Merciful One restore the Temple service to its rightful place for us, speedily in our days, amen.

QUESTIONS FOR DISCUSSION

Rabbi Simon Jacobson in his handbook *The Counting of the Omer* outlines forty-nine steps we can take to make the days between Passover and Shavuot, when the Jewish people received the Torah, more spiritually meaningful, relevant, and uplifting. How can we infuse our daily lives with more spirituality? More connection to God? Doing more good deeds?

REFLECTION

The Omer represents the counting of forty-nine days between when the sheaf of barley of the new crop (which was to be offered after Passover) began until Shavuot, the time of the giving of the Torah. In addition, tradition teaches us that when the Jews left Egypt, they were told that fifty days later they were going to receive the Torah. They were so excited that they began to count down the period until that day would arrive. Along with the joyful aspect of the countdown, this period of time has also taken on a more somber tone. During the time of Rabbi Akiva, a terrible plague killed thousands of his students and only abated on the thirty-third day of the Omer. Thus during this period of time until Shavuot, traditionally, weddings and other celebrations with music are avoided. Only on Lag b'Omer (the thirty-third day of the Omer, called Lag because the Hebrew letters *lamed-gimmel* signify thirty-three) is there a break in the sadness. Tradition teaches us that the students of Rabbi Akiva died in the plague because they didn't respect each other.

QUESTIONS FOR DISCUSSION

How could the students of the great Rabbi Akiva, whose most famous teaching was "*V'ahavta l'reiacha k'mocha*" (Love your fellow as yourself), not respect each other? What did they fail to learn from their teacher? Some have suggested that we add an additional version with a twist: *v'ahavta l'reiacha asher lo k'mocha* (love the person who isn't like you)!

Nirtzah: Concluding

LEADER: Having drunk the final cup of wine, we come to the concluding portion of our Seder, Nirtzah. May our prayers be accepted, our dreams fulfilled, our hopes realized. May the coming week of Pesach and thereafter be filled with inspiration, memory, liberation, and freedom. May we be truly freed from that which enslaves us, and may we experience the true redemption in the coming year in the holy and rebuilt city of Jerusalem.

חֲסַל סִדּוּר פֶּסַח כְּהִלְכָתוֹ,
כְּכָל מִשְׁפָּטוֹ וְחֻקָּתוֹ.
כַּאֲשֶׁר זָכִינוּ לְסַדֵּר אוֹתוֹ,
כֵּן נִזְכֶּה לַעֲשׂוֹתוֹ. זָךְ שׁוֹכֵן
מְעוֹנָה, קוֹמֵם קְהַל עֲדַת
מִי מָנָה. בְּקָרוֹב נַהֵל נִטְעֵי
כַנָּה, פְּדוּיִם לְצִיּוֹן בְּרִנָּה.

Chasal Sidur Pesach k'hilchato,
k'chol mishpato v'chukato. Ka-
asher zachinu l'sadeir oto, kein
nizkeh la-asoto. Zach shochein
m'onah, komeim k'hal adat mi
manah. B'karov naheil nitei chanah,
p'duyim l'Tzion b'rinah.

We've made another Seder just as we were told.

We followed all the rules laid down in days of old.

Just as we've been privileged to do it now with care,

May God grant us the chance to do it every year.

Pure-one, O pure Dweller-of-the-Realm-Above:

Restore Your countless people,

    bring them home with love;

Quickly take Your vine shoots and

    replant them strong

Back in Zion's vineyard,

    where they will sing Your song.

L'shanah haba-ah birushalayim.

Next year in the rebuilt Jerusalem!

לְשָׁנָה הַבָּאָה בִּירוּשָׁלָיִם:

REFLECTION

We have already pointed out earlier the rabbinic discussion regarding Moshe's absence from the Haggadah. Some point to places where he is alluded to, and here is one such place: the word *nirtzah*, the final step of the Seder, has the numerical value of 345 – the same numerology as the name Moshe!

REFLECTION

L'shanah haba'ah was added in the Middle Ages. This phrase is recited twice during the year: at the end of Yom Kippur services (at Neilah) and at the end of the Seder. On both occasions, we take note of what it means not to have a Temple in Jerusalem. On

Yom Kippur, there is no Kohen Gadol to perform the Avodah (service). On Passover, we are unable to bring the Korban Pesach, the Passover sacrifice. But what remains for us is the ever-present memory, the story brought to life, and always the hope for redemption.

See pp. 223–24 for reflections on "Next year in Jerusalem" from Dr. Mendy Ganchrow, Natan Sharansky, and Ethiopian Jews

Uv'chein Vay'hi Bachatzi Halaylah

This *piyyut*, "It Happened at Midnight," refers to events that occurred to different individuals in Jewish history, according to Jewish tradition, on the night of Passover. Dr. Yael Levine Katz in *Midreshei Bitya bat Pharaoh* has written two stanzas based on what occurred to female personalities on the first night of Passover.[90]

On the first night:

Uv'chein Vay'hi Bachatzi Halaylah	וּבְכֵן "וַיְהִי בַּחֲצִי הַלַּיְלָה"
Az rov nisim hifleita balaylah,	אָז רוֹב נִסִּים הִפְלֵאתָ בַּלַּיְלָה,
B'rosh ashmurot zeh halaylah,	בְּרֹאשׁ אַשְׁמוּרוֹת זֶה הַלַּיְלָה,
Geir tzedek nitzachto k'nechelak lo	גֵּר צֶדֶק נִצַּחְתּוֹ כְּנֶחֱלַק לוֹ
laylah, vay'hi bachatzi halaylah.	לַיְלָה, וַיְהִי בַּחֲצִי הַלַּיְלָה.
Danta melech g'rar bachalom	דַּנְתָּ מֶלֶךְ גְּרָר בַּחֲלוֹם הַלַּיְלָה,
halaylah, Hifchadta arami b'emesh	הִפְחַדְתָּ אֲרַמִּי בְּאֶמֶשׁ לַיְלָה,
laylah, Va-yashar Yisra-eil l'malach	וַיָּשַׂר יִשְׂרָאֵל לְמַלְאָךְ וַיּוּכַל
vayuchal lo laylah, vay'hi bachatzi	לוֹ לַיְלָה, וַיְהִי בַּחֲצִי הַלַּיְלָה.
halaylah. Zera b'chorei fatros	זֶרַע בְּכוֹרֵי פַתְרוֹס מָחַצְתָּ
machatzta bachatzi halaylah,	בַּחֲצִי הַלַּיְלָה, חֵילָם לֹא
Cheilam lo matz'u b'kumam	מָצְאוּ בְּקוּמָם בַּלַּיְלָה,
ba-laylah, Tisat n'gid charoshet	טִיסַת נְגִיד חֲרֹשֶׁת סִלִּיתָ

silita v'choch'vei laylah, vay'hi bachatzi
halaylah. Ya-atz m'chareif l'nofeif ivuy,
hovashta f'garav balaylah, Kara beil
umatzavo b'ishon laylah, L'ish chamudot
niglah raz chazot laylah, vay'hi bachatzi
halaylah. Mishtakeir bichlei kodesh
neherag bo balaylah, Nosha mibor
arayot poteir bi-atutei laylah, Sinah
natar agagi v'chatav s'farim laylah, vay'hi
bachatzi halaylah. Orarta nitzchacha
alav b'neded sh'nat laylah, Purah tidroch
l'shomeir mah mi-laylah, Tzarach
kashomeir v'sach ata voker v'gam laylah,
vay'hi bachatzi halaylah. Kareiv yom
asher hu lo yom v'lo laylah, ram hoda ki
l'cha hayom af l'cha halaylah, shom'rim
hafkeid l'ir'cha kol hayom v'chol
halaylah, ta-ir k'or yom cheshkat laylah,
vay'hi bachatzi halaylah.

בְּכוֹכְבֵי לַיְלָה, וַיְהִי בַּחֲצִי הַלַּיְלָה.
יָעַץ מְחָרֵף לְנוֹפֵף אִוּוּי, הוֹבַשְׁתָּ
פְגָרָיו בַּלַּיְלָה, כָּרַע בֵּל וּמַצָּבוֹ
בְּאִישׁוֹן לַיְלָה, לְאִישׁ חֲמוּדוֹת נִגְלָה
רָז חֲזוֹת לַיְלָה, וַיְהִי בַּחֲצִי הַלַּיְלָה.
מִשְׁתַּכֵּר בִּכְלֵי קֹדֶשׁ נֶהֱרַג בּוֹ
בַּלַּיְלָה, נוֹשַׁע מִבּוֹר אֲרָיוֹת
פּוֹתֵר בְּעֲתוּתֵי לַיְלָה. שִׂנְאָה
נָטַר אֲגָגִי וְכָתַב סְפָרִים
לַיְלָה, וַיְהִי בַּחֲצִי הַלַּיְלָה.
עוֹרַרְתָּ נִצְחֲךָ עָלָיו בְּנֶדֶד שְׁנַת
לַיְלָה, פּוּרָה תִדְרוֹךְ לְשׁוֹמֵר מַה
מִּלַּיְלָה, צָרַח כַּשֹּׁמֵר וְשָׂח אָתָא
בֹקֶר וְגַם לַיְלָה, וַיְהִי בַּחֲצִי הַלַּיְלָה.
קָרֵב יוֹם אֲשֶׁר הוּא לֹא יוֹם וְלֹא
לַיְלָה, רָם הוֹדַע כִּי לְךָ הַיּוֹם אַף לְךָ
הַלַּיְלָה, שׁוֹמְרִים הַפְקֵד לְעִירְךָ כָּל
הַיּוֹם וְכָל הַלַּיְלָה, תָּאִיר כְּאוֹר יוֹם
חֶשְׁכַת לַיְלָה, וַיְהִי בַּחֲצִי הַלַּיְלָה:

It Happened at Midnight

In times of yore You wrought most miracles at night. In the early
watches of this night; You granted Avraham victory at night;
It happened at midnight.

Gerar's king (Avimelech) You judged in a dream by night;

You startled Lavan in the dark of night;

Yaakov fought and bested an angel by night;

It happened at midnight.

Egypt's firstborn You smote at midnight;

They could not find their wealth when they rose at night;

Sisra You routed through stars of the night;

It happened at midnight.

Sancheriv's legions You devastated by night;

Babylon's god was overthrown in the dark of the night; Daniel was

Shown the secret of Your mysteries of the night;

It happened at midnight.

Drunken Belshatzar was killed this very night;

Daniel was saved from the lions' den at night;

Haman wrote evil decrees in the night;

It happened at midnight.

You arose and vanquished him by Achashverosh's sleepless night;

You will help those who ask: "What of the night?"

You will call: "Morning follows the night";

It happened at midnight.

Speed the day that is neither day nor night;

Most High, proclaim that Yours is the day and also the night;

Set guards over Your city all day and all night;

Make bright as day the darkness of the night;

It happened at midnight.

וַיְהִי בַּחֲצִי הַלַּיְלָה

בָּתֵּי תוֹסֶפֶת עַל נָשִׁים   יעל לוין

Brit hivtachta et rosh ha-imahot	בְּרִית הִבְטַחְתָּ אֶת רֹאשׁ הָאִמָּהוֹת לַיְלָה
laylah. Muvelet l'veit Paroh	מוּבֶלֶת לְבֵית-פַּרְעֹה
v'la-avimelech hitzalta laylah,	וְלַאֲבִימֶלֶךְ הִצַּלְתָּ לַיְלָה
M'shulat shoshanah ya-atzah	מְשׁוּלַת שׁוֹשַׁנָּה יָעֲצָה
l'hachlif ha-brachot balaylah,	לְהַחְלִיף הַבְּרָכוֹת בַּלַּיְלָה
Vay'hi bachatzi halaylah.	וַיְהִי בַּחֲצִי הַלַּיְלָה

Tza-akah ha-yoledet v'hikita	צָעֲקָה הַיּוֹלֶדֶת וְהִכִּיתָ
reishit onim laylah. B'chorah	רֵאשִׁית אוֹנִים לַיְלָה
milat'ta lo yichbeh neirah balaylah,	בְּכוֹרָה מִלַּטְתָּ לֹא יִכְבֶּה נֵרָהּ בַּלַּיְלָה
Hadassah asukah haitah b'se'udat	הֲדַסָּה עֲסוּקָה הָיְתָה
Haman balaylah.	בִּסְעוּדַת הָמָן בַּלַּיְלָה
Vay'hi bachatzi halaylah.	וַיְהִי בַּחֲצִי הַלַּיְלָה

It Was in the Middle of the Night

Additional verses by Yael Levine

You have promised a covenant to the head of the Matriarchs	at night.
She who has been taken to Pharaoh and Avimelech you have saved	at night.
She who has been likened to a rose suggested to exchange the blessings	at night.
It was in the middle of the night.	

The woman who gave birth cried out and you smote the firstborn	at night.
You saved a firstborn, her candle did not extinguish	at night.
Hadassah was busy with the feast of Haman	at night.
It was in the middle of the night.	

On the second night:

**Uv'chein va-amartem
zevach Pesach**

וּבְכֵן "וַאֲמַרְתֶּם
זֶבַח פֶּסַח"

Ometz g'vurotecha hifleita
ba-Pesach, B'rosh kol mo-adot
niseita Pesach, Gilita la-ezrachi
chatzot leil Pesach, Va-amartem
zevach Pesach. D'latav dafakta
k'chom hayom ba-Pesach, Hisid
notz'tzim ugot matzot ba-Pesach,
V'el ha-bakar ratz zeicher l'shor
eirech Pesach, Va-amartem
zevach Pesach. Zo-amu s'domim
v'lohatu ba-eish ba-Pesach,
Chulatz lot meihem, umatzot
afah b'keitz Pesach, Titeita admat
mof v'nof b'ovr'cha ba-Pesach,
va-amartem zevach Pesach.
Yah, rosh kol on machatzta b'leil
shimur Pesach, Kabir, al bein
b'chor pasachta b'dam Pesach,
L'vilti teit mashchit lavo vif-
tachai ba-Pesach, va-amartem

אֹמֶץ גְּבוּרוֹתֶיךָ הִפְלֵאתָ בַּפֶּסַח,
בְּרֹאשׁ כָּל מוֹעֲדוֹת נִשֵּׂאתָ
פֶּסַח, גִּלִּיתָ לָאֶזְרָחִי חֲצוֹת לֵיל
פֶּסַח, וַאֲמַרְתֶּם זֶבַח פֶּסַח.
דְּלָתָיו דָּפַקְתָּ כְּחֹם הַיּוֹם בַּפֶּסַח,
הִסְעִיד נוֹצְצִים עֻגוֹת מַצּוֹת
בַּפֶּסַח, וְאֶל הַבָּקָר רָץ זֵכֶר לְשׁוֹר
עֵרֶךְ פֶּסַח, וַאֲמַרְתֶּם זֶבַח פֶּסַח.
זֹעֲמוּ סְדוֹמִים וְלֹהֲטוּ בָּאֵשׁ
בַּפֶּסַח, חֻלַּץ לוֹט מֵהֶם, וּמַצּוֹת
אָפָה בְּקֵץ פֶּסַח, טִאטֵאתָ
אַדְמַת מֹף וְנֹף בְּעָבְרְךָ בַּפֶּסַח,
וַאֲמַרְתֶּם זֶבַח פֶּסַח.
יָהּ, רֹאשׁ כָּל אוֹן מָחַצְתָּ בְּלֵיל
שִׁמּוּר פֶּסַח, כַּבִּיר, עַל בֵּן בְּכוֹר
פָּסַחְתָּ בְּדַם פֶּסַח, לְבִלְתִּי
תֵּת מַשְׁחִית לָבֹא בִּפְתָחַי
בַּפֶּסַח, וַאֲמַרְתֶּם זֶבַח פֶּסַח.
מְסֻגֶּרֶת סֻגְּרָה בְּעִתּוֹתֵי
פֶּסַח, נִשְׁמְדָה מִדְיָן

zevach Pesach. M'sugeret sugarah b'itotei Pesach, Nishm'dah midyan bitzlil s'orei omer Pesach, Sorfu mishmanei pul v'lud bikad y'kod Pesach, va-amartem zevach Pesach. Od hayom b'nov la-amod, ad ga-ah onat Pesach, Pas yad kat'vah l'ka-akei-a tzul ba-Pesach, Tzafoh hatzafit aroch ha-shulchan ba-Pesach, va-amartem zevach Pesach. Kahal kinsah hadasah tzom l'shaleish baPesach, Rosh mibeit rasha machatzta b'eitz chamishim ba-Pesach, Sh'tei eileh rega, tavi l'utzit ba-Pesach, Ta-oz yad'cha v'tarum y'min'cha, k'leil hitkadeish chag Pesach, va-amartem zevach Pesach.

בִּצְלִיל שְׂעוֹרֵי עֹמֶר פֶּסַח, שָׂרְפוּ מִשְׁמַנֵּי פוּל וְלוּד בִּיקַד יְקוֹד פֶּסַח, וַאֲמַרְתֶּם זֶבַח פֶּסַח. עוֹד הַיּוֹם בְּנֹב לַעֲמוֹד, עַד גָּעָה עוֹנַת פֶּסַח, פַּס יָד כָּתְבָה לְקַעֲקֵעַ צוּל בַּפֶּסַח, צָפֹה הַצָּפִית עָרוֹךְ הַשֻּׁלְחָן, בַּפֶּסַח, וַאֲמַרְתֶּם זֶבַח פֶּסַח. קָהָל כִּנְּסָה הֲדַסָּה צוֹם לְשַׁלֵּשׁ בַּפֶּסַח, רֹאשׁ מִבֵּית רָשָׁע מָחַצְתָּ בְּעֵץ חֲמִשִּׁים בַּפֶּסַח, שְׁתֵּי אֵלֶּה רֶגַע, תָּבִיא לְעוּצִית בַּפֶּסַח, תָּעוֹז יָדְךָ וְתָרוּם יְמִינֶךָ, כְּלֵיל הִתְקַדֶּשׁ חַג פֶּסַח, וַאֲמַרְתֶּם זֶבַח פֶּסַח.

Thus you will say: This is the Passover offering

Your wondrous powers You displayed on Passover;

Above all festivals You set Passover;

You revealed Yourself to Avraham at midnight of Passover;

And you shall say: This is the Passover offering.

At Avraham's door You knocked at high noon on Passover;

You fed the angels matzot on Passover;

To the cattle he ran for the ox on Passover;

And you shall say: This is the Passover offering.

The Sodomites enraged God and were burned on Passover;

Lot was saved and he baked matzot on Passover;

You swept Egypt as You passed through on Passover;

And you shall say: This is the Passover offering.

God, You crushed the firstborn on Passover night;

But Your own firstborn You spared by the sign of the blood;

The Destroyer did not enter our homes on Passover;

And you shall say: This is the Passover offering.

Jericho was taken on Passover;

Gideon felled Midian through a barley-cake dream on Passover;

Assyria's legions were consumed on Passover;

And you shall say: This is the Passover offering.

Sancheriv halted to shun the siege on Passover;

A hand wrote Babylon's doom on the wall on Passover;

Feasting Babylon was conquered on Passover;

And you shall say: This is the Passover offering.

Esther assembled the people for a three-day fast on Passover;

You crushed Haman on a gallows tree on Passover;

You will punish Edom doubly on Passover;

Let Your might free us as it did then on the night of Passover;

And you shall say: This is the Passover offering.

On both nights continue:

Ki Lo Na-eh

Ki Lo Na-eh lists God's accolades. Some attribute its authorship to the eighth-century rabbi Eliezer Kallir and believe it was added to the Haggadah in the thirteenth century.

Ki Lo Na-eh

כִּי לוֹ נָאֶה

Adir bimluchah, bachur ka-halachah,

אַדִּיר בִּמְלוּכָה, בָּחוּר כַּהֲלָכָה,

g'dudav yomru lo.

גְּדוּדָיו יאמְרוּ לוֹ:

L'cha ul'cha, l'cha ki l'cha, l'cha af l'cha,

לְךָ וּלְךָ, לְךָ כִּי לְךָ, לְךָ אַף

l'cha Adonai hamamlachah.

לְךָ, לְךָ יְיָ הַמַּמְלָכָה.

Ki lo na-eh, ki lo ya-eh.

כִּי לוֹ נָאֶה, כִּי לוֹ יָאֶה.

Dagul bimluchah, hadur ka-halachah,

דָּגוּל בִּמְלוּכָה, הָדוּר כַּהֲלָכָה,

v'tikav yomru lo.

וְתִיקָיו יאמְרוּ לוֹ:

L'cha ul'cha, l'cha ki l'cha, l'cha af l'cha,

לְךָ וּלְךָ, לְךָ כִּי לְךָ, לְךָ אַף

l'cha Adonai hamamlachah.

לְךָ, לְךָ יְיָ הַמַּמְלָכָה.

Ki lo na-eh, ki lo ya-eh.

כִּי לוֹ נָאֶה, כִּי לוֹ יָאֶה.

Zakay bimluchah, chasin ka-halachah,

זַכַּאי בִּמְלוּכָה, חָסִין כַּהֲלָכָה,

tafs'rav yomru lo. L'cha ul'cha, l'cha

טַפְסְרָיו יאמְרוּ לוֹ:

ki l'cha, l'cha af l'cha, l'cha Adonai

לְךָ וּלְךָ, לְךָ כִּי לְךָ, לְךָ אַף

hamamlachah.

לְךָ, לְךָ יְיָ הַמַּמְלָכָה.

Ki lo na-eh, ki lo ya-eh.

כִּי לוֹ נָאֶה, כִּי לוֹ יָאֶה.

Yachid bimluchah, kabir ka-halachah,

יָחִיד בִּמְלוּכָה, כַּבִּיר כַּהֲלָכָה,

limudav yomru lo. L'cha ul'cha, l'cha

לִמּוּדָיו יאמְרוּ לוֹ:

ki l'cha, l'cha af l'cha, l'cha Adonai

לְךָ וּלְךָ, לְךָ כִּי לְךָ, לְךָ אַף לְךָ,

hamamlachah.

Ki lo na-eh, ki lo ya-eh.

Mosheil bimluchah, nora ka-
halachah, s'vivav yomru lo. L'cha
ul'cha, l'cha ki l'cha, l'cha af l'cha,
l'cha Adonai hamamlachah.
Ki lo na-eh, ki lo ya-eh.

Anav bimluchah, podeh ka-
halachah, tzadikav yomru lo.
L'cha ul'cha, l'cha ki l'cha, l'cha af
l'cha, l'cha Adonai hamamlachah.
Ki lo na-eh, ki lo ya-eh.

Kadosh bimluchah, rachum ka-
halachah, shinanav yomru lo.
L'cha ul'cha, l'cha ki l'cha, l'cha af
l'cha, l'cha Adonai hamamlachah.
Ki lo na-eh, ki lo ya-eh.

Takif bimluchah, tomeich ka-
halachah, t'mimav yomru lo. L'cha
ul'cha, l'cha ki l'cha, l'cha af l'cha,
l'cha Adonai hamamlachah.
Ki lo na-eh, ki lo ya-eh.

לְךָ יְיָ הַמַּמְלָכָה.

כִּי לוֹ נָאֶה, כִּי לוֹ יָאֶה.

מוֹשֵׁל בִּמְלוּכָה, נוֹרָא

כַּהֲלָכָה, סְבִיבָיו יֹאמְרוּ לוֹ:

לְךָ וּלְךָ, לְךָ כִּי לְךָ, לְךָ אַף

לְךָ, לְךָ יְיָ הַמַּמְלָכָה.

כִּי לוֹ נָאֶה, כִּי לוֹ יָאֶה.

עָנָו בִּמְלוּכָה, פּוֹדֶה כַּהֲלָכָה,

צַדִּיקָיו יֹאמְרוּ לוֹ:

לְךָ וּלְךָ, לְךָ כִּי לְךָ, לְךָ אַף

לְךָ, לְךָ יְיָ הַמַּמְלָכָה.

כִּי לוֹ נָאֶה, כִּי לוֹ יָאֶה.

קָדוֹשׁ בִּמְלוּכָה, רַחוּם

כַּהֲלָכָה, שִׁנְאַנָּיו יֹאמְרוּ לוֹ:

לְךָ וּלְךָ, לְךָ כִּי לְךָ, לְךָ אַף

לְךָ, לְךָ יְיָ הַמַּמְלָכָה.

כִּי לוֹ נָאֶה, כִּי לוֹ יָאֶה.

תַּקִּיף בִּמְלוּכָה, תּוֹמֵךְ

כַּהֲלָכָה, תְּמִימָיו יֹאמְרוּ לוֹ:

לְךָ וּלְךָ, לְךָ כִּי לְךָ, לְךָ אַף

לְךָ, לְךָ יְיָ הַמַּמְלָכָה.

כִּי לוֹ נָאֶה, כִּי לוֹ יָאֶה

It Is Fitting to Praise God

August in sovereignty, rightfully chosen,

God's angel-legions say to God: "Yours, only Yours, Yours alone,

O Holy One, is the sovereignty!"

It is fitting to praise God.

Preeminent in sovereignty, truly resplendent,

God's faithful say to God: "Yours, only Yours, Yours alone,

O Holy One, is the sovereignty!"

It is fitting to praise God.

Pristine in sovereignty, truly powerful,

God's disciples say to God: "Yours, only Yours, Yours alone,

O Holy One, is the sovereignty!"

It is fitting to praise God.

Exalted in sovereignty, truly awe-inspiring,

God's heavenly courtiers say to God: "Yours, only Yours, Yours alone,

O Holy One, is the sovereignty!"

It is fitting to praise God.

Humble in sovereignty, truly liberating,

God's upright say to God: "Yours, only Yours, Yours alone,

O Holy One, is the sovereignty!"

It is fitting to praise God.

Holy in sovereignty, truly merciful,

God's angels say to God: "Yours, only Yours, Yours alone,

O Holy One, is the sovereignty!"

It is fitting to praise God.

Mightily sovereign, truly sustaining,

God's faultless ones say to God: "Yours, only Yours, Yours alone,

O Holy One, is the sovereignty!"

It is fitting to praise God.

Adir Hu

Adir Hu follows the pattern of Ki Lo Na-eh, listing the accolades of God. It was added to the Haggadah in the fourteenth century.

Adir Hu

אַדִּיר הוּא

Adir Hu, yivneh veito b'karov,

אַדִּיר הוּא, יִבְנֶה בֵּיתוֹ

bimheirah bimheirah, b'yameinu

בְּקָרוֹב, בִּמְהֵרָה בִּמְהֵרָה,

b'karov. Eil b'neih, b'neih veitcha

בְּיָמֵינוּ בְּקָרוֹב. אֵל בְּנֵה,

b'karov.

בְּנֵה בֵיתְךָ בְּקָרוֹב.

Bachur Hu, gadol Hu, dagul Hu,

בָּחוּר הוּא, גָּדוֹל הוּא, דָּגוּל

yivneh veito b'karov, bimheirah

הוּא, יִבְנֶה בֵּיתוֹ בְּקָרוֹב,

bimheirah, b'yameinu v'karov. Eil

בִּמְהֵרָה בִּמְהֵרָה, בְּיָמֵינוּ

b'neih, Eil b'neih, b'neih veitcha

בְּקָרוֹב. אֵל בְּנֵה, אֵל בְּנֵה,

b'karov.

בְּנֵה בֵיתְךָ בְּקָרוֹב.

Hadur Hu, vatik Hu, zakay Hu,

הָדוּר הוּא, וָתִיק הוּא, זַכַּאי

chasid Hu, yivneh veito b'karov,

הוּא, חָסִיד הוּא, יִבְנֶה בֵּיתוֹ

bimheirah bimheirah, b'yameinu

בְּקָרוֹב, בִּמְהֵרָה בִּמְהֵרָה,

v'karov. Eil b'neih, Eil b'neih,

בְּיָמֵינוּ בְּקָרוֹב. אֵל בְּנֵה,

b'neih veitcha b'karov.

אֵל בְּנֵה, בְּנֵה בֵיתְךָ בְּקָרוֹב.

Tahor Hu, yachid Hu, kabir Hu, טָהוֹר הוּא, יָחִיד הוּא, כַּבִּיר הוּא,

lamud Hu, melech Hu, nora Hu, לָמוּד הוּא, מֶלֶךְ הוּא, נוֹרָא הוּא,

sagiv Hu, izuz Hu, podeh Hu, סַגִּיב הוּא, עִזּוּז הוּא, פּוֹדֶה הוּא,

tzadik Hu, yivneh veito b'karov, צַדִּיק הוּא, יִבְנֶה בֵיתוֹ בְּקָרוֹב,

bimheirah bimheirah, b'yameinu v'karov. בִּמְהֵרָה בִּמְהֵרָה, בְּיָמֵינוּ בְּקָרוֹב.

Eil b'neih, Eil b'neih, b'neih veitcha b'karov. אֵל בְּנֵה, אֵל בְּנֵה, בְּנֵה בֵיתְךָ בְּקָרוֹב.

Kadosh Hu, rachum Hu, shadai Hu, קָדוֹשׁ הוּא, רַחוּם הוּא, שַׁדַּי הוּא,

takif Hu, yivneh veito b'karov, bimheirah תַּקִּיף הוּא, יִבְנֶה בֵיתוֹ בְּקָרוֹב,

bimheirah, b'yameinu v'karov. Eil b'neih, בִּמְהֵרָה בִּמְהֵרָה, בְּיָמֵינוּ בְּקָרוֹב.

Eil b'neih, b'neih veitcha b'karov. אֵל בְּנֵה, אֵל בְּנֵה, בְּנֵה בֵיתְךָ בְּקָרוֹב.

August is God –

May God rebuild the Holy Temple very soon, in our time:

O God, build; O God, rebuild Your Temple soon.

Chosen is God, pure is God, preeminent is God;

May God rebuild the Holy Temple very soon, in our time:

O God, build; O God, rebuild Your Temple soon.

Magnificent is God, venerable is God, pristine is God;

May God rebuild the Holy Temple very soon, in our time:

O God, build; O God, rebuild Your Temple soon.

Benevolent is God, pure is God, One-alone is God;

May God rebuild the Holy Temple very soon, in our time:

O God, build; O God, rebuild Your Temple soon.

Mighty is God, wise is God, Ruler is God;

May God rebuild the Holy Temple very soon, in our time:

O God, build; O God, rebuild Your Temple soon.

Awesome is God, exalted is God, powerful is God;

May God rebuild the Holy Temple very soon, in our time:

O God, build; O God, rebuild Your Temple soon.

Redeemer is God, just is God, holy is God;

May God rebuild the Holy Temple very soon, in our time:

O God, build; O God, rebuild Your Temple soon.

Merciful is God, Almighty is God, potent is God;

May God rebuild the Holy Temple very soon, in our time:

O God, build; O God, rebuild Your Temple soon.

Echad Mi Yodei-a

Echad Mi Yodei-a was also incorporated into the Haggadah in the four-teenth century. Some think that due to its phrasing, it could keep the attention of children at the end of the Seder and prevent them from falling asleep. It follows the question-and-answer format that we see throughout the Haggadah.

Echad Mi Yodei-a	**אֶחָד מִי יוֹדֵעַ?**
Echad mi yodei-a? Echad ani yodei-a. Echad Eloheinu shebashamayim uva-aretz.	אֶחָד מִי יוֹדֵעַ? אֶחָד אֲנִי יוֹדֵעַ: אֶחָד אֱלֹהֵינוּ שֶׁבַּשָּׁמַיִם וּבָאָרֶץ.
Sh'nayim mi yodei-a? Sh'nayim ani yodei. Sh'nei luchot hab'rit, echad Eloheinu shebashamayim uva-aretz.	שְׁנַיִם מִי יוֹדֵעַ? שְׁנַיִם אֲנִי יוֹדֵעַ: שְׁנֵי לֻחוֹת הַבְּרִית, אֶחָד אֱלֹהֵינוּ שֶׁבַּשָּׁמַיִם וּבָאָרֶץ.

Sh'loshah mi yodei-a? Sh'loshah
ani yodei-a. Sh'loshah avot,
sh'nei luchot hab'rit, echad
Eloheinu shebashamayim uva-aretz.

שְׁלֹשָׁה מִי יוֹדֵעַ? שְׁלֹשָׁה
אֲנִי יוֹדֵעַ: שְׁלֹשָׁה אָבוֹת,
שְׁנֵי לֻחוֹת הַבְּרִית, אֶחָד
אֱלֹהֵינוּ שֶׁבַּשָּׁמַיִם וּבָאָרֶץ.

Arba mi yodei-a? Arba ani
yodei-a. Arba imahot, sh'loshah
avot, sh'nei luchot hab'rit, echad
Eloheinu shebashamayim uva-aretz.

אַרְבַּע מִי יוֹדֵעַ? אַרְבַּע אֲנִי
יוֹדֵעַ: אַרְבַּע אִמָּהוֹת, שְׁלֹשָׁה
אָבוֹת, שְׁנֵי לֻחוֹת הַבְּרִית, אֶחָד
אֱלֹהֵינוּ שֶׁבַּשָּׁמַיִם וּבָאָרֶץ.

Chamishah mi yodei-a? Chamishah ani
yodei-a. Chamishah chum'shei Torah,
arba imahot, sh'loshah avot,
sh'nei luchot hab'rit, echad
Eloheinu shebashamayim uva-aretz.

חֲמִשָּׁה מִי יוֹדֵעַ? חֲמִשָּׁה אֲנִי
יוֹדֵעַ: חֲמִשָּׁה חוּמְשֵׁי תוֹרָה,
אַרְבַּע אִמָּהוֹת, שְׁלֹשָׁה אָבוֹת,
שְׁנֵי לֻחוֹת הַבְּרִית, אֶחָד
אֱלֹהֵינוּ שֶׁבַּשָּׁמַיִם וּבָאָרֶץ.

Shishah mi yodei-a? Shishah ani yodei-a.
Shishah sidrei Mishnah, chamishah
chum'shei Torah, arba imahot, sh'loshah
avot, sh'nei luchot hab'rit, echad
Eloheinu shebashamayim uva-aretz.

שִׁשָּׁה מִי יוֹדֵעַ? שִׁשָּׁה אֲנִי יוֹדֵעַ:
שִׁשָּׁה סִדְרֵי מִשְׁנָה, חֲמִשָּׁה חוּמְשֵׁי
תוֹרָה, אַרְבַּע אִמָּהוֹת, שְׁלֹשָׁה
אָבוֹת, שְׁנֵי לֻחוֹת הַבְּרִית, אֶחָד
אֱלֹהֵינוּ שֶׁבַּשָּׁמַיִם וּבָאָרֶץ.

Shivah mi yodei-a? Shivah ani yodei-a.
Shivah y'mei shabata, shishah sidrei
Mishnah, chamishah chum'shei Torah,

שִׁבְעָה מִי יוֹדֵעַ? שִׁבְעָה אֲנִי יוֹדֵעַ:
שִׁבְעָה יְמֵי שַׁבַּתָּא, שִׁשָּׁה סִדְרֵי
מִשְׁנָה, חֲמִשָּׁה חוּמְשֵׁי תוֹרָה, אַרְבַּע

arba imahot, sh'loshah avot,

sh'nei luchot hab'rit, echad Eloheinu

shebashamayim uva-aretz.

אִמָּהוֹת, שְׁלֹשָׁה אָבוֹת,
שְׁנֵי לֻחוֹת הַבְּרִית, אֶחָד
אֱלֹהֵינוּ שֶׁבַּשָּׁמַיִם וּבָאָרֶץ.

Sh'monah mi yodei-a? Sh'monah ani

yodei-a. Sh'monah y'mei

milah, shivah y'mei shabata,

shishah sidrei Mishnah, chamishah

chum'shei Torah, arba

imahot, sh'loshah avot,

sh'nei luchot hab'rit, echad

Eloheinu shebashamayim uva-aretz.

שְׁמוֹנָה מִי יוֹדֵעַ? שְׁמוֹנָה
אֲנִי יוֹדֵעַ: שְׁמוֹנָה יְמֵי
מִילָה, שִׁבְעָה יְמֵי שַׁבַּתָּא,
שִׁשָּׁה סִדְרֵי מִשְׁנָה, חֲמִשָּׁה
חוּמְשֵׁי תוֹרָה, אַרְבַּע
אִמָּהוֹת, שְׁלֹשָׁה אָבוֹת,
שְׁנֵי לֻחוֹת הַבְּרִית, אֶחָד
אֱלֹהֵינוּ שֶׁבַּשָּׁמַיִם וּבָאָרֶץ.

Tishah mi yodei-a? Tishah

ani yodei-a. Tishah yarchei

leidah, sh'monah y'mei milah, shivah

y'mei shabata, shishah

sidrei Mishnah, chamishah

chum'shei Torah, arba

imahot, sh'loshah avot,

sh'nei luchot hab'rit, echad

Eloheinu shebashamayim uva-aretz.

תִּשְׁעָה מִי יוֹדֵעַ? תִּשְׁעָה
אֲנִי יוֹדֵעַ: תִּשְׁעָה יַרְחֵי
לֵדָה, שְׁמוֹנָה יְמֵי מִילָה,
שִׁבְעָה יְמֵי שַׁבַּתָּא, שִׁשָּׁה
סִדְרֵי מִשְׁנָה, חֲמִשָּׁה
חוּמְשֵׁי תוֹרָה, אַרְבַּע
אִמָּהוֹת, שְׁלֹשָׁה אָבוֹת,
שְׁנֵי לֻחוֹת הַבְּרִית, אֶחָד
אֱלֹהֵינוּ שֶׁבַּשָּׁמַיִם וּבָאָרֶץ.

Asarah mi yodei-a? Asarah

ani yodei-a. Asarah dib'raya, tishah

עֲשָׂרָה מִי יוֹדֵעַ? עֲשָׂרָה
אֲנִי יוֹדֵעַ: עֲשָׂרָה

yarchei leidah, sh'monah
y'mei milah, shivah y'mei shabata,
shishah sidrei Mishnah, chamishah
chum'shei Torah, arba imahot, sh'loshah
avot, sh'nei luchot hab'rit, echad
Eloheinu shebashamayim uva-aretz.

דְּבְרַיָּא, תִּשְׁעָה יַרְחֵי לֵדָה, שְׁמוֹנָה
יְמֵי מִילָה, שִׁבְעָה יְמֵי שַׁבַּתָּא,
שִׁשָּׁה סִדְרֵי מִשְׁנָה, חֲמִשָּׁה
חוּמְשֵׁי תוֹרָה, אַרְבַּע אִמָּהוֹת,
שְׁלֹשָׁה אָבוֹת, שְׁנֵי לְחוֹת הַבְּרִית,
אֶחָד אֱלֹהֵינוּ שֶׁבַּשָּׁמַיִם וּבָאָרֶץ.

Achad asar mi yodei-a? Achad
asar ani yodei-a. Achad asar
koch'vaya, asarah dib'raya, tishah
yarchei leidah, sh'monah y'mei milah,
shivah y'mei shabata, shishah
sidrei Mishnah, chamishah chum'shei
Torah, arba imahot, sh'loshah
avot, sh'nei luchot hab'rit, echad
Eloheinu shebashamayim uva-aretz.

אַחַד עָשָׂר מִי יוֹדֵעַ? אֶחָד
עָשָׂר אֲנִי יוֹדֵעַ: אַחַד עָשָׂר
כּוֹכְבַיָּא, עֲשָׂרָה דִּבְּרַיָּא, תִּשְׁעָה
יַרְחֵי לֵדָה, שְׁמוֹנָה יְמֵי מִילָה,
שִׁבְעָה יְמֵי שַׁבַּתָּא, שִׁשָּׁה
סִדְרֵי מִשְׁנָה, חֲמִשָּׁה חוּמְשֵׁי
תוֹרָה, אַרְבַּע אִמָּהוֹת, שְׁלֹשָׁה
אָבוֹת, שְׁנֵי לְחוֹת הַבְּרִית, אֶחָד
אֱלֹהֵינוּ שֶׁבַּשָּׁמַיִם וּבָאָרֶץ.

Sh'neim asar mi yodei-a? Sh'neim asar
ani yodei-a. Sh'neim asar shivtaya,
achad asar koch'vaya, asarah dib'raya,
tishah yarchei leidah, sh'monah y'mei
milah, shivah y'mei shabata, shishah
sidrei Mishnah, chamishah chum'shei
Torah, arba imahot, sh'loshah avot,

שְׁנֵים עָשָׂר מִי יוֹדֵעַ? שְׁנֵים עָשָׂר
אֲנִי יוֹדֵעַ: שְׁנֵים עָשָׂר שִׁבְטַיָּא,
אַחַד עָשָׂר כּוֹכְבַיָּא, עֲשָׂרָה דִּבְּרַיָּא,
תִּשְׁעָה יַרְחֵי לֵדָה, שְׁמוֹנָה יְמֵי מִילָה,
שִׁבְעָה יְמֵי שַׁבַּתָּא, שִׁשָּׁה סִדְרֵי
מִשְׁנָה, חֲמִשָּׁה חוּמְשֵׁי תוֹרָה, אַרְבַּע
אִמָּהוֹת, שְׁלֹשָׁה אָבוֹת, שְׁנֵי לְחוֹת

sh'nei luchot hab'rit, echad Eloheinu shebashamayim uva-aretz.

הַבְּרִית, אֶחָד אֱלֹהֵינוּ שֶׁבַּשָּׁמַיִם וּבָאָרֶץ.

Sh'loshah asar mi yodei-a?
Sh'loshah asar ani yodei-a.
Sh'loshah asar midaya, sh'neim asar shivtaya, achad asar koch'vaya, asarah dib'raya, tishah yarchei leidah, sh'monah y'mei milah, shivah y'mei shabata, shishah sidrei Mishnah, chamishah chum'shei Torah, arba imahot, sh'loshah avot, sh'nei luchot hab'rit, echad Eloheinu shebashamayim uva-aretz.

שְׁלשָׁה עָשָׂר מִי יוֹדֵעַ?
שְׁלשָׁה עָשָׂר אֲנִי יוֹדֵעַ:
שְׁלשָׁה עָשָׂר מִדַּיָּא, שְׁנֵים
עָשָׂר שִׁבְטַיָּא, אַחַד עָשָׂר
כּוֹכְבַיָּא, עֲשָׂרָה דִבְּרַיָּא,
תִּשְׁעָה יַרְחֵי לֵדָה, שְׁמוֹנָה
יְמֵי מִילָה, שִׁבְעָה יְמֵי
שַׁבַּתָּא, שִׁשָּׁה סִדְרֵי
מִשְׁנָה, חֲמִשָּׁה חוּמְשֵׁי
תוֹרָה, אַרְבַּע אִמָּהוֹת,
שְׁלשָׁה אָבוֹת, שְׁנֵי לֻחוֹת
הַבְּרִית, אֶחָד אֱלֹהֵינוּ
שֶׁבַּשָּׁמַיִם וּבָאָרֶץ

Who Knows One?

Who knows one? I know one!
One is Hashem, one is Hashem in the heaven and the earth.

Who knows two? I know two!
Two are the Tablets that Moshe brought;
One is Hashem, one is Hashem in the heaven and the earth.

Who knows three? I know three!

Three are the papas;

Two are the Tablets that Moshe brought;

One is Hashem, one is Hashem in the heaven and the earth.

Who knows four? I know four!

Four are the mamas;

Three are the papas;

Two are the Tablets that Moshe brought;

One is Hashem, one is Hashem in the heaven and the earth.

Who knows five? I know five!

Five are the books of the Torah;

Four are the mamas;

Three are the papas;

Two are the Tablets that Moshe brought;

One is Hashem, one is Hashem in the heaven and the earth.

Who knows six? I know six!

Six are the books of the Mishnah;

Five are the books of the Torah;

Four are the mamas;

Three are the papas;

Two are the Tablets that Moshe brought;

One is Hashem, one is Hashem in the heaven and the earth.

Who knows seven? I know seven!

Seven are the days of the week;

Six are the books of the Mishnah;

Five are the books of the Torah;

Four are the mamas;

Three are the papas;

Two are the Tablets that Moshe brought;

One is Hashem, one is Hashem in the heaven and the earth.

Who knows eight? I know eight!

Eight are the days to brit milah;

Seven are the days of the week;

Six are the books of the Mishnah;

Five are the books of the Torah;

Four are the mamas;

Three are the papas;

Two are the Tablets that Moshe brought;

One is Hashem, one is Hashem in the heaven and the earth.

Who knows nine? I know nine!

Nine are the months till a baby's born;

Eight are the days to brit milah;

Seven are the days of the week;

Six are the books of the Mishnah;

Five are the books of the Torah;

Four are the mamas;

Three are the papas;

Two are the Tablets that Moshe brought;

One is Hashem, one is Hashem in the heaven and the earth.

Who knows ten? I know ten!

Ten are the commandments of Sinai;

Nine are the months to childbirth;

Eight are the days to *brit milah*;

Seven are the days of the week;

Six are the books of the Mishnah;

Five are the books of the Torah;

Four are the mamas;

Three are the papas;

Two are the Tablets that Moshe brought;

One is Hashem, one is Hashem in the heaven and the earth.

Who knows eleven? I know eleven!

Eleven are the stars in Yosef's dream;

Ten are the commandments of Sinai;

Nine are the months to childbirth;

Eight are the days to brit milah;

Seven are the days of the week;

Six are the books of the Mishnah;

Five are the books of the Torah;

Four are the mamas;

Three are the papas;

Two are the Tablets that Moshe brought;

One is Hashem, one is Hashem in the heaven and the earth.

Who knows twelve? I know twelve!

Twelve are the tribes of Yisrael;

Eleven are the stars in Yosef's dream;

Ten are the commandments of Sinai;

Nine are the months to childbirth;

Eight are the days to *brit milah*;

Seven are the days of the week;

Six are the books of the Mishnah;

Five are the books of the Torah;

Four are the mamas;

Three are the papas;

Two are the Tablets that Moshe brought;

One is Hashem, one is Hashem in the heaven and the earth.

Who knows thirteen? I know thirteen!

Thirteen are the attributes of Hashem;

Twelve are the tribes of Yisrael;

Eleven are the stars in Yosef's dream;

Ten are the commandments of Sinai;

Nine are the months till a baby's born;

Eight are the days to brit milah;

Seven are the days of the week;

Six are the books of the Mishnah;

Five are the books of the Torah;

Four are the mamas;

Three are the papas;

Two are the Tablets that Moshe brought;

One is Hashem, one is Hashem in the heaven and the earth.

Echad Mi Yodei-a in Yiddish

מה אַספּרה

מה אַספּרה, מה אַדברה, אותך, אותך יום–טוב'אַריִע

ווער קען זאָגן, ווער קען רעדן

וואָס די איינס באַטייַט, וואָס די איינס באַטייַט?

איינער איז גאָט

און גאָט איז איינער, און ווייַטער קיינער!

מה אַספּרה, מה אַדברה, אותך אותך יום–טוב'אַרִיע
ווער קען זאָגן, ווער קען רעדן
וואָס די צוויי באַטײַט, וואָס די צוויי באַטײַט?
צוויי זענען די לוחות, און איינער איז דער גאָט
און גאָט איז איינער, און ווײַטער קיינער!

מה אַספּרה, מה אַדברה, אותך אותך יום–טוב'אַרִיע
ווער קען זאָגן, ווער קען רעדן
וואָס די דרײַ באַטײַט, וואָס די דרײַ באַטײַט?
דרײַ זענען די אָבֿות
און צוויי זענען די לוחות, און איינער איז דער גאָט
און גאָט איז איינער, און ווײַטער קיינער!

מה אַספּרה, מה אַדברה, אותך אותך יום–טוב'אַרִיע
ווער קען זאָגן, ווער קען רעדן
וואָס די פֿיר באַטײַט, וואָס די פֿיר באַטײַט?
פֿיר זענען די אמהות

און דרײַ זענען די אָבֿות, און צוויי זענען די לוחות, און איינער
איז דער גאָט

און גאָט איז איינער, און ווײַטער קיינער!

מה אַספֿרה, מה אַדברה, אותך יום־טובֿ׳אַרְיֶע

ווער קען זאָגן, ווער קען רעדן

וואָס די פֿינף באַטײַט, וואָס די פֿינף באַטײַט?

פֿינף זענען די חומשים

און פֿיר זענען די אמהות, און דרײַ זענען די אָבֿות, און צוויי
זענען די לוחות, און איינער איז דער גאָט

און גאָט איז איינער, און ווײַטער קיינער!

מה אַספֿרה, מה אַדברה, אותך יום־טובֿ׳אַרְיֶע

ווער קען זאָגן, ווער קען רעדן

וואָס די זעקס באַטײַט, וואָס די זעקס באַטײַט?

זעקס זענען די משניות

און פֿינף זענען די חומשים, און פֿיר זענען די אמהות, און דרײַ
זענען די אָבֿות, און צוויי זענען די לוחות, און איינער איז דער
גאָט

און גאָט איז איינער, און ווײַטער קיינער!

מה אַספֿרה, מה אַדברה, אותך יום־טובֿ׳אַרְיֶע

ווער קען זאָגן, ווער קען רעדן

וואָס די זיבן באַטײַט, וואָס די זיבן באַטײַט?

זיבן זענען די וואָכנטעג

און זעקס זענען די משניות, און פֿינף זענען די חומשים, און פֿיר
זענען די אמהות, און דרײַ זענען די אָבֿות, און צוויי זענען די
לוחות, און איינער איז דער גאָט

און גאָט איז איינער, און ווײַטער קיינער!

Mo Asapro

Mo asapro, mo adabro, oyskho, oyskho, yom-tov'ari'e

Ver ken zogn, ver ken redn

Vos di eyns batayt, vos di eyns batayt?

Eyner iz Got Un Got iz eyner, un vayter keyner!

Mo asapro, mo adabro, oyskho, oyskho, yom-tov'ari'e

Ver ken zogn, ver ken redn

Vos di tsvey batayt, vos di tsvey batayt?

Tzvey zenen di lukhes, un eyner iz der Got

Un Got iz eyner, un vayter keyner!

Mo asapro, mo adabro, oyskho, oyskho, yom-tov'ari'e

Ver ken zogn, ver ken redn

Vos di dray batayt, vos di dray batayt?

Dray zenen di oves, un tsvey zenen di lukhes, un eyner iz der Got

Un Got iz eyner, un vayter keyner!

Mo asapro, mo adabro, oyskho, oyskho, yom-tov'ari'e

Ver ken zogn, ver ken redn

Vos di fir batayt, vos di fir batayt?

Fir zenen di imoes, un dray zenen di oves, un tsvey zenen di lukhes, un einer iz der Got

Un Got iz eyner, un vayter keyner!

Mo asapro, mo adabro, oyskho, oyskho, yom-tov'ari'e

Ver ken zogn, ver ken redn

Vos di finf batayt, vos di finf batayt?

Finf zenen di khumoshim, un fir zenen di imoes, un dray zenen di

oves, un tsvey zenen di lukhes, un einer iz der Got

Un Got iz eyner, un vayter keyner!

Mo asapro, mo adabro, oyskho, oyskho, yom-tov'ari'e

Ver ken zogn, ver ken redn

Vos di zeks batayt, vos di zeks batayt?

Zeks zenen di mishnayes, un finf zenen di khumoshim, un fir zenen di

imoes, un dray zenen di oves, un tsvey zenen di lukhes, un eyner iz der

Got

Un Got iz eyner, un vayter keyner!

Mo asapro, mo adabro, oyskho, oyskho, yom-tov'ari'e

Ver ken zogn, ver ken redn

Vos di zibn batayt, vos di zibn batayt?

Zibn zenen di vokhnteg, un zeks zenen di mishnayes, un finf zenen

di khumoshim, un fir zenen di imoes, un dray zenen di oves, un

tsvey zenen di lukhes, un eyner iz der Got Un Got iz eyner, un vayter

keyner!

Chad Gadya

At first glance this song comes across as a child's rhyme, but it actually conveys a deeper meaning. It was incorporated into the Haggadah in the Middle Ages as well and is a metaphor for the many enemies who tried to wipe out the Jewish people; in the end God will vanquish these enemies (here the Angel of Death) and bring the final redemption.

Chad Gadya	חַד גַּדְיָא
Chad gadya, chad gadya	חַד גַּדְיָא, חַד גַּדְיָא
d'zabin aba bitrei zuzei,	דְּזַבִּין אַבָּא בִּתְרֵי זוּזֵי,
chad gadya, chad gadya.	חַד גַּדְיָא, חַד גַּדְיָא.
V'ata shun'ra, v'achlah	וְאָתָא שׁוּנְרָא, וְאָכְלָה
l'gadya, d'zabin aba bitrei	לְגַדְיָא, דְּזַבִּין אַבָּא בִּתְרֵי
zuzei, chad gadya, chad gadya.	זוּזֵי, חַד גַּדְיָא, חַד גַּדְיָא.
V'ata chalba, v'nashach l'shunra,	וְאָתָא כַלְבָּא, וְנָשַׁךְ לְשׁוּנְרָא,
d'achlah l'gadya, d'zabin aba bitrei	דְּאָכְלָה לְגַדְיָא, דְּזַבִּין אַבָּא בִּתְרֵי
zuzei, chad gadya, chad gadya.	זוּזֵי, חַד גַּדְיָא, חַד גַּדְיָא.
V'ata chutra, v'hikah l'chalba,	וְאָתָא חוּטְרָא, וְהִכָּה לְכַלְבָּא,
d'nashach l'shunra, d'achlah	דְּנָשַׁךְ לְשׁוּנְרָא, דְּאָכְלָה
l'gadya, d'zabin aba bitrei	לְגַדְיָא, דְּזַבִּין אַבָּא בִּתְרֵי
zuzei, chad gadya, chad gadya.	זוּזֵי, חַד גַּדְיָא, חַד גַּדְיָא.
V'ata nura, v'saraf l'chut'ra,	וְאָתָא נוּרָא, וְשָׂרַף לְחוּטְרָא,
d'hikah l'chalba, d'nashach l'shunra,	דְּהִכָּה לְכַלְבָּא, דְּנָשַׁךְ לְשׁוּנְרָא,
d'achlah l'gadya, d'zabin aba bitrei	דְּאָכְלָה לְגַדְיָא, דְּזַבִּין אַבָּא בִּתְרֵי
zuzei, chad gadya, chad gadya.	זוּזֵי, חַד גַּדְיָא, חַד גַּדְיָא.

V'ata maya, v'chavah l'nura,
d'saraf l'chutra, d'hikah
l'chalba, d'nashach l'shunra,
d'achlah l'gadya, d'zabin aba bitrei
zuzei, chad gadya, chad gadya.

וְאָתָא מַיָּא, וְכָבָה לְנוּרָא,
דְּשָׂרַף לְחוּטְרָא, דְּהִכָּה
לְכַלְבָּא, דְּנָשַׁךְ לְשׁוּנְרָא,
דְּאָכְלָה לְגַדְיָא, דְּזַבִּין אַבָּא
בִּתְרֵי זוּזֵי, חַד גַּדְיָא, חַד גַּדְיָא.

V'ata tora, v'shata l'maya,
d'chavah l'nura, d'saraf l'chutra,
d'hikah l'chalba, d'nashach l'shunra,
d'ach'lah l'gadya, d'zabin aba bitrei
zuzei, chad gadya, chad gadya.

וְאָתָא תוֹרָא, וְשָׁתָא לְמַיָּא,
דְּכָבָה לְנוּרָא, דְּשָׂרַף לְחוּטְרָא,
דְּהִכָּה לְכַלְבָּא, דְּנָשַׁךְ לְשׁוּנְרָא,
דְּאָכְלָה לְגַדְיָא, דְּזַבִּין אַבָּא
בִּתְרֵי זוּזֵי, חַד גַּדְיָא, חַד גַּדְיָא.

V'ata hashocheit, v'shachat l'tora,
d'shata l'maya, d'chavah l'nura,
d'saraf l'chutra, d'hikah l'chalba,
d'nashach l'shunra, d'achlah l'gadya,
d'zabin aba bitrei zuzei, chad gadya,
chad gadya.

וְאָתָא הַשּׁוֹחֵט, וְשָׁחַט לְתוֹרָא,
דְּשָׁתָא לְמַיָּא, דְּכָבָה לְנוּרָא,
דְּשָׂרַף לְחוּטְרָא, דְּהִכָּה לְכַלְבָּא,
דְּנָשַׁךְ לְשׁוּנְרָא, דְּאָכְלָה
לְגַדְיָא, דְּזַבִּין אַבָּא בִּתְרֵי
זוּזֵי, חַד גַּדְיָא, חַד גַּדְיָא.

V'ata Malach ha-Mavet,
v'shachat l'shocheit, d'shachat
l'tora, d'shata
l'maya, d'chavah l'nura,
d'saraf l'chutra, d'hikah
l'chalba, d'nashach l'shunra,

וְאָתָא מַלְאַךְ הַמָּוֶת,
וְשָׁחַט לְשׁוֹחֵט, דְּשָׁחַט
לְתוֹרָא, דְּשָׁתָא
לְמַיָּא, דְּכָבָה לְנוּרָא,
דְּשָׂרַף לְחוּטְרָא, דְּהִכָּה
לְכַלְבָּא, דְּנָשַׁךְ לְשׁוּנְרָא,

d'achlah l'gadya, d'zabin aba bitrei
zuzei, chad gadya, chad gadya.

דְּאָכְלָה לְגַדְיָא, דְּזַבִּין אַבָּא בִּתְרֵי
זוּזֵי, חַד גַּדְיָא, חַד גַּדְיָא.

V'ata Hakadosh Baruch Hu, v'shachat
l'Malach ha-Mavet, d'shachat
l'shocheit, d'shachat l'tora, d'shata
l'maya, d'chavah l'nura, d'saraf l'chutra,
d'hikah l'chalba, d'nashach l'shunra,
d'achlah l'gadya, d'zabin aba bitrei
zuzei, chad gadya, chad gadya.

וְאָתָא הַקָּדוֹשׁ בָּרוּךְ הוּא, וְשָׁחַט
לְמַלְאַךְ הַמָּוֶת, דְּשָׁחַט לְשׁוֹחֵט,
דְּשָׁחַט לְתוֹרָא, דְּשָׁתָא לְמַיָּא,
דְּכָבָה לְנוּרָא, דְּשָׂרַף לְחוּטְרָא,
דְּהִכָּה לְכַלְבָּא, דְּנָשַׁךְ לְשׁוּנְרָא,
דְּאָכְלָה לְגַדְיָא, דְּזַבִּין אַבָּא בִּתְרֵי
זוּזֵי, חַד גַּדְיָא, חַד גַּדְיָא.

One Kid

One kid, one kid,
That Father bought for two zuzim;
One kid, one kid.

Came a cat and ate the kid
That Father bought for two zuzim;
One kid, one kid.

Came a dog and bit the cat
That ate the kid
That Father bought for two zuzim;
One kid, one kid.

Came a stick and beat the dog
That bit the cat
That ate the kid

That Father bought for two zuzim;

One kid, one kid.

Came a fire and burned the stick

That beat the dog

That bit the cat

That ate the kid

That Father bought for two zuzim;

One kid, one kid.

Came the water and quenched the fire

That burned the stick

That beat the dog

That bit the cat

That ate the kid

That Father bought for two zuzim;

One kid, one kid.

Came an ox and drank the water

That quenched the fire

That burned the stick

That beat the dog

That bit the cat

That ate the kid

That Father bought for two zuzim;

One kid, one kid.

Came the butcher and killed the ox

That drank the water

That quenched the fire

That burned the stick

That beat the dog

That bit the cat

That ate the kid

That Father bought for two zuzim;

One kid, one kid.

Came the Angel of Death

And slew the butcher

Who killed the ox

That drank the water

That quenched the fire

That burned the stick

That beat the dog

That bit the cat

That ate the kid

That Father bought for two zuzim;

One kid, one kid.

Came the Blessed Holy One

And slew the Angel of Death

Who slew the butcher

Who killed the ox

That drank the water

That quenched the fire

That burned the stick

That beat the dog

That bit the cat

That ate the kid

That Father bought for two zuzim;

One kid, one kid

Appendix 1
Additional Songs and Readings

Songs and Readings for the Order of the Seder

The Order of the Seder

By Gary Teblum (Sung to the tune of "It's a Small World")

We wash our hands
And we bless the wine
Greens put in salt water
Dippings so fine
There's so much that we see
Celebrating we're free
It's our Pass-Over Seder.

Chorus:
It's our Pass-Over Seder
It's our Pass-Over Seder
It's our Pass-Over Seder
It's our Passover seder.

We break the matzah
Four questions are asked
We tell the story
About our past
The motzi we say
Because that is the way
Of our Pass-Over Seder.

(Chorus)[1]

We Didn't Start the Seder

By Bangitout.com (Sung to the tune of "We Didn't Start the Fire" by Billy Joel)

Kadesh, Orchatz
Karpas, Yachatz,
Maggid, Rachtza, Motzei Matzah.

Maror, Korech,
Shulchan Orech,
Tsafoon,
Baraich,
Hallel, Nirtzah!

We didn't start the seder,
The Haggadah has always been our script
Since the Jews left Egypt
We didn't steal the afikomen
No we didn't eat it
But we tried to hide it

(additional verses) Burn your Chometz, after you search,
Bedika, blowtorch,
Fill up, your first cup of wine,
Throw on your kittel,
Kiddush time

Stand up, say the prayer,
Shechiaunu, for the new year,
Lean to the left,
Drink it slow,
Realize you got four cups to go!

We didn't start the seder,
The Hagadah has always been our script
Since the Jews left Egypt
We didn't steal the afikomen
No we didn't eat it
But we tried to hide it

Chad Gad Ya, Who knows one,
That's it,
The seder's done.[2]

There's No Seder Like Our Seder

By Rabbi Daniel Liben (sung to the tune of "There's No Business Like Show Business")

There's no Seder like our Seder,
There's no Seder I know.
Everything about it is halachic
Nothing that the Torah won't allow.
Listen how we read the whole Haggadah
It's all in Hebrew
'Cause we know how.

---

1   Used by permission of Gary Teblum.

2   *The Bangitout Seder Sidekick, 2003,* http://www.bangitout.com/seder-sidekick-2003/#sthash.3GXoMhlV.dpuf. Used by permission of Bangitout.

There's no Seder like our Seder,
We tell a tale that is swell:
Moses took the people out into the heat
They baked the matzah
While on their feet
Now isn't that a story
That just can't be beat?
Let's go on with the show![3]

OUR PASSOVER THINGS

By Dr. Warren Tessler (Sung to the tune of "Our Favorite Things")

Cleaning and cooking and so many dishes
Out with the chametz, no pasta, no knishes.
Fish that's gefilted, horseradish that stings,
These are a few of our Passover things.

Matzah and karpas and chopped-up charoset.
Shankbone and Kiddush and Yiddish neuroses.
Tante who kvetches and uncle who sings,
These are a few of our Passover things.

Motzi and maror and trouble with Pharaohs.
Famines and locusts and slaves with wheelbarrows.
Matzah balls floating and eggshell that clings,
These are a few of our Passover things.

When the plagues strike
When the lice bite
When we're feeling sad
We simply remember our Passover things
And then we don't feel so bad.[4]

Songs and Readings for Yachatz

DON'T SIT ON THE AFIKOMEN

By Cantor Deborah Katchko-Gray (Sung to the tune of "Battle Hymn of the Republic")

My dad at every Seder breaks a matzah piece in two
And hides the afikomen half — a game for me and you
Find it, hold it ransom, for the Seder isn't through
till the afikomen's gone.

Chorus:
Don't sit on the afikomen.
Don't sit on the afikomen.
Don't sit on the afikomen.
Or the meal will last all night

One year Daddy hid it 'neath a pillow on a chair
But just as I raced over, my Aunt Sophie sat down there
She threw herself upon it — awful crunching filled the air
And crumbs flew all around

(Chorus)

There were matzah crumbs all over — oh, it was a messy sight
We swept up all the pieces though it took us half the night
So, if you want your Seder ending sooner than dawn's light,
Don't sit on the afiko-o-men

(Chorus)[5]

Songs and Readings for Maggid: Mah Nishtanah

TOP TEN MOST POPULAR JEWISH QUESTIONS

By Isaac and Seth Galena, Bangitout.com

10. Are you sure you had enough to eat?
 9. How long ago did we eat meat?
 8. Why aren't you married yet?
 7. Nebech...did you hear the news about (any name)?
 6. But is it a hot Kiddush?
 5. Can we get a scholarship?
 4. You paid how much?
 3. What kind of question is that?
 2. Mincha?
 1. Oh, you're from (fill in any city in the world). Do you know (fill in any random Jewish name)?[6]

---

3 Used by permission of Rabbi Daniel Liben.
4 Used by permission of Dr. Warren Tessler.

5 © Cantor Deborah Katchko-Gray, *Passover Seder Songs* (CD Baby, 2012), www.cantordebbie.com. Used by permission of Cantor Deborah Katchko-Gray.
6 Isaac and Seth Galena, *The Bangitout Seder Sidekick, 2017*, http://www.bangitout.com/wp-content/uploads/2017/04/Bangitout-SederSidekick2017.pdf. Used by permission of Bangitout.

Four Questions

By Yeshaya Douglas Ballon (Sung to the tune of "Twinkle, Twinkle")

Kiddush cups and candlelight,
How I wonder about this night.
On other nights we eat bread,
Tonight we eat matzah instead.
Kiddush cups and candlelight
How I wonder about this night.
Kiddush cups and candlelight,
How I wonder about this night.
It's nice that there's no babysitter,
But the herbs taste rather bitter.
Kiddush cups and candlelight
How I wonder about this night
Kiddush cups and candlelight,
How I wonder about this night.
On other nights we rarely dip,
Tonight it's twice, without a chip.
Kiddush cups and candlelight,
How I wonder about this night.
Kiddush cups and candlelight,
How I wonder about this night.
On other nights we align our spines,
Tonight is different, we recline.
Kiddush cups and candlelight,
How I wonder about this night.[7]

Songs and Readings for Maggid: Avadim Hayinu

Go Down, Moses

When Israel was in Egypt land,
Let my people go!
Oppressed so hard they could not stand,
Let my people go!

Chorus: Go down, Moses, way down in Egypt land
Tell old Pharaoh to let my people go!

Then God told Moses what to do
Let my people go!
To lead the children of Israel through
Let my people go!
(Chorus)

O, let us all from bondage flee
Let my people go!

And soon may all this world be free,
Let my people go!

Hi-Ho, I Will Not Let Them Go

By Gary Teblum (Sung to the tune of "Hi-Ho, Hi-Ho")

Oh no, oh no, I will not let them go
I will not let the Jews go free
Oh no, oh no, oh no.
Oh no, oh no, I will not let them go
Your people will not leave this land
Oh no, oh no.[8]

Frogs on His Nose

By Gary Teblum (Sung to the tune of "Zippedee Do Da")

Frogs on his nose now
Frogs in his hair
My, oh my
There were frogs everywhere.
Plenty of jumping
All round his bed
Pharaoh was feeling frogs round his head.
Mister bullfrog on his shoulder
It's the truth
It's frightnin'
All these plagues are knuckle whitenin'.
Frogs on his toes now
What do you say?
Terrible feeling,
Terrible day.[9]

Yesterday

By Gary Teblum (Sung to the tune of "Yesterday")

Yesterday
We were slaves in Egypt yesterday
Now be thankful that we're free today
We must remember yesterday.

Slavery
Pharaoh kept us all in slavery

We were working hard as hard can be
Oh, yesterday saw slavery.

---

7   Used by permission of Yeshaya Douglas Ballon.

8   Used by permission of Gary Teblum.
9   Used by permission of Gary Teblum.

Chorus:
Why we couldn't go, I don't know
He made us stay
Then God set us free
Now we teach 'bout yesterday.

Yesterday
We were brought forth so that we could pray
Now I need to teach the kids to say
We must remember yesterday.

(Chorus)
Yesterday
We were brought forth so that we could pray
At the Seder, teach the kids to say
Why we remember yesterday.[10]

YOU'LL BE SLAVES!

By Jonathan Glick, Doug Gordon, and Aaron Naparstek (Sung to the tune of "You'll Be Back" from Hamilton: An American Musical)

You say
Getting whipped is no fun and you're tired of slaving away.
You kvetch
"Let us go," which you really must know makes me just want to retch.
My advice?
You're happiest mortaring bricks on a very hot day
Now it's all frogs and lice
Remember despite your complaining, I'm your Pharaoh...

Chorus:
You are slaves!
Soon you'll see
You will never get across the Sea.
You are slaves!
That bread won't rise
Two stone tablets really won't suffice.

Oceans part, armies drown
And I'm certain you will turn around.
If you don't, it's your loss
I will send ten thousand of my chariots to remind you who's the boss.
 Oy oyoy oy oy
Oy oyoyoy oyyyoy

Oyoy oy oy oyyyoy
 Oy oyoy oy oy
Oy oyoyoy oyyyoy Oyoy oy oy oy

Bridge:
You say your God's the One and He'll set you free
Instead chillax, enjoy your slavery!

And, no, don't get all vague
With all these threats of plagues.
I'm not afraid of plagues
Your silly little plagues
Not ever not ever not ever not ever not ever...
 (Chorus)

Just be slaves
And worship Ra.
You'll build pyramids and we'll go far.
For your God
You'd depart?
Go ahead and get a good head start.

'Cause when you leave, you will find
That my armies will be right behind.
And when we meet, it's your loss
I'll kill every single Hebrew to remind you who's the boss

Oy oyoy oy oy
Oy oyoyoy oyyyoy
Oyoy oy oy oyyyoy

Oy oyoy oy oy
Oy oyoyoy oyyyoy
Oyoy oy

Everybody!

Oy oyoy oy oy
Oy oyoyoy oyyyoy
Oyoy oy oy oyyyoy

Oy oyoy oy oy
Oy oyoyoy oyyyoy
Oyoyoy oy oy oyyyoy[11]

---

10 Used by permission of Gary Teblum.

11 Used by permission of Aaron Naparstek.

Songs and Readings for Maggid: Amar Rabi Elazar ben Azaryah

TAKE US OUT OF EGYPT

By Dr. Ron Wolfson (Sung to the tune of "Take Me Out to the Ball Game")

Take us out of Egypt
Free us from slavery.
Bake us some *matzot* in a haste.
Don't worry about flavor –
Give no thought to taste.
Oh, it's rush, rush, rush to the Reed Sea,
If we don't cross, it's a shame!
It's Ten Plagues down and you're out,
At the *Pesah* History Game![12]

TOP TEN SIGNS THE GUY YOUR DAUGHTER BROUGHT HOME FOR THE PASSOVER SEDER ISN'T GOING TO WORK OUT

By Isaac and Seth Galena, Bangitout.com

10. Hides the afikomen in his pants.
9. Won't stop asking when the latkes are going to be served.
8. When welcoming Elijah, he checks the chimney.
7. After fourth time calling your wife "'Ma Nishtanah," stills hopes to get a laugh.
6. In return for the afikomen, he asks to see your tax returns.
5. To comply with the Haggadah, he punches the person who reads the "wicked child" in the mouth.
4. You are at the third cup, he's on number nine.
3. After the afikomen is stolen, he starts pocketing silverware.
2. When everyone points to the maror, he points directly at you.
1. As a gift, he brings fresh-baked challah.[13]

---

12 Dr. Ron Wolfson with Joel Lurie Grishaver, *Passover: The Family Guide to Spiritual Celebration*, 2d ed. (Woodstock, VT: Jewish Lights, 2003), 12. Used by permission of Jewish Lights.

13 Isaac and Seth Galena, *The Bangitout Seder Sidekick, 2016*, http://www.bangitout.com/wp-content/uploads/2016/04/Bangitout-SederSidekick-2016.pdf. Used by permission of Bangitout.

Songs and Readings for Maggid: The Ten Plagues

LET US GO

By Rabbi Howard Goldsmith (Sung to the tune of "Let It Go" from Disney's *Frozen*)

The sands glow white on the Nile tonight
(The snow glows white on the mountain tonight)
Not a ripple to be seen
(Not a footprint to be seen)
A kingdom that has enslaved us
(A kingdom of isolation)
And they really are so mean
(And it looks like I'm the queen)

But now the bush burns and it isn't yet consumed
(The wind is howling like this swirling storm inside)
God calls from it, says Pharaoh is doomed
(Couldn't keep it in – heaven knows I tried)

We worked so hard, no break to pee
(Don't let them in, don't let them see)
We moaned to God and now God sees
(Be the good girl you always have to be)
We'll soon be free, Pharaoh must know
(Conceal, don't feel, don't let them know)
Pharaoh's God's foe!
(Well, now they know)

Let us go! Let us go!
(Let it go, let it go)
We won't be slaves anymore
(Can't hold it back anymore)
Let us go! Let us go!
(Let it go, let it go)
We're walking to the shore
(Turn away and slam the door)

We don't care
(I don't care)
And we won't plea
(What they're going to say)
Let the plagues come on
(Let the storm rage on)
Israelites just wanna be really free
(The cold never bothered me anyway)

It's funny how a Moses
(It's funny how some distance)

Saved from river when so small
(Makes everything seem small)
Has grown to lead a nation
(And the fears that once controlled me)
Stands before the Pharaoh tall
(Can't get to me at all)

This time he'll see what God can do
(It's time to see what I can do)
With ten plagues God'll see us through
(To test the limits and break through)
Yeah, we will go, Moses will lead
(No right, no wrong, no rules for me)
We're free
(I'm free)

Let us go! Let us go!
(Let it go, let it go)
We won't be slaves anymore
(I am one with the wind and sky)
Let us go! Let us go!
(Let it go, let it go)
We're walking to the shore
(You'll never see me cry)

Here we stand
(Here I stand)
At the Sea of Reeds
(And here I'll stay)
Let the plagues rage on
(Let the storm rage on)

The chariots race and rumble all across the
ground (My power flurries through the air into
the ground)
The sea's in front of us just like a jail cell we will
drown (My soul is spiraling in frozen fractals all
around)
But wait, it's splitting down the middle with dry
land (And one thought crystallizes like an icy
blast)
We're really outta here
(I'm never going back)
Through split sea on the sand
(The past is in the past)

Let us go! Let us go!
(Let it go, let it go)
We won't be slaves anymore
(And I'll rise like the break of dawn)
Let us go! Let us go!
(Let it go, let it go)
We're walking to the shore

(That perfect girl is gone)
We don't care
(Here I stand)
And we won't plea
(In the light of day)
Let the plagues come on
(Let the storm rage on)
Israelites just wanna be really free
(The cold never bothered me anyway)[14]

LEAVING ON A DESERT PLANE

**By Randi and Murray Spiegel (Sung to
the tune of "Leaving on a Jet Plane")**

All our bags are packed, we're ready to go
We're standing here outside our doors
We dare not wake you up to say goodbye.

But the dawn is breakin' this early morn'
Moses is waiting, he's blowing his horn
We're planning our escape so we won't die.

You'll miss me, as you will see
You've been dealt a harsh decree
You held us like you'd never let us go.

We're leaving from this great strain
We pray we won't be back again
God knows, can't wait to go.
There's so many times you've let us down
Your many crimes have plagued our town
I tell you now they were all mean things.

Every place I go, you'll shrink from view,
Every song I sing will be 'gainst you
I won't be back to wear your ball and chain.

You'll miss me, as you will see
You've been dealt a harsh decree
You held us like you'd never let us go.

We're leaving through a wet plain
We hope we won't be back again
God knows, can't wait to go.

Now the time has come to leave you
One more time, let me diss you
Close your eyes, we'll be on our way.

Dream about the days to come
When you'll be left here all alone
About the time when I won't have to say.
You'll miss me, as you will see

14 Used by permission of Rabbi Howard Goldsmith.

You've been dealt a harsh decree
You held us like you'd never let us go.

We're leaving all our bread grain
We know we won't be back again
God knows, can't wait to go.[15]

Songs and Readings for Maggid: Dayeinu

DAYEINU

By Yeshaya Douglas Ballon (Sung to the tune of "The Wheels of the Bus")

Had God brought us out of Egypt,
But not parted the sea,
Parted the sea, parted the sea,
Had God brought us out of Egypt, but not parted the sea,
Dayeinu!

Had God parted the sea,
But not given us Shabbat,
Given us Shabbat, given us Shabbat,
Had God parted the sea, but not given us Shabbat,
Dayeinu!

Had God given us Shabbat,
But not given us Torah,
Given us Torah, given us Torah,
Had God given us Shabbat, but not given us Torah,
Dayenu![16]

Songs and Readings for Maggid: Pesach, Matzah, U-maror

THE THREE SYMBOLS

By Yeshaya Douglas Ballon (Sung to the tune of "Baa Baa Black Sheep")

Said Gamliel, "It's not enough,
until you talk about this stuff!"
One is the Matzah, another is the Bone,
And finally the Maror that makes you groan.

Said Gamliel, "It's not enough,
until you talk about this stuff!"

The Matzah is the bread we made in flight.
It didn't have time to rise that night.
Said Gamliel, "It's not enough,
until you talk about this stuff!"

The lamb bone reminds us of the sacrifice.
We're sad that so many paid such a price.
Said Gamliel, "It's not enough,
until you talk about this stuff!"

The Maror is so bitter; you must be brave.
It reminds us that we once were slaves
Said Gamliel, "It's not enough,
until you talk about this stuff!"[17]

Songs and Readings for Maggid: Hallel

THROUGH THE RED SEA

By Gary Teblum (Sung to the tune of "Under the Sea")

Our people were running quickly
Not stopping to even bake.
They dreamed about a new homeland
Not simply for their own sake.
They saw what must lie before them
The Red Sea they could not pass.
They all turned to look at Moses
He needed to move quite fast.
Through the Red Sea.
Through the Red Sea
Clearing a pathway
It was a great day
Take it from me.
Yes, a miracle this may be
You can tell from all the glee
Quickly they scampered
Couldn't be hampered
Through the Red Sea.
Egyptians followed behind them
And into the path they go.
But no sooner were they in there
Than G-d did close down the show.
Egyptians were not so lucky
They drowned on the water's floor.

15 Lyrics copyright © 2000 by Randi and Murray Spiegel, http://sedersforyou.tripod.com/. Used by permission of Randi and Murray Spiegel.
16 Used by permission of Yeshaya Douglas Ballon.
17 Used by permission of Yeshaya Douglas Ballon.

Such wonderful things did happen
What more could we ask God for?
Under the sea
Under the sea
That's where Egyptians
Are having conniptions
Now we are free.
Yes, it's a miracle that this may be
You can tell from all the glee
We were all saved there
That's why you should care
'Bout the Red Sea.[18]

Songs and Readings for Maror: Bitter Herbs

A SPOONFUL OF CHAROSET

By Barbara Sarshik (Sung to the tune of "A Spoonful of Sugar")

Every Seder, every year,
There is an element of fear
When I must eat a bitter herb.
And in the moment that I dread,
The heat goes to my head,
I cough! I sneeze! I whimper and I wheeze!
But…
Chorus:
A spoon of charoses helps the bitter herb go down,
The bitter herb go down, bitter herb go down,
Yes, a spoon of charoses helps the bitter herb go down
In the most delightful way.

So you should keep it in your mind,
If there's a moment when you find
There's something dreadful you must do.
It will be better if you add
A thing that's not so bad,
A song! A sweet! A favorite toy or treat! Cause…

(Chorus)[19]

DISCO DELIVERANCE: WE WILL SURVIVE

By Anna Morrison Markowitz (Sung to the tune of Gloria Gaynor's "I Will Survive")

Moses:
First I was afraid –
I was petrified.
Kept thinking I'm just not a public speaking kind of guy.
But then I spent too many nights
Seeing how you'd done them wrong,
And I grew strong.
Yes, I learned how to get along!

Pharaoh:
So now you're here,
Back in my face.
You've brought us pestilence and famine,
Now I want you off my case!
I should have let your people go
When the locusts ate our grain.
Now our firstborn have been taken,
And you've caused us so much pain!

Go on, now, go!
Walk out the door.
Don't turn around now –
You're not welcome anymore.
Weren't you the ones to bite the hand that held your pie?
Without me, you'll crumble –
You'll all lie down and die!

Chorus:
No, we've got Chai –
We will survive!
As long as we trust in our God,
We know we'll stay alive.
Our numbers will be countless
As the stars up in the sky.
Yes, we'll survive…
We will survive!

Moses:
It took all the strength we had
Not to fall apart.
Now God has heard the weeping
Of our broken hearts.
You know we spent too many years
Sweating, hungry, and abused.
We used to cry –
But now we hold our heads up high!

---

18 Used by permission of Gary Teblum.
19 © 2008 Barbara Sarshik, www.barbarasarshik.com. Used by permission of Barbara Sarshik.

So now you'll see
Somebody new.
We're not that chained-up little people
Once enslaved by you.
So if you decide to chase us,
Don't expect it to be free.
Our God will surely save us,
Guide us through the parted sea!

Pharaoh:
Go on, now, go!
Walk out the door.
Don't turn around now –
You're not welcome anymore.
Weren't you the ones to bite the hand
that held your pie?
Without me, you'll crumble –
Yeah, you'll lie down and die!

Chorus:
No, we've got Chai –
We will survive!
As long as we trust in our God,
We know we'll stay alive.
Our numbers will be countless
As the stars up in the sky.
Yes, we'll survive…
We will survive!

Yeah, we've got Chai –
We will survive!
These miracles of freedom
God delivered long ago –
Still we tell our children,
So the story they will know.
We will survive!
We have survived!!!!
HEY, HEY![20]

Songs and Readings for Barech: Sh'foch Hamatcha

ODE TO ELIJAH

By Barbara Sarshik (Sung to the tune of "Be Our Guest")

Be our guest! Be our guest!
Put our Seder to the test!
All you have to do is come on in

And we'll provide the rest.
Here's some wine in a cup!
Just recline and drink it up!
It will be your favorite flavor
If it's Concord grape you favor!
Life is sweet! Life is good!
When you're in our neighborhood!
And when you are here, Elijah, we are blessed!
Just park your golden chariot.
You don't need a Marriot!
Be our guest! Be our guest! Be our guest![21]

LES MISELIJAH

By Stuart Malina (Sung to the tune of "Do You Hear the People Sing" from *Les Misérables*)

Do you hear the doorbell ring,
And it's a little after ten?
It can only be Elijah
Come to take a sip again.
He is feeling pretty fine
But in his head a screw is loose.
So perhaps instead of wine
We should only give him juice![22]

ELIJAH

By Rabbi Daniel Liben (Sung to the tune of "Maria" from *West Side Story*)

Elijah!
I just saw the prophet Elijah.
And suddenly that name
Will never sound the same to me.
Elijah!
He came to our Seder
Elijah!
He had his cup of wine,
But could not stay to dine
This year –
Elijah!
For your message all Jews are waiting:
That the time's come for peace
and not hating.
Elijah –
Next year we'll be waiting.
Elijah![23]

---

20 © 2008 Anna Morrison Markowitz, benannas4u@rochester.rr.com. Used by permission of Anna Morrison Markowitz.

21 © 2008 Barbara Sarshik, http://www.thoseroses.com/barb/Sedersongs2010.pdf. Used by permission of Barbara Sarshik.

22 Used by permission of Stuart Malina.

23 Used by permission of Rabbi Daniel Liben.

WELCOMING ELIJAH

Rabbi Shlomo Carlebach told the following story: Once there was a rich man who wanted to give Elijah his due and purchased an exquisite silver goblet in his honor. He and his wife enjoyed using it at the Seder for many years. One year, he lost all his money and had to sell off all of his possessions. But he did not want to sell the silver cup, although it was worth a lot of money.

Spring came, and there was no money to buy matzah and wine for Pesach. Reluctantly, he decided to sell the cup. He told his wife his plans, adding, "Why do we need the cup if we will not have a Seder?"

His wife did not agree.

"We can't even have the mitzvah of eating matzah, and you are not allowing me to sell the cup." He was very angry. On the morning before Pesach he told her, "This is our last chance: let's sell the cup."

"No," she said without hesitation.

"Then I am leaving the house and going to shul. There is nothing left for me to do here." He left.

In a little while, there was a knock at the door. A rich-looking man was standing at the entrance. "Is this the house of Reb Chaim the great scholar? I came from very far and would like to be with his family for the Seder."

"I wish we could invite you," said the wife, "but it looks like this year we won't have a Seder; we have no money."

"This is no problem," the rich man said. "Here is money. Run and buy food for the whole Pesach. I'll return in time for the Seder."

That evening, the husband walked home dejectedly and was greatly surprised when he opened the door and saw that the table was set in a way that he remembered from his affluent years.

"Dear husband, we have to wait for the rich man," his wife told him, and she explained what had happened.

They waited and waited, but the afikomen had to be eaten before midnight, so they began sadly without the guest.

It was time to fill Elijah's Cup, and the husband dozed off. The wife went to open the door for Elijah, and a man entered; it was the rich man.

"Thank you for not selling my cup," he said, and he blessed her before he left.

The husband woke. "What happened? I feel I missed something very great."

When he was told what happened, he said, "You held on, therefore you had the great merit and you were the one who saw the prophet."

Reb Shlomo concludes his story: My dearest friends, Hold on, hold on![24]

---

24 Carlebach Shul Bulletin, Pesach 1984. Used by permission of Shy Held, President, Carlebach Shul.

SEDER READING OF REMEMBRANCE

Adapted from the Seder Ritual Committee of the American Jewish Congress

On this night of the Seder we remember with reverence and love the six million of our people of the European exile who perished at the hands of a tyrant more wicked than the Pharaoh who enslaved our ancestors in Egypt. Come, said he to his minions, let us cut them off from being a people, that the name of Israel may be remembered no more. And they slew the blameless and pure, men and women and children, with vapors of poison and burned them with fire. But we abstain from dwelling on the deeds of the evil ones lest we defame the image of God in which humanity was created.

Many chose spiritual resistance, continuing to learn Torah at penalty of death, like the martyred rabbis of the Hadrianic period. We recall them tonight as well as the remnants of our people who were left in the ghettos and camps of annihilation that rose up against the wicked ones for the sanctification of the Name, and slew many of them before they died.

It was on the first night of Passover that the holy souls in the ghetto of Warsaw rose up against the adversary, even as in the days of Judah the Maccabee. They were lovely and pleasant in their lives, and in their death they were not divided, and they brought redemption to the name of Israel through all the world.

And from the depths of their affliction the martyrs lifted their voices in a song of faith in the coming of the Messiah, when justice and brotherhood will reign among all. *Ani ma-amin be-emunah sh'leimah b'viat ha-mashiach; v'af al pi she-yit-ma-meiah im kol zeh achakeh lo be-chol yom she-yavo* (I believe with perfect faith in the coming of the Messiah; and, though he tarry, nonetheless I will wait for him every day until he arrives).

Reflection from Dr. Mendy Ganchrow

In the 1960s, Dr. Mendy Ganchrow served as a physician on an army base during the Vietnam War. One year, he was tapped to lead the base Seder with four hundred soldiers participating. The first half of the Seder was filled with singing and warmth and enthusiasm and a hot kosher meal. When everyone had finished eating, the soldiers began drifting out of the room, to smoke or catch a movie on a large outdoor screen. Dr. Ganchrow assumed that the majority of them would not be returning for the concluding part of the Seder, as very few were from observant backgrounds. Suddenly, he heard a loud woosh, which signified incoming rocket fire and missiles, landing perhaps five or six hundred yards from the area where the Seder was being held. Most of those who came to the Seder had arrived from other bases and had no idea where the shelters were located. Not knowing if the rocket fire would start up again, Dr. Ganchrow knew that protocol required him to direct everyone to evacuate to the shelters. But he knew if he did that, they would be there for hours until the source of the missiles could be detected; and as a result, he realized that the Seder would never resume.

He just couldn't bear to have the Seder end. Recalling the rabbinic maxim that the person who performs a mitzvah will be protected, he announced, "Men, I am the ranking officer in this room. I give you my solemn word that God will allow no harm to befall you if you now perform the mitzvah of sitting back down and finishing the Seder." He would realize afterwards that what he did was neither wise nor morally correct, contravening both US Army regulations (which could have led him to be court martialed) and the Jewish moral imperative to safeguard and protect and preserve life at all costs.[25] Yet, he said, the hundreds of soldiers stayed in the Seder hall and completed the Seder in surreal tranquility. At the conclusion, he rose from his seat and began dancing while singing *L'shanah haba-ah birushalayim*. Soon hundreds of men joined in the singing and dancing, with tears rolling down their eyes, professing their shared love from the jungles of Vietnam for far-off Jerusalem. At that moment he could see that everyone in the room – whether observant or not – felt that they were "participating in a transcendent moment that felt truly miraculous."

Reflection from Natan Sharansky

Mr. Sharansky, the past head of the Jewish Agency in Israel, was a longtime prisoner in the Soviet Gulag. He had applied in 1973 to emigrate to Israel and in 1977 was arrested for "treason," the day after his marriage to his wife Avital. On the fortieth anniversary of his sentencing by a Soviet court, he released the following statement:

Forty years ago today, I stood before three Soviet judges and said the following words:

"For two thousand years the Jewish people, my people, have been dispersed all over the world and seemingly deprived of any hope of returning. But still, each year Jews have stubbornly...said to each other, *Le'shana haba'a b'Yerushalayim!* And today, when I am further than ever from my dream, from my people, and from my Avital, and when many difficult years of prisons and camps lie ahead of me, I say to my wife and to my people, *Le'shana haba'a b'Yerushalayim*.

"And to the court, which has only to read a sentence that was prepared long ago – to you I have nothing to say."

As I stood trial in that Moscow court room, my wife Avital marched with thousands of Jews in Amsterdam and the Hague, London and Paris. She heard of my final remarks, and my sentencing, as she landed in Washington, DC. In the eight years that followed, she went on marching, and the Jews of the world marched on with her. It is because of them that eight years after that bleak July 14th in Moscow I finally made it to Jerusalem, and touched the Western Wall.

Today, the Soviet empire is gone, and the Jewish story which it tried to repress – the story of those people who prayed to reach Jerusalem – lives on. And today, forty years after my sentencing, my family is preparing to bring our seventh grandchild into the "Brito shel Abraham Avinu" and the Jewish story – in Jerusalem.

Avital and I thank all of you who marched with us and for us. May the Jewish People continue marching together from strength to strength.[26]

---

25 He says that through his "arrogance and stupidity I could have gotten us all killed." Dr. Mandell Ganchrow, *Journey through the Minefields: From Vietnam to Washington* (Savage, MD: Eshel Press, 2004), 5. Used by permission.

26 Natan Sharansky, Facebook, July 14, 2018. Used by permission of Natan Sharansky.

REFLECTION FROM ETHIOPIAN JEWS

In 1993, over fourteen thousand Ethiopian Jews were airlifted to Israel as part of Operation Solomon, the second wave of bringing Ethiopian Jews to Israel. For hundreds of years, Ethiopian Jews were cut off from the world Jewish community and Jewish traditions and history. As part of her Israeli army service, Keren Gottlieb was serving in a teacher's unit at an absorption center for Ethiopian Jews. In addition to teaching secular subjects, she spent time teaching these new immigrant children recent Jewish history, of which they were totally ignorant. When the month of Nisan arrived, she began teaching about Pesach. She told her students that on Passover, the Jewish people used to visit the Beit Hamikdash, the Temple. One of the students asked her if she had ever been to the Temple. She answered him, "No, of course not. That was a *very* long time ago!" He persisted in asking if she had visited the Temple, and the other students joined in demanding to know if she was ever there. She tried to calm them down but finally she said, "Listen, everyone – there is no Temple! There used to be a Temple many years ago, but today we don't have a Temple. It was destroyed, burned down. I have never been to it, my father's never been to it, and my grandfather has never been to it! We haven't had a Temple for two thousand years!"

The class became more and more agitated. Keren couldn't understand what her students were saying to each other in Amharic nor why they were so bothered by this information. The next day when she came to back to the school, a huge crowd of parents was waiting for her at the gate, as agitated as their children had been the day before. They confronted Keren and asked her why she would tell their children that the Beit Hamikdash had been destroyed. "What's all the fuss about?" Keren asked, explaining that she had merely told the children what had happened two thousand years ago. "What?' said the parents, shocked. "What are you talking about?"

Now, a different scene commenced: one woman fell to the ground, a second broke down in tears. A man standing by them just stared at the teacher in disbelief. A group of men began quietly talking amongst themselves, very fast, in confusion and disbelief. The children stood on the side, looking on in great puzzlement. Another woman suddenly broke into a heart-rending cry. Her husband came over to hug her.

"I felt as if I had just brought them the worst news possible," writes Keren. "It was as if I had just told them about the death of a loved one. I stood there across from a group of Jews who were genuinely mourning the destruction of the Temple."[27]

27 Keren Gottlieb, "The Heart-Rending Cry," August 2, 2003, www.aish.com/h/9av/aas/The_Heart_Rending_Cry.html. Used by permission of Aish.com.

Fifteen Suggestions for the Intermediate Days and End Days of Passover

1. **Shir Hashirim.** It is customary after the Passover Seder to read the Song of Songs. This is one of the most beautiful liturgical works in Jewish tradition, reflecting an allegory of God's love for the Jewish people. If a post-Seder reading doesn't happen, try to find time during the Passover week.

2. **Baal Shem Tov Seudah.** The Baal Shem Tov, founder of the Chasidic movement, had a custom to hold a "Seudah Mashiach" on the afternoon of the last day of Passover, echoing the theme of the concluding days of Passover, when we hope for the ultimate redemption. Today, many follow this custom, gathering together with friends and family, serving a light meal along with four cups of wine (just one blessing) and matzah, interspersed with other foods, songs, and stories. Think of it as beautiful way to end the Passover holiday!

3. **No more chametz.** When you put away your Passover dishes or, if you were away, when you put away your suitcases, make a wish that the only chametz that will permeate your environment after Passover will be a culinary one. Whatever spiritually weighed you down, try not to let it reenter your environment and your soul.

4. **Journal.** Write down lists of what you bought and used or didn't use and any memorable moments or comments from the Seder or Passover week that will help you the following year when planning your Seders and week-long celebration of the holiday.

5. **Donate.** Give any leftover matzah and food to a food bank.

6. *Schlissel challah.* There is a custom to bake a challah with a key (the Yiddish word for key is *schlissel*) inside (wrapped of course in foil) – on the eve of the first Shabbat after Passover. We hope that this key will be a source of blessing, a symbol of opening the gates of heaven not only for economic sustenance but also the bringing of the redemptive age.

7. **Omer count.** Beginning on the second night of Passover and continuing for forty-nine evenings, we count the Omer, a reminder of the counting till the spring harvest as well as the period of time until Shavuot when we received the Torah. This nightly ritual is also a wonderful opportunity to dedicate each night to a different theme of self-improvement.

Here is a song that can be taught to children together with counting the Omer:

We are counting the days of the week – day after day, the weeks are going by until we stood at Har Sinai!

8. **Birkat Ha'ilanot.** During the Hebrew month of Nisan, there is a meaningful tradition to bless trees that are budding. The Bostoner Rebbe who lived in Boston would travel in the 1930s to the suburbs with his Chasidim to find fruit trees to bless. On one occasion, they saw a house with many fruit trees, and he had his driver knock on the door and ask the woman who answered if they could come into her backyard and make a blessing on the trees. She happily said yes. As they were leaving and thanking her, she asked the Rebbe if he could also bestow a blessing on one of the other trees in the corner that had stopped producing apples. He readily agreed, and the owner of the house, who was Catholic, was very grateful. The following fall, the woman came by to his home and left with his assistant a basket filled with beautiful red apples with a note that the apples were from the barren tree he had blessed![28]

9. **Yom Hashoah.** Following Passover there are four commemorations on the Jewish calendar. The first is Yom Hashoah on 27 Nisan. This is the date set aside to recall the six million Jews, including one million children, who were systematically murdered during the Holocaust. Light a candle, attend a memorial service, but most of all make sure not to forget. In some communities there are all-night readings of the names of Holocaust victims.

10. **Yom Hazikaron.** Shortly after Yom Hashoah, on the fourth of Iyar, we commemorate Yom Hazikaron, the date when we recall the thousands of Israeli soldiers who fell in defense of the State of Israel. In many communities there are communal commemorations as well that you can participate in.

11. **Yom Haatzmaut.** Immediately after Yom Hazikaron, we celebrate Israel Independence Day on the fifth of Iyar. If there is a community-wide celebration, don't miss it. No matter what your political point of view, use it as an occasion to toast the miracle that after two thousand years, we have an independent Jewish state!

12. **Pesach Sheni.** On the fifteenth of Iyar, we observe the "second Passover." During the time of the Temple, this was the period when people who had been unable to bring the Passover sacrifice on the original date could come and do so. Today, in the absence of the Beit Hamikdash, we mark the occasion by eating matzah – some use any part of the afikomen that was put aside, representing the idea that we all wish for a second chance.

13. **Yom Yerushalayim.** On the twenty-eighth of Iyar, we have the chance to mark the reunification of Jerusalem.

From 1948 until the June 1967 Six-Day War, Jews were forbidden to visit the Western Wall or to live in the Old City.

14. **Mind your health.** With Passover several weeks behind us, some of us may realize that all those wonderful tasty morsels took a toll. If you need to get in physical shape, join a gym and embrace a healthful diet if not already a part of your lifestyle.

15. **Rejuvenate your spiritual diet.** Finally, from a spiritual point of view, if a Passover Seder is one of the few Jewish activities you engage in throughout the year, think of other ways to enhance your spiritual diet. For example, stay up all night on the eve of Shavuot to study Jewish texts or hear interesting speakers, have a picnic on Shavuot (don't forget the cheesecake), buy a lulav and etrog and have a meal in a sukkah during the Sukkot festival. Most of all, remember to rejoice in the festivals and every day to appreciate even the small joyful moments of life.

28 Yitzhak Buxbaum, *A Person Is Like a Tree: A Sourcebook for Tu BeShvat* (New Jersey: Jason Aaronson, 2000), 164–66.

APPENDIX 2
Recipes for the Seder

By Amy Rosen, Cooking By Design

(Make sure to check and clean all vegetables and herbs for bugs.)

SEPHARDIC CHAROSET

Serves 10–15

Ingredients
> ½ cup pitted dates
> 2 cups peeled, cored, and thinly sliced apples
> ½ cup dried apricots
> ½ cup chopped walnuts

Directions
In a medium pan, combine the dates, apples, and apricots.

Add water to cover the fruit and bring to a boil over high heat. Lower the heat and simmer until mixture is tender enough to mash with a fork, about 5 minutes.

Remove from the heat, let cool slightly, and process in a blender, leaving some texture.

Just before serving, fold in the walnuts.

NOT YOUR MOTHER'S MATZAH BALLS

Makes approximately 20–25 small matzah balls

Ingredients
> 6 tablespoons (¾ stick) unsalted pareve margarine
> ⅓ cup packed finely chopped leeks (white and pale green parts)
> ¼ cup finely chopped fresh chives
> 4 eggs
> 2 tablespoons ginger ale
> 1½ teaspoons kosher salt
> ¼ teaspoon ground pepper
> ¼ teaspoon finely grated fresh ginger root (or powdered ground ginger)
> 1 tablespoon kosher for Passover vodka
> 1 cup unsalted matzah meal

Directions
Melt margarine in heavy sauté pan over medium heat. Add leeks and sauté for 5 minutes. Do not allow to brown – stir occasionally.

Remove from heat. Stir in the ½ cup fresh chives.

Beat eggs, ginger ale, vodka, salt, pepper, and fresh (or powdered) ginger in a bowl. Mix in the matzah meal and blend together. Then fold in the leek mixture. Cover and chill until firm, at least 2 hours.

Line large baking sheet with wax paper. Using moistened palms, roll a rounded tablespoon of matzah mixture into balls. Place on prepared baking sheet. Chill 30 minutes.

Bring large pot of salted water to boil. Drop in matzah balls and cover pot. Cook matzah balls until tender and evenly colored throughout (approximately 40 minutes). Transfer matzah balls to bowl. Cover and chill.

PASSOVER CHICKEN ROULADES

Serves 12

Ingredients
> 6 pounds chicken cutlets, pounded
> 4 large eggs, beaten
> 2 cups matzah meal, seasoned with 2 tablespoons onion powder, 2 tablespoons garlic powder, 1 tablespoon pepper

Filling
> 1½ cups dried apricots, cut into thirds lengthwise
> 1 cup whole pecans, chopped
> 4 medium whole onions, cut apple style
> 6 garlic cloves, sliced
> 6 tablespoons apricot spreadable fruit
> salt and pepper to taste

Glaze
> 8 tablespoons apricot spread
> ½ cup chicken broth
> Any extra filling from above

Directions
Chicken and Filling
Pound the chicken and set aside.

In a sauté pan, sauté onions and garlic until translucent. Add the dried apricots, chopped pecans, and 6 tablespoons of apricot spread over low heat. Add salt and pepper to taste. Let the mixture cook for another 5 minutes and remove from heat.

To assemble, spray a cookie sheet with nonstick cooking spray. Then place approximately 1 tablespoon of the filling in center of each pounded cutlet (there will be leftover filling that will be added to the glaze), roll and dip into beaten eggs and then into matzah meal. Place on prepared

cookie sheet seam side down. Spray the stuffed chicken with olive oil cooking spray. Bake at 350° F for 25 minutes. Remove the chicken from the oven and spread the glaze (see below) on top of the chicken. Bake for another 5 minutes. Cut each chicken cutlet into 3 roulades.

Glaze

Heat the apricot spread and add the chicken broth slowly in a saucepan. Stir until it is a little thicker than a syrupy consistency. Add in the remaining filling mixture and stir together.

ROASTED VEGETABLE STACKS WITH ROSEMARY SPRIGS

Serves 8–10

Ingredients

2 each red, yellow, and orange bell pepper
12 cherry tomatoes
3 portabella mushrooms, sliced
3 zucchini, sliced lengthwise
2 large eggplants, sliced into ¼" rounds
13 fresh rosemary sprigs (save one to sprinkle leaves onto vegetables before roasting)
olive oil
kosher salt

Directions

Slice the peppers in half and remove all seeds and membranes. Then slice each half again so you have 4 quarters. Place the sliced peppers, sliced mushrooms, tomatoes, eggplant, and zucchini on a cookie sheet. Brush with olive oil and sprinkle with kosher salt and rosemary leaves. Roast in oven uncovered for 50 minutes. Remove from heat.

Slice the zucchini into 3" lengths. Slice the larger eggplant rounds in ½. Then stack alternating pepper, mushroom, zucchini, eggplant, pepper, mushroom, zucchini, and eggplant. Top with the cherry tomatoes.

Stick a rosemary sprig through the center and plate.

DECADENT SUNFLOWER, MATZAH, AND APPLE PUDDING

Serves 12

Ingredients

4 cups matzah farfel
4 cups boiling water
4 eggs
½ cup sugar
1 cup brown sugar
¼ cup chopped walnuts
¼ cup chopped almonds
¼ teaspoon salt
1 tablespoon cinnamon
1 tablespoon nutmeg
1 tablespoon mace
3 tablespoons margarine (plus a few pats for the top)
2 teaspoons vanilla extract
2 apples, sliced
1 orange rind for zest
1 tablespoon golden raisins
1 tablespoon dried cranberries
1 tablespoon currants
3 tablespoons apricot spreadable fruit

Directions

Put the farfel in a colander that can fit in a large mixing bowl and cover farfel with boiling water. Let soak until saturated and drain immediately. Then put the farfel in a large mixing bowl. Add beaten eggs, sugar, salt, and margarine. Mix in cinnamon, nutmeg, and mace. Add vanilla to mixture. In a small bowl, mix together the raisins, cranberries, and currants, and set aside.

For a spring form pan

Grease the bottom of the pan; lay one of the sliced apples in the bottom of the pan in a circular pattern. Then add the matzah mixture to the baking dish and smooth out. Add raisin mixture on top of the matzah mixture in the center only. Next lay the other sliced apple in concentric circles starting on the outer rim of the pan for the first layer and overlapping the outer layer, working your way in to the center where the raisin mixture is to make a sunflower. Scatter with chopped nuts and add pats of margarine and spreadable apricot fruit on top of the sunflower apple design.

For a molded baking dish (or Bundt pan)

Grease the bottom of the pan (which will be the top of the cake when it is turned over after it is cooked). Add the raisin mixture to the bottom of the dish. Next lay one of the sliced apples in the bottom of the pan in a circular pattern, overlapping each apple slice by a small amount. Then add matzah mixture to baking dish and smooth out, then add the other sliced apple in concentric circles.

Bake at 350° F for 30 minutes

Serve on a cake pedestal and slice like a piece of cake!

BEEF BRISKET WITH FIG, BALSAMIC AND MERLOT

Serves 8-10

Ingredients

1 (8–10-pound) beef brisket
8 garlic cloves
salt and pepper to taste
2 tablespoons fresh thyme
2 tablespoons fresh rosemary
½ cup dry red wine, such as Merlot, Shiraz, or Malbec
⅓ cup balsamic vinegar
¾ cup beef stock
1 (15-ounce) can diced tomatoes
1 tablespoon tomato paste
4 large onions, sliced into rings
4 stalks celery, with leaves
4 parsnips, peeled
6 fresh carrots, peeled
½ cup dried figs, halved (optional)

Directions

Season brisket with salt and pepper and place into a shallow baking dish. Combine the red wine, tomato paste, and balsamic vinegar, and pour in with the brisket. Cover and marinate in the refrigerator for at least 2 hours.

Preheat oven to 300° F.

Arrange onion rings in the bottom of the roasting pan. Season with garlic, thyme, and rosemary. Pour the marinade into the bottom of the pan along with beef stock and stewed tomatoes, and lay the roast on top of the onions, using them as a roasting rack. Cover tightly with foil or a lid.

Bake for 3 hours in the preheated oven, then peel back the aluminum foil and add carrots, parsnips, and celery (as well as the figs if using) to the pan. Cover the pan again and continue roasting for an additional 1–2 hours (or until you can pull apart with a fork). Slice and serve.

ROASTED BOSC PEARS WITH POMEGRANATE GLAZE

Serves 12

Ingredients

1½ cups dry red wine, such as Syrah, Malbec, or Merlot
1½ cups pomegranate juice
¾ cup sugar
2 cinnamon sticks
3 teaspoons grated orange peel
12 Bosc pears with stems, peeled
pareve vanilla ice cream
kosher for Passover biscotti (or substitute almond cookies)

Directions

Pre heat oven to 350° F. Stir wine, pomegranate juice, sugar, cinnamon stick, and orange peel in medium saucepan over medium heat until sugar dissolves, about 3 minutes.

Using small melon baller, core pears from bottom of wide end. Trim bottoms flat and stand upright in 2-inch-deep 8x8 inch baking dish. Pour pomegranate-wine sauce over the pears.

Roast pears until tender when pierced with knife, basting pears with sauce every 20 minutes, about 1 hour. Using spatula, transfer roasted pears to serving platter.

Transfer pan juices to small saucepan. Simmer until reduced to 1 cup, about 5 minutes. (Can be made 4 hours ahead. Let sauce and pears stand at room temperature. Rewarm sauce before continuing.)

Spoon glaze over pears. Serve warm or room temperature with pareve vanilla ice cream and biscotti or almond cookies.

PASSOVER BANANA CHOCOLATE CHIP BREAD OR MUFFINS

Serves 12

Ingredients

3–4 overripe bananas
1 cup sugar
1 egg
½ cup (1 stick) unsalted margarine
1 cup matzah meal
1 teaspoon salt
1 teaspoon baking soda
1 cup (6 ounces) semisweet (pareve) chocolate chips

Directions

Preheat oven to 325° F.

Melt the margarine in a pan.

Mix bananas, sugar, and eggs with a fork (don't mix too much).

Mix in matzah meal, salt, baking soda, and melted margarine.

Fold in chocolate chips.

For Banana Bread

Spray loaf pan with nonstick spray. Powder dish with matzah meal and shake off extra. Pour mixture into loaf pan and bake for one hour. Let cool on wire rack. Take out of loaf pan and serve. Can slice and then slice each piece again in half.

For Muffins

Spray muffin tin with nonstick spray. Place cupcake foils in the pan. Fill the foils ¾ of the way up. Bake for 25 minutes or until toothpick inserted in the middle comes out clean. Let cool on wire rack.

CHOCOLATE-DIPPED MATZAH PLACE CARDS

Serves 24

Ingredients

8 ounces semisweet (pareve) chocolate
1 (1-pound) box matzah

Directions

Melt chocolate in a double boiler over hot water (not boiling). Stir occasionally.

Break matzah into 3 rectangular pieces on the perforations.

Dip both ends of the pieces into the melted chocolate, using tongs or fingers. Place on wax paper.

After all matzah pieces have been dipped, put the rest of the chocolate in a plastic squeeze bottle or a cake/pastry decorating bag with a round opening, and write the name of one of your guests on each piece.

Refrigerate to harden for 5–10 minutes, then remove from wax paper.

Set in front of wine glasses or directly on plate as place cards.

MATZAH S'MORES

Serves 12

Ingredients

3–4 matzot, cut up into 2" squares
1 cup (6 ounces) semisweet (pareve) chocolate chips
12 marshmallows or 12 heaping tablespoons marshmallow fluff
pareve dark chocolate bars, broken into 1½ inch squares
kosher salt

Directions

Melt chocolate chips in a double boiler.

Put pieces of matzah on a cookie sheet and drizzle with chocolate. Sprinkle with kosher salt. Place in the refrigerator for 5 minutes.

Place marshmallows or a heaping tablespoon of fluff on a cookie sheet and broil until brown. Layer matzah squares with a piece of chocolate, a broiled marshmallow, and then another piece of matzah.

Serve on platter.

CHOCOLATE MATZAH BRITTLE

Serves many!

Ingredients

3–4 whole matzot
1 cup (2 sticks) unsalted margarine
1 cup brown sugar
2 cups (12 ounces) semisweet (pareve) chocolate chips
½ cup chopped pecans
½ cup chopped walnuts
½ cup chopped pistachios
kosher salt

Directions

Preheat oven to 325° F. Place foil on a cookie sheet, grease foil with margarine, and then lay the matzot flat on the cookie sheet (fill in where needed with broken pieces of matzah).

In a saucepan, melt margarine with brown sugar and stir until dissolved.

Spread the mixture on the matzah.

Bake 8 to 10 minutes.

Turn off oven and remove pan.

Sprinkle chocolate chips to cover the matzah, then put back into the turned-off but still warm oven for 8 minutes.

Remove from oven and spread the now-melted chocolate chips. Then sprinkle over the chocolate kosher salt and a variety of chopped nuts.

Variations

You **can** just use the kosher salt and not nuts, or use chopped dried fruit instead of or in addition to nuts.

Glossary of Commentators

Abarbanel (or Abravanel), Rabbi Don Yitzchak (1437–1508). Biblical scholar and commentator who served as financial advisor to King Ferdinand and Queen Isabella prior to the expulsion from Spain.

Alshich, Rabbi Moshe (1508–1593). Mystical biblical commentator from Safed, Israel.

Aruch HaShulchan (1829–1908). Lithuanian rabbi Yechiel Epstein, author of Aruch HaShulchan (by which he became known), which discusses the origins and sources of each Jewish law and custom.

Bnei Yissaschar (1783–1841). Rabbi Zvi Elimelech Shapiro of Dinov, Chasidic master, student of the Seer of Lublin, and author of the *Bnei Yissaschar*, by which he became known.

Carlebach, Rabbi Shlomo (1925–1994). Pioneered reaching out to Jews disconnected from Judaism. Composed and sang hundreds of songs which created a unique genre in Jewish music.

Chidushei Harim (1799–1866). Rabbi Yitzhak Meir Rotenberg-Alter. Known as the Chidushei Harim for his Torah interpretations, this descendant of Rashi and the Tosafist Rabbi Meir Rothenberg was the first Rebbe of the Ger Chasidic dynasty.

Falk, Rebbetzin Baileh Edels (sixteenth–seventeenth centuries). Married to Rabbi Joshua Falk, a well-known halachic authority, Rebbetzin Falk was a scholar in her own right. Her explanation of why we light candles differently on festivals is quoted in Rabbi Falk's commentary (the Derisha) on the *Arba'ah Turim*, the basis for the *Shulchan Aruch* (Code of Jewish Law).

Grate, Rabbi Abraham of Prague (eighteenth century). Author of *Beer Avraham*, a 1708 mystical commentary on the Passover Haggadah.

Hirsch, Rabbi Samson Raphael (1808–1888). Founder in Germany of the Torah im Derech Eretz school of Orthodox Judaism and author of *The Nineteen Letters* and *Horev*, as well as a commentary on the Torah.

Kasher, Rabbi Menachem (1895–1983). Best known for his multi-volume encyclopedia, the *Torah Sheleimah* (the complete Torah), which he began in 1927 and continued writing up until his death.

Kli Yakar (1550–1619). Rabbi Shlomo Ephraim ben Aaron Luntschitz, a rabbi in Prague, is best known for his homiletical commentary on the Torah, the *Kli Yakar*, the name by which he became known.

Lubavitcher Rebbe (1902–1994). Rabbi Menachem Mendel Schneerson, charismatic Chasidic Rebbe and scholar who pioneered outreach to Jews throughout the world.

Maharal ([1512–1526]–1609). Rabbi Judah Loewe, known by the acronym Maharal, which stands for Moreinu HaRav Loewe (our teacher, Rabbi Loewe), wrote *Gur Aryeh al HaTorah*, a commentary on Rashi's Torah commentary. He created the legend of the Golem of Prague, a statue of clay that came to life and was designed to protect the Jewish community.

Maimonides (c. 1135–1204). Rabbi Moses ben Maimon (or Rambam, which is an acronym of his title, Rabbenu Moshe ben Maimon). Physician to the sultans of Morocco and Egypt, author of the *Guide for the Perplexed* and the fourteen-volume codification of Talmudic law the *Mishneh Torah*, he is acknowledged as the preeminent arbiter of Jewish law and philosophy.

Mordechai (1250–1298). Rabbi Mordechai ben Hillel Hakohen. Author of the *Mordechai*, a commentary on the Code of Jewish Law, after which he is known.

Nachman, Rabbi of Breslov (1772–1810). The great-grandson of the Baal Shem Tov, the founder of Chasidism. He emphasized the spiritual kabbalistic side of Judaism, being close to God and spending time alone in contemplation.

Orenstein, Rabbi Yaakov (1774–1839). Chief rabbi of Lemberg, noted scholar, author of *Yeshuat Yaakov*.

Rashi (1040–1105). Rabbi Shlomo Yizchaki. Known by the acronym for his name, Rashi was a medieval French rabbi who is renowned for his clear commentary on and explanations of both the Torah and Talmud texts.

Rashbam (1085–1158). Rabbi Shmuel ben Meir. Known by the acronym for his name, Rashbam was a grandson of Rashi and a leading French Tosafist, who wrote commentaries on the Torah (focused on the plain meaning of the text) and on the Talmud.

Rema (1520–1572). Rabbi Moshe Isserles. Known by the acronym for his name, the Rema was a renowned Polish scholar, halachic authority, and codifier. His commentary on the Sephardic rabbi Yosef Karo's *Shulchan Aruch* (Code of Jewish Law) serves as the Ashkenazic corollary to the Code of Jewish Law.

Rosh (c. 1250–1327). Rabbi Asher ben Jehiel, Known by the acronym for Rabbeinu Asher, the Rosh was a leading German rabbi, scholar, commentator, and Talmudist whose abstract of Jewish law is printed in almost every edition of the Talmud.

Sefat Emet (1847–1905). Rabbi Yehudah Aryeh Leib Alter. A Gerer Rebbe known by the title of his work the *Sefat Emet*, a commentary on the weekly Torah portions and holidays.

Sacks, Rabbi Jonathan (b. 1948). Chief Rabbi of the United Hebrew Congregations of the British Commonwealth from 1991 to 2013. A prolific author, theologian, and PhD philosopher, he is a member of the British House of Lords.

Salanter, Rabbi Israel (1810–1883). A Talmudist and famed *rosh yeshiva* in Lithuania, he is considered the father of the Musar movement, which emphasized the importance not only of ritual requirements in Judaism but ethical and spiritual development and interpersonal relationships with others.

Soloveitchik, Rabbi Yosef Dov (1820–1892). From Brisk, Lithuania, this rabbi, scholar, and author of the *Beis Halevi* (by whose name he is known) was the first of what became known as the Soloveitchik dynasty and the "Brisker" method.

Soloveitchik, Rabbi Joseph B. (1903–1993). Scion of the Soloveitchik dynasty, *rosh yeshiva* at Yeshiva University, eminent Talmudist, and deep thinker with a PhD in philosophy, he became known as "the Rav." He stressed in his lectures and writings the idea of *Torah u'madah*, the synthesis of Torah and secular knowledge.

Vilna Gaon (1720–1797). Rabbi Elijah ben Solomon Zalman, known as the Vilna Gaon or HaGra (haGaon Rabbenu Eliyahu), was the leading Lithuanian Talmudist, halachist, and commentator on the Torah, Mishnah, and *Shulchan Aruch*. He is also known for being a vehement opponent (*mitnaged*) of the Chasidic movement.

Endnotes

1 Rav Hisda was a third-century Amora (Talmudic scholar). Rav Zeira said to Rav Hisda, "Come and teach!" Rav Hisda responded, "I have not even learned Birkat Hamazon properly, and you want me to teach?" Rabbi Zeira said, "What are you talking about?" Rav Hisda responded, "When I visited the house of the Exilarch, and I recited Birkat Hamazon, Rav Sheshet uncoiled his neck at me like a snake [he was very angry]. And why? Because I did not say *brit* [covenant of circumcision] and Torah and [David's] kingship." "And why didn't you say them?" "I followed Rav Hananel in the name of Rav: Whoever did not say 'covenant' and 'Torah' and 'kingship' [nevertheless] fulfilled the obligation. I omitted 'covenant' because it is not applicable to women, I omitted 'Torah' and 'kingship' because they are not applicable to women and slaves." Rabbi Zeira exclaimed, "And you rejected all the Tannaim and Amoraim and followed Rav?" Rav Hisda's version was not accepted by the majority of the rabbis and I am not following it here. However, his sensitivity to all who recite Grace after Meals and his desire to avoid language that doesn't apply to all is admirable.

2 Kobi Nahshoni, "Revolutionary Ruling: 'Yes' to Kitniyot on Pesach," March 30, 2007, http://www.ynetnews.com/articles/0,7340,L-3382886,00.html.

3 For further insight on the origins of the Seder and comparison with Greek custom, see Baruch M. Bokser, *The Origins of the Seder: The Passover Rite and Early Rabbinic Judaism* (Oakland, CA: University of California Press, 1984).

4 Leo Adler had traveled with the Mir Yeshiva, which was saved by visas issued by the Japanese diplomat Chiune Sugihara and the Dutch consul Jan Zwartendik. His wife Bella ended up in a Soviet labor camp in Karaganda in Kazakhstan, and they were miraculously reunited in New York after the Holocaust. See Barbara Sofer, "Passport to Freedom," *Jerusalem Post*, April 11, 2003.

5 *Sotah* 11b.

6 See *Pesachim* 114b, Rav Huna.

7 Yael Levine, "Placing a Cooked Food on the Seder Table in Commemoration of Miriam," in *All the Women Followed Her: A Collection of Writings on Miriam the Prophet and The Women of the Exodus*, ed. Rebecca Schwartz (Mountain View, California: Rikudei Miriam Press, 2001), 235–51; quoted by Lisa Schlaff, Tammy Jacobowitz, and Andrea Sherman, "A Place at the Table: An Orthodox Feminist Exploration of the Seder," *JOFA Journal* 5, no. 1 (spring 2004): 3, referencing a medieval collection of responsa that preserves this tenth-century dialogue. Used by permission of Yael Levine.

8 *Ma'aseh Roke'ach* 59.

9 *Shemot Rabbah* 6:4 and *Pesachim* 117b.

10 *Pesachim* 117b.

11 Jerusalem Talmud, *Pesachim* 10:1, 37c.

12 Maharal, *Gevurat HaShem* 48.

13 Ibid.

14 "Miriam died there...and there was no water for the congregation" (Exodus 20:1–2).

15 Rashi, Numbers 20:2; *Ta'anit* 9a; *Song of Songs Rabbah* 4:14, 27.

16 *Shemot Rabbah* 1.

17 Based on the teachings of the Lubavitcher Rebbe, Rabbi Menachem Mendel Schneerson, adapted by Yanki Tauber. Cited in Carol Kaufman Newman, "Sing a New Song," *JOFA Journal* 5, no. 1 (spring 2004): 1.

18 This fast takes place on the eve of Passover, or if Passover begins on a Saturday night, either the preceding Thursday or Friday.

19 *Pesikta d'Rav Kahana* 7; *Exodus Rabbah* 18:3.

20 *Shulchan Aruch*, Orach Chaim, siman 470, 1.

21 *Shulchan Aruch*, Orach Chaim, siman 470, 5.

22 *Pesachim* 108.

23 Tosafot, *Pesachim* 108.

24 *Pesachim* 108a.

25 *Shulchan Aruch*, Orach Chaim, siman 472:4.

26 In Yiddish the terms would be *kratzen* (scouring), *shobben* (scraping), *rieben* (rubbing), and *kasheren* (making kosher). Rabbi Binyamin Adler, *The Vintage Haggadah: Yeinah Shel Torah; A Collection of Explanations, Interpretations, Profound Insights and Thoughts on the Haggadah* (Jerusalem: Feldheim, 1993), 70. Used by permission of Feldheim Publishers.

27 *Pesachim* 1:1. The *Aruch Hashulchan* (437:7) notes that women nowadays are even more scrupulous in searching than men.

28 Rabbi Yitzchak Meir Goodman, *And There Was Light: A Treasury of Commentaries on Sefer Shemos* (Southfield, MI: Targum Press, 2004), 312.

29 *Aruch Hashulchan*, Orach Chaim 473:6.

30 Cited in M. Stein, *Pesach: Passover—Its Observance, Laws and Significance, A Presentation Based on Talmudic and Traditional Sources* (Brooklyn, NY: Mesorah, 1994), 107.

31 See David Golinkin, ed., *The Responsa of Professor Louis Ginzberg* (New York: JTS Press, 1996), 130–31; Hannah Sprecher, "Let Them Drink and Forget Our Poverty: Orthodox Rabbis React to Prohibition," *American Jewish Archives* 43, no. 2 (1991):135–79, http://americanjewisharchives.org/publications/journal/PDF/1991_43_02_00_sprecher.pdf.

32 See Eli Ginzberg, *Louis Ginzberg: Keeper of the Law* (Philadelphia: Jewish Publication Society, 1966), 221. Was he being threatened by the Mafia or individual bootleggers? Some posit that a "price" was put on his head, but the Jewish gangster Bugsy Siegel said it wouldn't look nice to murder a rabbi, and the "hit job" was removed!

33 See Rabbi David Feinstein, *Kol Dodi* (New York: Tiferet, 1970), 5–6.

34 Used by permission of Alan Morinis. Cited by Alan Morinis in *Yashar*, e-newsletter of the Mussar Institute, April 2010, http://mussarinstitute.org/apr2010-lens.htm.

35 Shmuly Yanklowitz, "The Forgotten Story of Cesar Chavez and the Jews," *Huffington Post*, May 12, 2016, http://www.huffingtonpost.com/rabbi-shmuly-yanklowitz/the-forgotten-story-of-ce_b_7260814.html.

36 Fragments found in the Cairo Geniza point to the custom of dipping eggs in salt water. Rav Yosef Zvi Rimon, in his contemporary Haggadah, discusses eating other foods to stave off hunger, enabling one to concentrate on the Haggadah. See Rabbi Yosef Zvi Rimon, *The Seder Night: Kinor David* (Jersey City, NJ: Ktav, 2014), 70.

37 Noam Zion, Seder Stories, 2014, http://www.templeisaiah.net/Portals/0/Attachments%20-%20Learning/Adult%20Learning/Seder%20Stories%202014.pdf. See also Gloria Hollander Lyon, *Mommy, What's That Number on Your Arm? A6374; My Holocaust Memoir* (Xlibris, 2016).

38 Rabbi Lev Meirowitz Nelson, ed., *The Other Side of the Sea: A Haggadah on Fighting Modern-Day Slavery* (New York: T'ruah, 2015), 33, http://www.truah.org/pesach.html, forward.com/food/368254/chocolate-at-passover-not-so-fast/.

39 See Associated Press, "Israel Reinforces Troops, Steps Up Humanitarian Aid to Syria," *New York Times*, July 1, 2018, https://www.nytimes.com/aponline/2018/07/01/world/middleeast/ap-ml-israel-syria.html; Anna Ahronheim, "On the Border with Syrians Brought to Israel for Medical Treatment," *Jerusalem Post*, January 19, 2018, https://www.jpost.com/Israel-News/On-the-border-with-Syrians-brought-to-Israel-for-medical-treatment-538160.

40 See the medieval commentary of Rav Manoach Hendel of Prague on Maimonides' *Hilchot Chametz U'matzah* 8:5. Before we even get to matzah, Rav Manoach reminds us that it was this first act of dipping the coat that led to slavery and redemption. See Rabbi Eliezer Muskin, "The Karpas Connection," *Insights to the Pesach Seder from the Rabbinic Alumni Committee of the Rabbi Isaac Elchanan Theological Seminary*, YU Torah Pesach-to-Go, April 2016, 41–42.

41 Rabbi Zev Schostak, *Why Is This Night Different? The Family Passover Haggadah*, 3d ed., rev. (Brooklyn, 1994), 34.

42 Rabbi Chagai Vilosky, *Pesach Haggadah: The Answer Is...* (New York: ArtScroll Mesorah, 2014), 55.

43 Rabbi Jonathan Sacks, *The Jonathan Sacks Haggada* (Jerusalem: Koren Publishers, 2013), 22–25. Used by permission of Koren Publishers.

44 See Rav Pinchas Kehati's commentary on the Mishnah, *Pesachim* 10:3.

45 For further discussion, see Gedaliah Alon, *The Jews in Their Land in the Talmudic Age, 70–640 CE* (Jerusalem: Magnes Press, 1977).

46 See Rabbi J. David Bleich, "Korban Pesach Bazman Hazeh: A Review of Halakhic Literature Pertaining to the Reinstitution of the Sacrificial Order," in Steven F. Cohen and Kenneth Brander, eds., *The Yeshiva University Haggada* (New York: Student Organization of Yeshiva, 1985), 34 (originally appeared in *Tradition*, fall 1967).

47 "In Modern First, Passover Sacrifice to Take Place in Old City," *Times of Israel*, April 5, 2017, https://www.timesofisrael.com/in-first-passover-sacrifice-to-take-place-in-old-city/.

48 See Rabbi Nosson Scherman, ed., *The Haggadah Treasury: A Seder Companion with Insights and Interpretations for Inspiration and Retelling* (New York: ArtScroll Mesorah, 1986), 40–41.

49 See "Vezot HaBerakha/Simchat Torah: How Can We Be Happy?" in Rabbi Norman Lamm, *Derashot Ledorot: Deuteronomy* (Jerusalem: Koren Maggid Books/OU Press, 2014), 154.

50 Donald Sheff, "Izzy, Did You Ask a Good Question Today?" *New York Times*, January 19, 1988, http://www.nytimes.com/1988/01/19/opinion/l-izzy-did-you-ask-a-good-question-today-712388.html.

51 Rabbi Joseph Elias, *Passover Haggadah* (Brooklyn: ArtScroll/Mesorah, 2000), 40.

52 Rabbi Abraham R. Besdin, *Reflections of the Rav*, vol. 1, *Lessons in Jewish Thought* (Hoboken, NJ: Ktav, 1979, 1993), 190–91.

53 "And it shall be, when you draw nigh unto the battle, that the priest shall approach and speak to the people and shall say to them: 'Hear, O Israel, you draw nigh this day unto battle against your enemies; let not your heart faint; fear not, nor be alarmed, neither be afraid of them; for the Lord your God goes with you, to fight for you against your enemies, to save you'" (Deuteronomy 20:2–

4). See Rabbi Avrohom Gordimer, "Parshas Shoftim – The Kohen Mashuach Milchamah and His Message," YU Torah, August 10, 2009, http://www.yutorah.org/lectures/lecture.cfm/736663/rabbi-avraham-gordimer/parshas-shoftim-the-kohen-mashuach-milchamah-and-his-message/.

54 See *Likutei Moharan* 2:44, cited in Rabbi Yehoshua Starret and Chaim Kramer, *The Breslov Haggadah*, edited by Moshe Mykoff (Jerusalem: Breslov Research Institute, 1989), 46–48.

55 Letter of the Lubavitcher Rebbe, 11 Nissan 5737, cited in Rabbi Yosef Marcus, *The Passover Haggadah: With Commentary from the Classic Commentators, Midrash, Kabbalah, the Chasidic Masters and the Haggadah of the Lubavitcher Rebbe* (New York: Kehot and Merkos, 2011), 2:578ff.

56 See Rabbi Eliyahu Touger, *The Chassidic Haggadah: An Anthology of Commentary and Stories for the Seder* (New York: Moznaim, 1988), 49.

57 Sefat Emet, cited in Rabbi Yissachar Dov Rubin, *Talelei Oros: The Haggadah Anthology* (Jerusalem: Arazim, 2004), 161.

58 Touger, *Chassidic Haggadah*, 54.

59 See Professor Louis Finkelstein, "The Oldest Midrash: Pre-Rabbinic Ideals and Teachings in the Passover Haggadah," *Harvard Theological Review* 31 (1938): 29; Mitchell First, "Arami Oved Avi: Uncovering the Interpretation Hidden in the Mishnah," *Hakirah, The Flatbush Journal of Jewish Law and Thought* 13 (spring 2012): 127–44, http://www.hakirah.org/vol13first.pdf.

60 Heard from Rabbi Simcha Lyons.

61 *Pirkei de-Rabi Eliezer* 48; *Exodus Rabbah* 5:13.

62 Rav Yitzchak Sender, *The Commentators' Pesach Seder Haggadah* (New York: Feldheim, 2004), 171–72. Used by permission of Feldheim Publishers.

63 Rubin, *Talelei Oros: The Haggadah Anthology*, 185.

64 Heard from Rabbi Zev Brenner.

65 Cited in Jenni Frazer, "Wiesel: Yes, We Really Did Put God on Trial," *The JC*, September 19,

2008, *www.thejc.com/news/uk-news/wiesel-yes-we-really-did-put-god-trial*.

66 Sender, *Commentators' Hagaddah*, 152–53.

67 Touger, *Chassidic Haggadah*, 66.

68 *Bangitout Seder Sidekick 2016*. Used by permission of Bangitout.

69 *Pirkei de-Rabbi Eliezer*, chapter 43.

70 "The Science of the 10 Plagues," Live Science, April 11, 2017, https://www.livescience.com/58638-science-of-the-10-plagues.html. Used by permission of Live Science.

71 Nahum M. Sarna, editor, *The JPS Torah Commentary: Exodus* (Philadelphia: Jewish Publication Society, 1991), 61.

72 Shanna Silver, "The Ten Modern Plagues of Today," *Kveller*, March 26, 2016, https://www.kveller.com/the-10-modern-plagues-of-today/amp/.

73 Their research showed that bystanders will more likely get involved when there are few or no other witnesses. If individuals are part of a larger group, they are socially influenced by looking around and seeing the behavior of others, rather than coming to their own decisions. This theory was inspired by the 1964 murder in Queens, New York, of Kitty Genovese. She was raped and stabbed to death near her apartment in the presence of several witnesses. Reports vary wildly as to the actual number of witnesses, and until recently it was believed no one called for help. But the overwhelming reports of witnesses' inaction (one witness said he just didn't want to get involved) prompted research into possible explanations, which helped develop the concepts of diffusion of responsibility and the bystander effect. See "Bystander Effect," *Psychology Today*, https://www.psychologytoday.com/us/basics/bystander-effect.

74 Steven F. Cohen and Kenneth Brander, eds., *The Yeshiva University Haggada* (New York: Student Organization of Yeshiva, 1985), 19.

75 Rabbi Sharon Cohen Anisfeld, Tara Mohr, and Catherine Spector, eds., *The Women's Seder Sourcebook: Rituals and Readings for Use at the Passover Seder* (Woodstock, VT: Jewish Lights, 2003), 151–52. Used by permission of Jewish Lights.

76 Cited in Elie Wiesel, *Souls on Fire: Portraits and Legends of Hasidic Masters*, translated by Marion Wiesel (New York: Summit Books, 1972), 167–68.

77 Jeffrey M. Cohen, *Prayer and Penitence: A Commentary on the High Holy Day Machzor* (Northvale, NJ: Jason Aronson, 1994), xxv.

78 Lynn Zinseraug, "Summer 2004 Games – Sailing: Men's Mistral; Israelis Revel in First Taste of Gold," *New York Times*, August 26, 2004.

79 David Ben-Gurion, statement, Public Hearing before the Anglo-American Committee of Inquiry, Jerusalem, March 11, 1936 (Jerusalem: Government Printing Office), http://cojs.org/wp-content/uploads/Public_Hearings_3.11.46.pdf.

80 Jodi Rudoren, "Proudly Bearing Elders' Scars, Their Skin Says 'Never Forget,'" *New York Times*, September 30, 2012, http://www.nytimes.com/2012/10/01/world/middleeast/with-tattoos-young-israelis-bear-holocaust-scars-of-relatives.html?pagewanted=all.

81 Lois K. Solomon, "Nurse Gets Tattoo to Honor Holocaust Patients," *Sun Sentinel*, December 9, 2014, http://www.sun-sentinel.com/local/palm-beach/boca-raton/fl-holocaust-tattoo-20141207-story.html.

82 See Yael Levine, *Midrashim of Bitya, the Daughter of Pharaoh: A Study Companion for the Seder Night* (Jerusalem, 2004).

83 "Prayer for Eating Chametz on Passover – in Bergen Belsen 1944," https://www.shabboshouse.org/mendels-messages/prayer-for-eating-chametz-on-passover-in-bergen-belsen-1944/.

84 Rabbi Binny Freedman, "Shemittah's Role in Terror Halt, and Atonement," *Jewish Star*, October 2, 2014, http://thejewishstar.com/stories/Shemittahs-role-in-terror-halt-and-atonement,5358. Used by permission of the author.

85 Adapted from Rabbi Tuvia Bolton, "The Feast: A Seder Story," http://www.chabad.org/library/article_cdo/aid/273207/jewish/The-Feast.htm. Used by permission of Chabad.org.

86 See Bokser, *The Origins of the Seder*, 65.

87 The origin of this custom is that the rabbis of old had advised people to eat salt with their

meals, and often a very strong type of salt called *melech S'domit* (salt of Sodom) was used. This salt could blind people if it got into their eyes. Therefore, the rabbis ruled that hands must be washed after the meals. Today, since this salt is no longer used, many do not follow this custom.

88 Jeffrey Cohen, *1001 Questions and Answers on Pesach* (Northvale, NJ: Jason Aronson, 1996), 158–59.

89 Marnie Winston-Macauley, *A Little Joy, A Little Oy 2005 Calendar: A Banquet of Jewish Humor and Wisdom* (Kansas City, MO: Andrews McMeel Publishing, 2004). Used by permission of Marnie Winston-Macauley.

90 Yael Levine, "It Was in the Middle of the Night," *JOFA Journal* 5, no. 1 (spring 2004): 8. Used by permission of Yael Levine.